United in Discontent

United in Discontent

Local Responses to Cosmopolitanism
and Globalization

Edited by
Dimitrios Theodossopoulos and
Elisabeth Kirtsoglou

Berghahn Books
NEW YORK • OXFORD

First published in 2010 by

Berghahn Books

www.berghahnbooks.com

©2010, 2013 Dimitrios Theodossopoulos and Elisabeth Kirtsoglou

First paperback edition published in 2013

Library of Congress Cataloging-in-Publication Data

United in discontent : local responses to cosmopolitanism and globalization
/ edited by Dimitrios Theodossopoulos and Elisabeth Kirtsoglou.
    p. cm.
Includes bibliographical references and index.
ISBN 978-1-84545-630-6 (hbk.)--ISBN 978-0-85745-809-4 (pbk.)
1. Cosmopolitanism--Cross-cultural studies. I. Theodossopoulos,
Dimitrios. II. Kirtsoglou, Elisabeth, 1973-

JZ1308.U64 2009
306--dc22

2009033131

British Library Cataloguing in Publication Data

A catalogue record for this book is available
from the British Library

Printed in the United States on acid-free paper.

ISBN 978-0-85745-809-4 (paperback)   ISBN 978-85745-833-9 (retail ebook)

CONTENTS

PREFACE TO THE PAPERBACK EDITION

Six years after the conception of this book, the topic it addresses – local discontent with globalizing and homogenizing processes – remains timely, even more so in the context of the global financial crisis. Public indignation with the visible inequalities in the global economy has grown. The new global media has contributed to this visibility and encouraged the development of anti-globalization as a worldwide ideological movement. The voices of discontent have spread via the Internet to inspire local, ephemeral and diachronic, emplaced, but also cosmopolitan communities of 'indignants' in Madrid, Athens, London and New York (to name but a few). Public protest is voiced in the 'here and now', and spread, with lightening speed, in the 'everywhere'.

Within the current global sense of indignation, it has become apparent that globalization can encourage its own critique across conventional and established boundaries. This is the argument promoted by this book and supported by ethnographic and comparative evidence. In the peripheries of economic and political power, local actors, unhappy with the dominant cosmo-politics, visualize a global community in discontent, imagining that they are not alone in the world. They see others in discontent answering back, through Facebook, Twitter and Skype. Anti-globalization imagines itself in global terms.

The concept of a community in discontent – imagined, temporarily actualized in protest, re-imagined at a global scale – is offered here as a tool to aid analysis in a time when anti-globalization and counter-cosmopolitanism have increased their appeal to the global peripheries. This is also a time when local expressions of discontent find unsuspecting sympathizers – fellows in protest – in unusual contexts; far away but close enough. We have seen discontent becoming a trope of engaging with a homogenizing world – a common disposition – even though the emerging critiques or protests share different cultural and historical referents. We are not intimidated by the many voices in discontent, voices that have increased since the hardback edition of this book was published. On the contrary, we are fascinated to see that the communities of the discontented have multiplied – in virtual spaces, in squares and on highways.

We have tried to prioritize the local point of view on resistance and discontent. Local discontent may be dynamic and unpredictable, seeking wider recognition, representing a desire to reach out to the world, take advantage of global flows, and bring that advantage home. But there are also dissident voices that reproduce conventional religious and nationalist attachments, desiring to be heard globally, reaching out for support among imagined communities of unhappy co-believers and ideologues. The imagined communities of discontent are many, but they increasingly come into conversation with each other. As they do so they engender new local, anti-global, counter-cosmopolitan arguments and positions: ideological, imagined, indignant, resisting.

We wait with anticipation to see the academic community engage, more directly, with the local meaningfulness of such views. This book provides some inspiration to aid in this endeavour.

Dimitrios Theodossopoulos, Canterbury
and Elisabeth Kirtsoglou, Durham
November 2012

PREFACE

This volume emerged out of the 2006 ASA conference on 'Cosmopolitanism and Anthropology' and it has been greatly inspired by the conversations and thoughts exchanged during that conference. Our initial concern with counter-cosmopolitanism was soon expanded to encompass the broader theme of discontent with globalizing processes. We soon realized that the thrust of the local critique of cosmopolitanism was directed towards its globalized, elite dimension, a hegemonic version of (primarily Western) cosmopolitan values distributed through globalization. Paradoxically, we also realized that the anti-global, anti-cosmopolitan critique, as this is articulated in local contexts, often assumes a global and cosmopolitan perspective. The cases of anti-cosmopolitanism that we explore in the volume share a certain degree of cosmopolitan empathy, and rely on the imagination of alternative communities of resisting peripheral actors, who might turn global processes to their advantage in an attempt to voice their critical views, or to communicate their discontent to others imagined as equally peripheral and marginalized. This is the community in discontent that we examine in this volume.

We want to thank the organizers and participants of the ASA 2006 conference and our contributors in this volume, Andrew and Pamela, Bill, Iain and David, Àngels, Victoria, and John. We also want to thank our publisher Marion Berghahn for her commitment to a serious anthropology that engages with timely political processes, and our colleagues in Bristol and Durham for their continuous intellectual stimulation. Finally, we would like to thank our partners Michaela Benson and Constantine Christou for their continuous support during the period of writing, while Elisabeth Kirtsoglou would like to thank Dimitrios Theodossopoulos for his perseverance and dedication.

Dimitrios Theodossopoulos
and Elisabeth Kirtsoglou

September 2008

Chapter 1

INTRODUCTION:
UNITED IN DISCONTENT

Dimitrios Theodossopoulos

In the minds of most people who do not profess to be specialists in academic epistemology, globalization – like the concept 'society' – has been broadly discussed as a reified entity: as a super-organic creature that grows and expands (often in an insatiable manner); one that is hungry and very much alive; and, more conveniently, one that can be addressed in local conversation, criticized, condemned and convicted as the guilty party responsible for global disparity and injustice. This lay 'organic analogy' – the conceptualization of globalization as a living thing – allows us to confront the monster face to face,[1] to give it an identity, treat it in metaphorical terms and thus 'move *it* about affectively by adornment and disparagement' (Fernandez 1986: 39). The scary creature we call globalization is out there, as many among us can testify; it is real and it is substantial. We can follow in its footsteps with caution, take advantage of it or prepare ourselves (and our arguments) for the inevitable confrontation. In daily life, the popular metaphor of a living, organic globalization facilitates a tangible conceptualization of the term and, simultaneously, its own critique.

And so everyday discourse tackles large-scale political experiences in concrete terms: the super-organism called globalization has been growing very quickly, taking up too much space, penetrating too many domains of everyday life. Such an unprecedented growth of this phenomenon has brought about an explosion of complaints. It has also facilitated the emergence of a new global awareness, which in many cases has given birth to discontent with the world order and inspired a new ideological orientation, often referred to as anti-globalization. What is very interesting to note here is that those feeling discontented often use the very technologies of globalization to pursue their critique. Inspired by new global possibilities, they imagine themselves as part of a much broader community in discontent. And, as anti-globalization becomes global, a number of related processes, such as westernisation, commoditisation, and the predominance of a neoliberal cosmopolitan ethos, are debated in everyday contexts, and are subsequently tolerated, resisted or rejected.

These observations bring us closer to the very subject matter of this volume: that of growing discontent with homogenizing global processes, and the scores of complaints from local actors displeased with international politics who turn against the global order (to which they refer in a generalizing manner as 'globalization') and its perceived representatives (national or international elites, endorsing a neoliberal, cosmopolitan political orientation). We are also concerned in this volume with the mutual sympathies generated by diverse versions of anti-globalization, the counter-cosmopolitanism defined in opposition to cosmopolitan elites and the imagination of a worldwide anti-global community in discontent. We investigate these expressions of local disapproval as they emerge in particular contexts, in 'culturally occupied locales' (Comaroff and Comaroff 2001: 14), in the words of situated actors who share some awareness of their peripheral positions but voice their complaints with confidence, resentment or indignation. Their critical discourse is mostly unofficial, not very systematic or articulate, but in all cases meaningful within its own cultural specificity.

In this introduction and the chapters that follow, we explore these local and peripherally positioned sets of meaningfulness, compelled to pay serious attention to their complexity. But, before we start this journey, I would like first to clarify our use of two terms that appear in the title of this book – globalization and cosmopolitanism.

Globalization is an ill-defined notion, too vague and too generalizing to convey the intricacies and local specificity of global processes. Other anthropologists use more flexible terms, such as 'transnational flows' (Eriksen 2003) or 'a world of flows' (Appadurai 1996, 2001), or prefer to highlight how globalization continuously unfolds as an ongoing process (Lewellen 2002). The flows in circulation involve goods, technologies, ideas, people and economic capital moving in all directions, and – as Inda and Rosaldo (2002) stress – not merely from the West to the rest, but also between peripheral destinations. I see some advantages in the broad, all-purpose conceptualization of globalization: its semantic vagueness and all-inclusiveness encapsulates very accurately the dynamic of local complaints against global processes. Globalization here could be regarded as responsible for all kinds of disaffections with the world order; it is easily transformed into a category of blame, one that is more effective when it is deliberately maintained as all-encompassing and ill-defined as possible. As we shall see in the ethnographic cases presented in this volume, local critiques of globalization exploit this semantic imprecision to its limits.

Cosmopolitanism, too, encapsulates different and contradictory political positions, attitudes and involvements (see Werbner 2006). Those who practise it are not necessarily the same as those who preach it or those who are labelled 'cosmopolitans' (Werbner 1999; Vertovec and Cohen 2002: 5). And those who resist it, the 'counter-cosmopolitans' (Appiah 2007), often advocate their opposition in terms of alternative, but equally cosmopolitan, visions; they frequently treat cosmopolitanism as a condition comparable to globalization, associated with the emergence of a global, rootless culture and mass consumerism (see Vertovec and Cohen 2002: 9–10). While some can view cosmopolitanism as 'an emancipatory project', offering liberation from 'the collective and the categorical' (Rapport 2006, 2007: 225), others feel threatened by its transformative potential or detest those who are trying to enforce it. I argue here that cosmopolitanism can be realized both through 'living together with difference' (Werbner 2008: 2) and also while consuming it, sometimes in a top-down manner (Hannerz 2004), without really establishing roots or sharing a commitment. As with globalization, the all-inclusiveness of the term inspires critical remarks, arguments and resistance. Once more, local critics make full use of the uncertainty surrounding cosmopolitanism's definition and turn it to their advantage. In this volume, we are particularly interested in this flexible and vague local use of the term, which is stretched beyond its refined academic treatment.

In local conversation, globalization is often closely associated with westernization and neoliberalism (Eriksen 2003), and cosmopolitanism with global governance (Hannerz 2004). These associations capture the imagination of local critics, who make the most of the broad semantic possibilities provided by these two terms and chart their ideological and political subversion, that is, anti-globalization and counter-cosmopolitanism. The authors of this process, the everyday life critics of politics and power, benefit from the wider global awareness that is fostered by globalization and cosmopolitanism themselves; and so do their ensuing critiques. In their interpretations of injustice and inequality in the world, local critics set the parameters for imagining a broader community of many others who feel the same kind of discontent.

Imagining a Community in Discontent

An emancipatory force in globalization, argues Arjun Appadurai (1996, 2001), is the work of imagination in social life. Appadurai extends Benedict Anderson's (1983) notion of the 'imagined community' to one that encompass the challenges and the abundance of information made available by an increasingly globalized world. He talks about 'imagined worlds' – a level of imagining more global than 'imagined communities' – which result from a variety of historically constituted imaginations. Some (more particular) imagined worlds are set in opposition 'to the imagined worlds of the official mind and the entrepreneurial mentality that surrounds them' (Appadurai 1996: 33); such are the imagined worlds of our anthropological respondents in this volume, those discontented with the global status quo, those who are simply critically predisposed and those who wish to subvert other, more established, imagined worlds perceived as powerful, unjust and imposed from the outside or from above.

In the same manner that the citizens of the nation imagine many others like them sharing similar cultural ideals – a process described by Anderson (1983) – the disenfranchised around the globe sometimes imagine themselves as parts of a larger community in discontent. They imagine that they share their unhappiness about contemporary global politics with other individuals in the world who are equally dissatisfied with the dominant Western civilization order or its neoliberal cosmopolitan representatives. And they visualize those sympathizers as inhabiting their very own or parallel (but comparable) communities of discontent. This is how sometimes symbolic alliances are redrawn between groups that are culturally diverse or separated by previous disagreements and ideological polarities.

It is in this respect that the imagined community of the discontented is paradoxically globalized in its own imagination. It is in fact the growth of the opportunities provided by globalization that has engendered the possibility for its own critique: along with cosmopolitan awareness comes the imagination of a world that does not comply with the established parameters of the existing global order. A growing global awareness, here, sustains an intensification of global discontent and its multiple – but increasingly interconnected, reciprocally encouraged – expressions. The very technologies that have facilitated the global flow of ideas also provide the inspiration for conceiving and articulating an anti-globalization critique at the global scale. Within this critique the partnership of those in discontent slowly emerges as a growing community with its own worldwide consciousness, an 'imagined world' in Appadurai's words.

We have so far stressed the link between an increasing global awareness and an increasing global discontent, but we do not, by any means, suggest that a unified, homogenizing process is at play here. Critical stances on globalization in principle object to homogenization. They emerge from culturally specific understandings of global processes

– local versions of global awareness – and represent the views of communities that imagine the world differently. Disenfranchised actors around the world prefer to imagine global discontent in locally meaningful terms. And their imagination – inspired by local histories and the politics of everyday life – matters. Imagination in the globalized world is no longer the prerogative of leaders, artists, elite cosmopolitans or ritual practitioners, explains Appadurai; it is a social process at the hands of ordinary people (Appadurai 1996: 5, 31).

With his appreciation of imagination as a social practice, Appadurai (1996), more than any other theorist of globalization, has facilitated our conceptualization of the community of the discontented. But, despite the insightfulness of his approach, I feel compelled to depart from it in two critical respects. The first regards Appadurai's focus on the various 'landscapes' of globalization – ethnoscapes, mediascapes, technoscapes, financescapes, ideoscapes – which I see as redirecting analytical attention to surface phenomena. Like other examples of theorizing in terms of landscapes (see Abramson 2000), the risk here lies with taking too lightly those deeply embedded relationships of power. Dwelling too much on the landscapes of global disjuncture can have such unwelcome consequences. As Lewellen pinpoints, Appadurai's emphasis on fragmentation miscalculates the intricate connections between various fragmented parts: 'what appears on the surface as disorganisation, disjuncture, fragmentation, and postmodern chaos is really quite systematic if we take the time to understand the larger system' (Lewellen 2002: 98; see also Friedman 1994: 211).

My second point of departure concerns Appadurai's view that globalization does not encourage its own criticism (Appadurai 2001: 4). This Appadurai attributes to 'a growing disjuncture between the globalization of knowledge and the knowledge of globalization' (Appadurai 2001: 4, 14). I am inclined to agree that globalization as a primarily apolitical flow of ideas and goods does not directly promote an awareness of global power and inequality. But at the same time it is not difficult to see that some of the ideas in circulation might have political consequences when they reach certain widely distributed audiences. As I have explained already, it is the global awareness promoted by globalization that has inspired the imagining of resisting communities and has enabled the spread of anti-globalization. In other words, despite the denial of political responsibility by the technologies that sustain the global flow, the knowledge in circulation and the mechanisms of circulation make possible the development of unexpected (and potentially anti-hegemonic and anti-homogenizing) political orientations (see Gledhill, this volume).

Cosmopolitan Counter-cosmopolitans

It is in the very nature of globalization that the complaints against it often assume global proportions. With the breaking down of communication barriers, Gledhill observes, global inequalities become visible enough to inspire transnational networks both between North and South, and between different communities in the South (2004: 343–44). But Gledhill also points to a second parallel possibility: soon after their birth, the networks assisted by the technologies of globalization become subject to re-colonization by 'the agencies of neoliberal global governmentality' (ibid.: 344). In these paradoxical circumstances, which give rise not only to the critique but also to the proliferation of neoliberal capitalism, ethnically and socially diverse communities, unhappy with the dominant cosmopolitics, develop an acknowledgement of their common position vis-à-vis a Western, 'universalist' point of view. Their discontent gives rise to a silent recognition of other peripheral people's introversion and closure, an acknowledgement of the universal community of those feeling discontented.

The recognition of parallel grounds for dissatisfaction among the universal community of the disenfranchised entails a degree of appreciation or respect for other cultures, an appreciation that can potentially develop out of the same political predicament, a shared sense of being dispossessed. In this type of anti-cosmopolitanism we can observe a certain degree of cosmopolitan empathy.

Hannerz (2004) has identified two faces of cosmopolitanism: its aesthetic, intellectual, consumerist dimension (a cosmopolitanism with a happy face); and its critical, political dimension (a cosmopolitanism with a worried face). The ethnographic cases presented in this volume testify that political cosmopolitanism is often seriously concerned with its counterpart, the aesthetic and consumerist cosmopolitanism. Peripheral actors in discontent target in their critique the neoliberal, global face of cosmopolitanism (its happy, apolitical face). And, along with this they attack older and recent cosmopolitan elites, those who are perceived to benefit from its commoditized artefacts, able to afford its acquired tastes, travel and consume other cultures (see also Hannerz 2004; Vertovec and Cohen 2002). Suspected of collaboration with established hierarchies of power, consumerist cosmopolitanism and the consuming cosmopolitan elites both become subjected to the critical scrutiny of political cosmopolitanism.

Appiah (2007) starts his chapter on 'the counter-cosmopolitans' with a portrait of a new (but somewhat unfamiliar to the Western audience) global community: They are young, he writes, and use the Internet; they resist Western consumerism, nationalism and traditional local allegiances; they aspire to make the world a better place; but, as Appiah explains, *they* are not the heirs of Cynic philosophy but members of the *Ummah*, the community of the faithful. 'They are young, global Muslim fundamentalists' (Appiah 2007: 138), some of them American, others children of Algerian immigrants in France, and most of them communicate with their global comrades in English. Like Christian fundamentalists, with whom they share the same anti-cosmopolitan world view, they do not plan to kill anybody or participate in any terrorist act (Appiah 2007: 137–40). They are first and foremost dissatisfied with the predominance of a Western, cosmopolitan ethos in the global world.

The community of young, Muslim, transnational counter-cosmopolitans, sketched by Appiah, represents a more privileged – paradoxically cosmopolitan – orientation of discontent in the Islamic world. Other, more ordinary, everyday actors in Indonesia, whose lives and mundane responsibilities confine them to well-circumscribed local contexts, share, when the opportunity permits, some similar worries. When they do find the time, they read *Sabili*, a widely circulated, fortnightly magazine, authored by the supporters of a Muslim political party (see Watson, this volume). *Sabili* contains articles with strong anti-Western views, which include a variety of recurring topics, such as the dangers posed by westernization, the consequences of Western intervention in Iraq, and the threat of Zionism or Christian missionary activity for the Muslim world.

The authors of *Sabili*, like Appiah's counter-cosmopolitans, have a strong awareness of the links (and IT networks) uniting Muslim communities at the global level, but the rhetorical thrust of their articles is targeting a local audience with an unwavering Muslim consciousness. In this respect, as Watson (in this volume) vividly describes, they are preaching to the converted, the ordinary reader who will briefly engage with the content of the magazine and agree, shake their head, 'mutter a religious quotation or two, and go about their everyday business in no way changed'. Many in Indonesia, those who are less or more religious, will understand (if not necessarily agree with) the nature of the discontent articulated in the pages of *Sabili*. This understanding is dependent upon an awareness of the local context: contextualizing local views 'within an international political moment, within an evolving national history and within a variety of local discourses', Watson argues, could help 'us' (anthropologists, westerners, subjects of the Enlightenment) to understand too.

Other groups in the Islamic world share a more confrontational vision of discontent. Ian Edgar and David Henig (this volume) pay careful attention to the Islamic night dream culture and its use as a global medium of mobilization by militant Islam. In contrast to the dream interpretation that conforms to the Western, Freudian psychoanalytic tradition (which focuses on lived experiences from the past), dreams in

Islam are interpreted as being mostly about the future, as being a way of divination. Particular dream motifs unravel the belief in a shared visionary world, which brings the believers of the past closer to the believers of the present, the mythical reality closer to mundane, everyday life. In this manner, dreams in Islam can transcend the dimensions of time and unite different Islamic groups across the Islamic world.

From the Philippines to West Africa, Edgar and Henig argue, dreams provide a uniting thread that can mobilize the community of Islam. It is in this respect that prophetic dreams can work as a global Islamic language, an inspiration for imagining a worldwide Islamic community. For militant Islam, the inner imagined unity of the Islamic dreamworlds works as another global communication medium, which, along with the contemporary technologies of globalization, facilitates the spread of ideas that put under critical perspective the dominant Western civilizational order. This is how, in the course of their anti-globalization critique, militant Muslim counter-cosmopolitans rely on a cosmopolitan brotherhood of believers, who share similar critical subjectivities and a similar relationship of mediation between dreams and political action.

We can trace similar paradoxes of cosmopolitan counter-cosmopolitanisms in less confrontational and less explicitly politicized contexts. `Angels Trias i Valls (in this volume) focuses on a rural town in Japan, 'a seemingly harmonious place', which came into existence recently after the merging of neighbouring villages under one administrative authority. The town includes two different types of residents: the older inhabitants of the area, people who have struggled in the past to attain the benefits of modernity; and a number of more recent arrivals, Japanese citizens from diverse backgrounds who seek a rural way of life as an antidote to the ills of modernity and globalization. The latter were welcomed in the town, supposedly because they would enhance its cosmopolitan ethos, but, ironically, the ideological orientation of the newcomers is counter-cosmopolitan in perspective: they maintain an explicitly critical view of entrepreneurial economic activities and a strong inclination towards anti-globalization.

'We came here to find a place away from the modern Japanese obsession with moneymaking, to return to a more sustainable living,' the counter-cosmopolitan respondents of Trias i Valls clarify. Discontented with the 'evils' of the global society, they look towards their organic gardens and reject consumerist values. At the same time, however, they maintain a cosmopolitan empathy for other destitute and underprivileged subjects and, in comparison with the indigenous majority in the town, a more enduring tolerance of difference. This example can help us appreciate, as Trias i Valls points out, how different discourses about agency and political power can merge in the same town, and how local attitudes towards cosmopolitanism and globalization cannot be reduced to a single one-dimensional narrative about (Japanese) identity. Even within the same locality we can see a cosmopolitan context with counter-cosmopolitan orientations that include, in their ideological articulation, some cosmopolitan points of view.

Cosmopolitics and Disbelief

From the point of view of its critiques in the periphery, cosmopolitanism, like globalization, can be regarded as a form of domination, 'a burden for ordinary people' (Hannerz 2004: 74). Although many ordinary people are forced by necessity – migration, or life in a multi-ethnic homeland – to become cosmopolitans (Appiah 2007), cosmopolitanism, when it is approached in a critical manner (especially in everyday conversation), is dissociated from its concrete representatives (people seen as cosmopolitans) and is treated as a condition rather than a political philosophy (Vertovec and Cohen 2002: 9–12). It is then that ordinary people address the condition of cosmopolitanism – reifying it in a manner similar to globalization – and denounce its neoliberal corollaries.

In her contribution to this volume, Goddard sheds some light on the nature of dissatisfaction with neoliberal cosmopolitics. Her chapter focuses on Argentina at two different, but comparable, points of time: the economic crisis at the beginning of the twentieth century, and the recent crisis at the beginning of the twenty-first. She looks at the dynamic social history of Argentina, the early encouragement of European migration, the ensuing multiculturalism and social inequalities, the infiltration of foreign capital as one empire (US) replaced another (UK). Goddard also considers the economic problems, the discrepancies in wealth and the development of parallel types of cosmopolitanism: that of the bourgeoisie, who could afford long visits to Paris, and that of the workers in the multicultural, impoverished, urban neighbourhoods. She also traces the growth of two parallel anti-cosmopolitanisms, a nationalist one (with racist, xenophobic or simply populist elements) and a radical one (which targeted the growing economic empire of the US). Goddard puts side by side the early discontents, such as terrorist attacks on North American banks, with contemporary reactions to globalization and the new cosmopolitanism of 'boundary-less' identities.

In 2001 the images of discontent were epitomized by armoured vehicles in the streets, angry demonstrators outside banks and long queues outside embassies. There was disillusionment with local leaders and global institutions (such as the IMF), anger directed against the banks and anti-American graffiti on the walls (written in English). The country was in disarray, its citizens were vulnerable and powerless, their confidence in the most fundamental (neoliberal) economic values was fading away. The emerging discontent was mixed with an emerging sense of powerlessness, an 'acute awareness of the slippery quality of truth, of certainty, of what one might have taken for granted' (Goddard, this volume). Faced with unexpected circumstances like these, the victims of the crisis in Argentina looked beyond the sterile, mechanical explanation provided by economic rationality. 'The difference between Latin Americans and the citizens of Northern liberal democracies', Gledhill has argued, 'is that the former are less inclined to suspend their disbelief about the way power actually works' (1999: 209). There are many similar examples in other peripheral contexts.

In Greece for example, we see a consistent and widespread disbelief in cosmopolitan and multicultural politics and a strong sympathy for anti-globalization (Kirtsoglou and Theodossopoulos, this volume). In everyday conversation, as this unravels itself in urban contexts, many in Greece discuss international politics and the involvement of the powerful in those politics. During such conversations, our Greek respondents do not hesitate to move beyond previously established rivalries. The Turks, the significant others of the Greeks (see Theodossopoulos 2007a), but also other people of the Middle East, who are discussed in terms of prejudiced and patronizing criteria during other conversations, are now approached with a cosmopolitan empathy that contradicts earlier stereotypes.

When the topic of conversation focuses on the power of the United States and its allies, or more specifically the Western military interventions in the Muslim world, our respondents in Greece look towards an alternative, 'culturally intimate' audience (Herzfeld 1997), one that includes those who can understand politics from a point of view that does not conform with the official explanation of events by the West. The people of the Balkan and Middle Eastern periphery – the lands with a long history that is a not, strictly speaking, a Western European history – are perceived as sharing such an understanding. These are the same people who are traditionally seen as enemies, bad neighbours or points of reference in negative categorizations (see Brown and Theodossopoulos 2004); but, in the 'analogical thinking' (Sutton 1998) of many Greeks, history is reworked in the present, and the present is evaluated in terms of the past. The cosmopolitan allegiances of our respondents, Kirtsoglou and I argue, are historically constituted, and their particular histories recommend caution and disbelief towards the politics of the powerful.

Reaching Out to the World

In their chapter in this volume, Strathern and Stewart identify a tendency among people who see themselves as peripheral to reach out towards the wider community of the disadvantaged. This, they argue, is 'an outward movement of thought and action tending towards a universalism of identification with peoples in parallel positions to oneself around the world'. This identification can inspire knowledge about how to pursue certain advantages from the wider world, or even encourage the development of arguments and practices that combine the rhetoric of indigenous identities with cosmopolitan traits. In Taiwan, for example, members of the indigenous Austronesian tribes – a small minority that pre-dates waves of subsequent colonization from China – reclaim their distinct cultural identities through a cosmopolitan awareness 'strongly geared to local interests'. Some Austronesian speakers would not hesitate to use Google Earth to validate their land claims, trace connections with other Austronesian groups outside Taiwan or use the Internet to advertise locally produced artefacts. Their brand of cosmopolitanism – representing the point of view of a very small minority – seeks out recognition and support by turning to the wider world and using it to the advantage of the local community (Strathern and Stewart, this volume).

There are similar examples from other parts of the world in which indigenous groups engage with the international community in such a confident manner. The Kayapo in Brazil have not hesitated to use audio-visual technologies, not merely to record their own cultural practices, but also to safeguard land rights and achieve wider political representation (see Turner 1992, 2002). The use of videos has served 'such an outreach function', Terence Turner explains, by creating links with non-Kayapo publics (2002: 238). What is interesting to note here is the confidence of the Kayapo in the advantages of becoming known to an international audience; their belief that the global community can provide them with assistance in their struggle against state agencies and those who want to extract the resources of their land, including fellow Kayapo who selfishly collaborate with developers (Turner 2002).

In Panama, several Embera communities are breaking away from a long-established tradition of avoiding European penetration (Kane 2004, Williams 2005), and are now welcoming contact with Western tourists. Like the Astronesian speakers in Taiwan, the Embera construct artefacts, using both strictly traditional patterns and more innovative designs, and select aspects of their indigenous culture to present to Western visitors in carefully controlled cultural presentations – for example, dance, music, knowledge about the medicinal properties of plants. When opportunity permits, some Embera communities do not hesitate to engage with tourism on a full-time basis, but in a manner that ensures a certain degree of control over the tourism exchange. Other, less fortunate communities in inaccessible locations resent their inability to attract a flow of tourists and struggle to learn the secrets of the tourist economy (Theodossopoulos 2007b, 2009).

The development of this 'touristy' type of indigenous cosmopolitanism is directly linked with the desire of a global audience to consume images of indigenous culture. Similar responses from around the world – in Vanuatu (Tilley 1997), in Indonesia, in Africa and in the Middle East (Bruner 2005) – show how local communities respond to a globalized type of consumerist exoticism. In many cases, they succeed in their response, turning the interaction to their own advantage. The consumption of indigenous images by global audiences enhances the visibility of peripheral minorities and provides – as in the cases of the Embera and the Astronesians of Taiwan – opportunities for claiming rights or achieving a certain degree of political representation. In other cases, and especially when the local community is deprived of control over the tourist exchange, the local actors end up feeling disenfranchised, and complain that their culture has been appropriated or taken away (see Kirtsoglou and Theodossopoulos 2004).

Under such circumstances, local actors feel puzzled, estranged, betrayed by the illusive promises of neoliberal capitalism. This is 'a capitalism that presents itself as the gospel of salvation; a capitalism that if rightly harnessed, is invested with the capacity wholly to transform the universe of the marginalized and disempowered' (Comaroff and Comaroff 2001: 2). Failure to do so brings disenchantment with the attractions of the neoliberal world economy, and so the rationality of the global market is challenged by the spread of innovative occult practices, such as the endeavour to conjure wealth or the attempt to produce an explanation for its accumulation (ibid.: 2, 19). The Comaroffs name several types of occult economic activity: pyramid schemes; email divination; prosperity gospel denominations; and fee-for-service religious movements (ibid.: 20–24). They represent economies of the occult and proliferate in the age of Millennial Capitalism (ibid.).

We have seen older, but similar, practices in the highlands of New Guinea, where cargo cults attempted to turn difficult-to-explain global changes to local benefit. The red box money cult found around Mount Hagen involved a certain degree of reordering of the local moral universe to incorporate the political processes of the white people and their material wealth (Strathern and Stewart, this volume). New, exogenous symbols were integrated into the local cosmology to account for the awareness of the wider world: the local ancestors turned into trans-local spirits of the wind able to travel (like aeroplanes) to the capital; a female leader (reconfigured as 'Queen') replaced male figures of authority; red boxes from Chinese trade stores (the containers of goods from the world outside) were transformed into objects of ritual activity (Strathern and Stewart, this volume). Similar movements, in other parts of the Papua New Guinea, involved attempts to redefine the origins of humanity in local terms by incorporating white people – as descendants of ancestral kin – into the local cosmology.[2]

Such 'mythopoetic constructions of solidarity and affinity with perceived centres of wealth and power', explain Strathern and Stewart, can be seen as responses to everyday life changes imposed from the outside – including the introduction of new technologies (for example computers, mobile phones and television) – and a growing awareness of the local community's interconnection with and dependence on a wider world. As I highlighted in the previous sections, some of the complex ways of adjusting to these new challenges involve the work of imagination and an attempt to make a connection with a universe of parallel subjectivities among the disadvantaged. They represent examples of peripheral and disenfranchised communities in discontent, which are reaching out to the world and are sometimes rewarded, while at other times they are not.

Resistance in Discontent

The stronger parties in the global power constellation prefer to underestimate local resistance movements by labelling them – in a convenient and patronizing manner – as pathological. According to this treatment, 'systemic effects of global transformation', including dissatisfaction and resistance, are sorted out (or ignored) as anomalies, pathologies 'rooted in purely local conditions' (Gledhill 1999: 201–2). This attitude, Gledhill explains, perpetuates an 'old North Atlantic habit of projecting perceptions of internal crisis onto an eternally "othered" periphery' (ibid.: 246). In his chapter in this volume, Gledhill focuses on subaltern versions of cosmopolitanism and movements that challenge neoliberal globalization in Brazil and Mexico. The new subaltern cosmopolitan visions that emerge, he argues, are still deeply entangled in global relations of power, but they do have the potential to diverge from established cosmopolitics in new and unpredictable ways. It is this unexpected element in local discontent that presents challenges to the structures that sustain hierarchies of class, race and gender in Latin America (Gledhill, this volume).

Gledhill's view of counter-cosmopolitan movements strikes a balance between the appreciation of local imagination and creativity, on the one hand, and the awareness of the constraints set by the global distribution of power, on the other. The first is important if we aspire not to underestimate the agency of our resisting respondents and their capacity to recombine old ideas in new forms and sometimes to challenge the status quo in surprising ways. As Ortner insightfully puts it, 'resistance can be more than opposition, can be truly creative and transformative' (1995: 191). But an acknowledgement of the limitations set by the broader distribution of power is equally fundamental if we do not wish to lose sight of the histories that inspire the imagination of our discontented respondents, the wider social processes that mould their world views, their political consciousness and the meaningfulness of their protest.

To achieve the balance mentioned above is not an easy task – especially when the researcher is overwhelmed by the resourceful expressions of discontent at the local level. Very often, capturing the logic of the local response, however accurate that is, entails the danger of de-emphasizing the connections with the wide-ranging hierarchies of power. James Scott (1985) provides us with a classic example of that type when he describes in detail the mechanics of a subculture of indirect opposition. His discontented respondents in Malaysia employ a number of everyday tactics – weapons of the weak – to undermine the power of their landlords.[3] Inspired by classic anthropological fieldwork, Scott, a political scientist, charted on the academic map the local dynamics of routine and non-dramatic confrontation; he sketched the pragmatic rationality of actors resisting at the local level and their 'hidden transcripts', an off-stage critique of the powerful (Scott 1990).

Nevertheless, and despite the accomplishments described above, Scott's close emphasis on the instrumental rationality of indirect resistance hides from our view the extent to which context-specific responses (and their logics) are shaped by broader (or more difficult to observe) processes. These include, to mention only a few, participation in organized popular movements, the lessons of personal histories, the authority of nationalized histories and the colonization (or recolonization) of subaltern consciousness. As Gledhill has argued, it is hard to identify 'spaces of subaltern social life that are completely uncolonised by power relations' (Gledhill 1994: 68).

It is in such terms that the concept of resistance poses a number of problems that are difficult to solve. How much (direct or indirect) opposition qualifies as recognizable resistance? How conscious does this opposition have to be? To what extent does resistance reproduce, or work against, the structures of domination? Bearing these difficulties in mind, Ortner (1995) emphasizes the ambiguous character of the notion, its social and political complexity. In a rather similar manner, Keesing (1992) identifies its metaphorical properties, its imprecision and idealized associations. The conceptual prototype of resistance, he clarifies, communicates the concrete image of pushing against a physical force, a power encroaching upon the human body, an imposing burden that one wishes to expel or drive back (ibid.: 219). This and similar concrete images – e.g. comrades standing united at the barricades – foster an irresistible romanticized identification with the subaltern other and a proclivity to essentialize domination and resistance. In most cases, resisting groups engage in less dramatic confrontation; they uphold many and diverse motives, sometimes hidden from one another, which are deeply embedded in social life. 'If the concept of resistance is to serve us well,' Keesing maintains, 'it will have to be through its flexibility and metaphoric richness, not its analytical precision' (ibid.: 6).

In this respect, then, the concept of resistance shares the same imprecision of definition with globalization and cosmopolitanism. As Kirtsoglou argues (in this volume), 'social actors around the world "resist", but not essentially to the same events, not necessarily for the same reasons, and invariably not in the same manner'. In the context of informal, local discourse about politics, the semantic imprecision of several core concepts – such as resistance, anti-globalization, counter-cosmopolitanism – has many advantages: it allows space for an impressive amount of argumentative combinations that articulate diverse kinds of dissatisfaction, as well as the freedom to engage in new and unusual types of opposition. It also allows for the possibility of resisting globalization and cosmopolitanism and imagining their subversion in global and cosmopolitan terms.

One Step Closer to Understanding Anti-global Discontent

In this volume we have taken the first steps towards an anthropology that focuses on the views of local actors unhappy with the dominant visions of globalization and cosmopolitanism. We trace such views of discontent in marginal contexts, when local communities attempt to address global processes, and, in particular, when local actors express their deep concern about power, justice and injustice in the global order. We also recognize that the emerging local critique has been facilitated by the flow of ideas and the cosmopolitan ethos that sustains globalization – that is, by the very source of the expressed discontent. In this respect, the local critique of globalization and cosmopolitanism is intimately connected with a growing global and cosmopolitan awareness.

It is, in fact, this growing awareness of the globalized world that has enabled the possibility of imagining a wider community in discontent. This particular type of imagining is authored by communities on the peripheries of global power, by social actors who see themselves as sharing similar predicaments with other disenfranchised and unhappy people. United by the same aversion to neoliberal cosmopolitan globalization, they perceive themselves as able to see a truth that is obvious to the dispossessed, but is left out of the discourses of the powerful. These same disenchanted actors situate themselves within imagined global communities of discontent, 'imagined worlds' (Appadurai 1996) that are set in opposition to global forces and cosmopolitan elites.

Resistance within these emerging imagined worlds is not always explicit, and takes many unprecedented and unpredictable forms, but it is also deeply rooted in cultural meaning and informed by local understandings of historical causality. As such, the resulting communities of discontent represent historically constituted reactions to the prevailing versions of global justice. Their subversive cosmopolitanisms, despite their unpredictability, remain intertwined in global relations of power (Gledhill, this volume), and very often are pervaded by an awareness of power imbalances. Then, in the pursuit of new global interconnections, particular disenfranchised communities reach out to the world, wishing to share global goods or seeking new alliances against the status quo (Strathern and Stewart, this volume), and, very often, retain a remarkable confidence in the idea that potential allies exist within other, similarly disenfranchised, communities. The imagined worlds that emerge out of such views make available, in turn, new allegiances of resistance.

The protagonists of the ethnography presented in the following chapters have limited resources and, in most cases, are aware of their own disempowerment. Their idiosyncratic versions of counter-cosmopolitanism make possible unpredictable rhetorical partnerships and forge new cosmopolitan connections; their anti-global sentiments are permeated by an alternative empathy towards others imagined as oneself; their pointed remarks and critical spirit appear persuasive in the context of everyday life, but do not reach far beyond local conversation. Having recognized the failure of such views to enter into official discourse, the contributors to this book felt compelled to look at them carefully and investigate their social history. In the chapters that follow we begin this task by putting into use the skills of the anthropologist's trade: by registering the complaints of our respondents, spending time with them and listening to their views, we have come, step by step, closer to understanding their discontent.

Notes

1. The use of such an organic analogy is also reminiscent of an older anthropology inspired by Durkheim and Radcliffe-Brown, an approach determined to take social phenomena at face value. Non-specialist discourse has caught up with this older anthropology, and has become sociologically sophisticated in its desire to confront and analyse wider political and social processes.
2. Strathern and Stewart (this volume) refer to Brutti's (2000) work on the Okspmin.
3. They use slander, rumours and malicious gossip (versions of what Scott calls character assassination), foot-dragging, pilfering and numerous other, often anonymous, minor acts of insubordination.

References

Abramson, A. 2000. Mythical Land, Legal Boundaries: Wondering about Landscape and Other Tracts. In A. Abramson and D. Theodossopoulos (eds) *Land, Law and Environment*. London: Pluto, pp. 1–30.

Anderson, B. 1983. *Imagined Communities: Reflections on the Origins and Spread of Nationalism*. London: Verso.

Appadurai, A. 1996. *Modernity at Large: Cultural Dimensions of Globalization*. Minneapolis: University of Minnesota Press.

——— 2001. Grassroots Globalization and the Research Imagination. In A. Appadurai (ed.) *Globalization*. Durham, N.C: Duke University Press, pp. 1–21.

Appiah, K.A. 2007. *Cosmopolitanism: Ethics in a World of Strangers*. New York: Norton.

Brown, K.S. and D. Theodossopoulos. 2004. Others' Others: Talking about Stereotypes and Constructions of Otherness in Southeast Europe. *History and Anthropology*, 15 (1), 3–14.

Bruner, E.M. 2005. *Culture on Tour: Ethnographies of Travel*. Chicago: University of Chicago Press.

Brutti, L. 2000. Afek's Last Son: Integrating Change in a Papua New Guinean Cosmology. *Ethnohistory*, 47 (1), 101–111.

Comaroff, J and J.L. Comaroff. 2001. Millennial Capitalism: First Thoughts on a Second Coming. In J. Comaroff and J.L. Comaroff (eds) *Millennial Capitalism and the Culture of Neoliberalism*. Durham, N.C: Duke University Press, pp. 1–56.

Eriksen, T.H. 2003. Introduction. In T.H. Eriksen (ed.) *Globalization: Studies in Anthropology*. London: Pluto, pp. 1–17.

Fernandez, J.W. 1986. *Persuasions and Performances: the Play of Tropes in Culture*. Bloomington: Indiana University Press.

Friedman, J. 1994. *Cultural Identity and Global Process*. London: Sage.

Hannerz, U. 2004. 4. Cosmopolitanism. In D. Nugent and J. Vincent (eds) *A Companion to the Anthropology of Politics*. Oxford: Blackwell, pp. 69–85.

Herzfeld, M. 1997. *Cultural Intimacy; Social Poetics in the Nation State*. New York: Routledge.

Inda, J.X. and R. Rosaldo. 2002. Introduction: a World in Motion. In J.X. Inda and R. Rosaldo (eds) *The Anthropology of Globalization: a Reader*. Oxford: Blackwell, pp. 1–34.

Gledhill, J. 1994. *Power and its Disguises: Anthropological Perspectives on Politics*. London: Pluto Press.

――― 1999. Official Masks and Shadow Powers: Towards an Anthropology of the Dark Side of the State. *Urban Anthropology*, 28 (3–4), 199–251.

――― 2004. Neoliberalism. In D. Nugent and J. Vincent (eds) *A Companion to the Anthropology of Politics*. Oxford: Blackwell, pp. 332–48.

Kane, S.C. 2004. *The Phantom Gringo Boat*. Christchurch, New Zealand: Cybereditions Corp.

Keesing, R.M. 1992. *Custom and Confrontation: The Kwaio Struggle for Cultural Autonomy*. Chicago: University of Chicago Press.

Kirtsoglou, E. and D. Theodossopoulos. 2004. 'They are Taking our Culture Away': Tourism and Culture Commodification in the Garifuna Community of Roatan. *Critique of Anthropology*, 24 (2), 135–57.

Lewellen, T.C. 2002. *The Anthropology of Globalization: Cultural Anthropology Enters the 21st Century*. Westport: Bergin and Garvey.

Ortner, S.B. 1995. Resistance and the Problem of Ethnographic Refusal. *Comparative Studies in Society and History*, 37 (1), 173–93.

Rapport, N. 2006. Anthropology as a Cosmopolitan Study. *Anthropology Today*, 22 (1), 23–24.

――― 2007. A Cosmopolitan Turn? *Social Anthropology*, 15 (2), 223–35.

Scott, C.J. 1985. *Weapons of the Weak: Everyday Forms of Peasant Resistance*. New Haven: Yale University Press.

――― 1990. *Domination and the Arts of Resistance: Hidden Transcripts*. New Haven: Yale University Press.

Sutton, D. 1998. *Memories Cast in Stone: The Relevance of the Past in Everyday Life*. Oxford: Berg.

Tilley, C. 1997. Performing Culture in the Global Village. *Critique of Anthropology*, 17 (1), 67–89.

Theodossopoulos, D. 2007a. Introduction: The 'Turks' in the imagination of the 'Greeks'. In D. Theodossopoulos (ed.) *When Greeks Think about Turks: The View from Anthropology*. London: Routledge, pp. 1–32.

――― 2007b. Encounters with Authentic Embera Culture in Panama. *Journeys*, 8 (1–2), 93–115.

――― 2009. Tourism and Indigenous Culture as Resources: Lessons from the Embera Cultural Tourism in Panama. In J. Carrier and D. Macleod (eds) *Tourism, Power and Culture: Anthropological Perspectives*. Clevedon: Channel View.

Turner, T. 1992. Defiant Images: The Kayapo Appropriation of Video. *Anthropology Today*, 8 (6), 5–16.

――― 2002. Representation, Polyphony and the Construction of Power in a Kayapo Video. In K.B. Warren and J.E. Jackson (eds) *Indigenous Movements,*

Self-representation, and the State in Latin America. Austin: University of Texas Press, pp. 229–50.

Vertovec, S. and R. Cohen. 2002 (eds). *Conceiving Cosmopolitanism: Theory, Context and Practice*. New York: Oxford University Press.

Werbner, P. 1999. Global Pathways: Working Class Cosmopolitans and the Creation of Transnational Ethnic Worlds. *Social Anthropology,* 7 (1), 17–35.

——— 2006. Vernacular Cosmopolitanism. *Theory, Culture and Society,* 23 (2–3), 496–98.

——— 2008. Introduction: Towards a New Cosmopolitan Anthropology. In P. Werbner (ed.) *Anthropology and the New Cosmopolitanism: Rooted, Feminist and Vernacular Perspectives*. Oxford: Berg, pp.1–29.

Williams, C.A. 2005. *Between Resistance and Adaptation: Indigenous Peoples and the Colonisation of the Choco 1510–1753*. Liverpool: Liverpool University Press.

Chapter 2

SHIFTING CENTRES, TENSE PERIPHERIES: INDIGENOUS COSMOPOLITANISMS

Andrew Strathern and Pamela J. Stewart

Cosmopolitanism as a term of topical analysis in anthropology is in the air as we write this chapter (January 2007). Volume 47 (5) for May 2006 of the American Anthropological Association's *Anthropology News* (AN) has pieces on a cluster of themes under the heading of 'Global Networks': human rights, vernacular cosmopolitanism, cosmopolitanism and being digital, reimagining globality, neoliberalism, diasporic practices and the transnationalizing of care for refugee youths. A great mixture of issues is found together here, but the overall focus is on movement, change, the crossing of boundaries and the opportunities and dilemmas these crossings produce. Pnina Werbner, in her contribution to this AN array of short essays (Werbner 2006), identifies the mediating concept of 'vernacular cosmopolitanism', which joins together 'contradictory notions of local specificity and universal enlightenment' (ibid.: 7), and she notes challenges made to cosmopolitanism as an ideology of the metropolitan elites of the world. She also mentions work by Kwame Anthony Appiah, who argues for a cosmopolitan tolerance that is rooted in the realization that mixtures are a regular part of cultural processes and that conversations across cultural boundaries are normal ways of producing transformations (see, for example, Appiah 2006: 37).

Appiah is evidently concerned to propose a kind of cosmopolitan ethics of liberal tolerance, while other scholars are more concerned simply to identify cosmopolitanism as a phenomenon or set of phenomena. The universalizing ethical dimension in this debate goes back to Stephen Toulmin's identification and critique of the notion of the cosmopolis in European thought as a utopian ideal of universal rationality and social order (Toulmin 1990). Contemporary discussions, since Toulmin's work, follow to some extent his critical approach, adding to it their own viewpoints. Nigel Rapport, focusing on 'the supranational city', perhaps refers obliquely to Toulmin's discussion of cosmopolis (i.e., the 'world-city'), but goes on to link the notion of the contemporary cosmopolite to an open-ended notion of society that escapes the framework of the nation state (Rapport 2006).

In our chapter here, our focus is similar to the theme of Pnina Werbner's discussion of 'vernacular cosmopolitanism' as a set of phenomena, and we seek to link cosmopolitanism with indigeneity, in a way that shows how people do actually combine their local concerns with a sense of global outreach. Christal Whelan, in the AN issue referred to above, notes that, in her view, 'being cosmopolitan means having a sense of history and of place by virtue of which it is possible to appreciate what it means to be Other' (Whelan 2006: 8). Our chapter here follows the spirit of this observation also. Whelan further notes that digital technology, which gives such easy access to information on a global scale, needs to 'be embedded in a broader moral and spiritual universe' (ibid.: 8). This 'embeddedness' within a broader moral and spiritual universe is precisely what some indigenous movements seek to achieve, whether by means of digital technology, as many have begun to do, or without it.

Although, then, cosmopolitanism, with its aura of liberalism and multicultural tolerance, is sometimes contrasted with movements for indigeneity and the separate identities of peoples, this contrast ignores a number of complications, relating to the ambiguity of definitions inherent in centre/periphery models of the world. Even within these models, certain discontents of the 'periphery' with the perceived 'centre' can be identified as occurring at a number of levels, from the local level through to the level of the 'global order'. Such discontents, further, can produce a sense of parallel subjectivities among those who see themselves as disadvantaged. In a different modality, peripheralized peoples sometimes make mythopoetic constructions of solidarity and affinity with perceived centres of wealth and power, as happened in some of the social movements labelled as 'cargo cults' in New Guinea. Such claims can be seen as the aspirant cosmopolitanisms of the dispossessed.

In Taiwan, the indigenous Austronesian speakers have been successively colonized by European explorers, Han colonists from China, the Japanese and the Kuomintang refugees from the conflict with Communist forces in China in 1949. In recent years, however, their peripheralized position has been ideologically reversed, with the advent of a political move towards separatism in Taiwan. They are now sometimes seen as emblematic of Taiwan's 'difference' from the mainland of China, because they are regarded as the 'authentic' people of the land. They themselves, moreover, are using this new status to reach out internationally to cultural movements in other Austronesian-speaking areas in the Pacific, South-East Asia and the Philippines, connections which they further extend in terms of imputed shared aspects of history to North American Indian or Native American populations. Whether these cultural revival movements of the indigenous groups in Taiwan will successfully continue following the anticipated return to power of the Kuomintang Party in 2008 remains to be seen. Their cultural revival, or assertion of identity, is thus based on a kind of cosmopolitanism of indigeneity. They, like many other 'indigenous' groups, use the Internet as a means of pursuing their international projects. 'Cosmopolitanism', therefore, does not necessarily belong only to the multicultural metropolitan contexts of life. It has to been seen in broader terms, and we have to recognize the ways in which peoples of the periphery both express their discontents with the centre and work to redefine new centres in which their peripheral status can be overcome.

These peripheral claims to significance in terms of centres of power may embody two different strategies. In one, the periphery asserts its own 'difference from' the centre. From this strategy springs the impetus to assertions of local, regional and national levels of indigeneity. Indigeneity in this sense is opposed to assimilation into or mimesis of the 'core' or centre. The numerous movements for indigenous rights and identities around the world attest to the popularity of such a strategy. The second strategy, however, is to assert 'connection with' the centre in some privileged way. Such a strategy may in turn take the form of asserting that the periphery actually constitutes a centre of its own and is therefore a crucial part of an 'alternative cosmopolitanism'. Graeme Were's study of a Baha'i movement in New Ireland, Papua New Guinea, provides an example of this second strategy, as practised in the Nalik area, where Baha'i teachings of 'unification' were combined with a policy of permitting the local people to revive customary rituals earlier proscribed by Christian missionaries. The movement thus resembled a movement for 'indigeneity', but it also claimed a kind of cosmopolitanism, because its members in the year 2000 'made monetary donations to the Ark Fund so that their names would be placed in a purpose-built temple in Haifa, Israel, the spiritual centre of the Baha'i faith' (Were 2005: 671). Were goes on to note that the ultimate aim involved is the 'unification of the world under the leadership of the Baha'is' (ibid.). 'Unification' here is a specific version of cosmopolitan ideology. This New Ireland case, combining as it does an ideal of indigeneity with one of world unity, indicates that different versions of cosmopolitanism can emanate from perceived peripheries and stake claims on 'centres' outside their immediate localities.

Case studies from our extensive work in the Highlands of Papua New Guinea are included in this chapter, as well as materials from our work in

Taiwan, over the last seven years, among the Austronesian-speaking peoples, which we will discuss in terms of their 'cultural revival' movements, which model themselves on global motifs of 'indigenous activism', from locales such as the Philippines and North America, as noted earlier.

Peoples who perceive themselves or are perceived by others as belonging to peripheries are likely to develop particular stances towards the issue of cosmopolitanism, because in effect cosmopolitanism is usually seen as belonging to some central metropolis. For example, in parts of Scotland, London is often seen in this light, especially by adherents of the Scottish Nationalist Party, and this perception becomes the focus of counter-assertions of Scottish identity. Cairns Craig has explored this topic in the field of literature, noting a process analogous to that we have described for Papua New Guinea. Referring to the work of the literary critic Donald Davie, he notes that his writings, like those of poets whom he cites, 'have sought to combine the experimentalism of the cosmopolitans with the values of the nativists … each new venture leaning as far out as it dares from a high wire which is up in the air with the "cosmopolitans" and yet rooted in the earth of the "nativists"' (Craig 1996: 182). Craig develops a view that the most constant feature of such genres of writing is their 'in-between' character: between peripheries and centres, between English and Scottish ways of writing. Such a vision of the dual and complex character of peripheral identities provides yet another pathway to an 'alternative cosmopolitanism': the cosmopolitanism of hybridity, of belonging to more than one world. In developing this point here we shall further draw briefly on materials from our work in Scotland itself, and in County Donegal, Ireland, on the Ulster-Scots movement there (Strathern and Stewart 2005a).

All of our case study examples are relevant in one way or another to the now somewhat overworked topic of globalization. Globalized currents of influence across the world produce both opportunities and discontents: opportunities for creative participation in change, and discontents because of the inherent inequities of power and agency that are built into such opportunities. Neoliberalism in turn, as an ideology, tends to facilitate the unbalanced terms of exchange between indigenous peoples and the political and economic worlds around them. If they have resources of commercial value, more can be extracted from them than they can receive back. However, our cases from Papua New Guinea and Taiwan show how people ingeniously attempt to overcome or circumvent such inequities. Their resourceful strategies in doing so are constitutive of what we have called here indigenous cosmopolitanisms.

We begin with materials that may appear to be rather different from the usual pathways of discussion of cosmopolitanism, but are crucial to our concept of the cosmopolitanism of the dispossessed: the 'cargo cults' in

New Guinea, specifically in Mount Hagen, Papua New Guinea, prior to
Papua New Guinea's independence from Australia in 1975.

Movements of Change in Highlands Papua New Guinea: Attractions and Repulsions of the Global

Many of the ritualized movements of change in the recent history of the
people of Highlands Papua New Guinea and Irian Jaya (West Papua) have
encoded a complex awareness of how local ways of living were being
irrevocably and violently altered through a sudden and enforced
acquaintance with the outside world (for Highlands Papua New Guinea,
see, for example, Stewart and Strathern 2002; Strathern and Stewart 2000a,
2004). The ritualized responses to these pressing turbulences reveal the
same sort of ambivalence that appears to characterize contemporary
responses to cosmopolitanism on a wider scale. There is an attempt to
reach out and grasp the changes, turning them to local benefit. But there
is also a wary recognition of the danger to local integrity and identity that
is encountered in doing so. Which element predominates depends on the
historical stage and geographical location of those involved.

One of the contexts in which this ambivalence was enacted was the
rash of so-called cargo cult movements that sprang up across the
Highlands of Papua New Guinea following Australian colonial
explorations and pacification in the 1930s and 1940s. Subsequently, overt
cargo movements were replaced by the enthusiastic adoption of forms of
Christianity. Chronologically speaking, Christian evangelization began
from the earliest colonial times, and Christian practices have both
intermingled with, and been in competition with cargo movements, as
elsewhere in Papua New Guinea. In broader terms, both cargo
movements and Christianity have functioned as complex ways of
adjusting to changes. Cargo movements explicitly aimed to obtain access
to the wealth of outsiders by local ritual means, while Christianity, with its
promises of salvation from sin and heaven as a form of utopia, offered a
globalized and mediated vision of a similar kind. Christianity may appear
to people as a direct exemplification of universal values, offering itself as
a kind of cosmopolitan image, while cargo movements in the Highlands
offered themselves as a new means of attaining existing local values (this
point is discussed further in Strathern and Stewart 2009).

A recurrent feature of the imagery associated with social changes in
Highlands Papua New Guinea history is the prevalence of representations
of movement itself, the transgressive movement of entities and powers
across local places. Given that aircraft were involved early on in colonial
exploration, this is not surprising. Wind is the image often invoked. In the

Eastern Highlands, Ronald and Catherine Berndt noted the arrival of the idea of a strong wind (*zona tetei*) that was said to herald strange new events linked to the advent of Australian explorers, Christian missionaries and government officials (Berndt 1952).

This image of the wind as a vector of power, positive or negative, also emerges in the history of the red box money cult in Mount Hagen, dating from 1968 to 1971 (Strathen 1979–80; Stewart and Strathern 2000a). An important part of the imagery of this cult movement was that in it the ancestors, who were expected to provide wealth for its adherents in the form of state money, were renamed. Instead of being simply *kor wamb* (spirit people, in the local Melpa language), they were said to demand that they be addressed now as *köpkö wamb* (wind people). The meaning of this expression was that these local ancestors, like their latter-day descendants who travelled on planes, had now learned to fly down to the national capital on the southern coast, Port Moresby, and in so doing had obtained the secrets of the 'white' people's wealth. These cult adherents also organized themselves around a woman, married into their group, who was the sister of a local Member of the House of Assembly, which met on the coast in Port Moresby, and was the forerunner of the Parliament after Papua New Guinea became an independent nation in 1975. This woman was described as the Queen of the movement, and she was said to wear a wig that made her hair look like that of a white woman. The adherents held meetings in Port Moresby, at which they addressed the 'wind people', asking for guidance on how to secure wealth for themselves. The day when the boxes, supposedly full of money, were to be opened was marked by dancing in full regalia, and the female leader was the most elaborately decorated of all. When the boxes were opened and only stones and metal pieces were found inside them, the cult disbanded.

The 'red box' theme itself was a historical marker of patterns and processes of labour migration, since migrants from coastal plantation work, who brought goods back home for distribution among their kin, kept their treasures in wooden boxes, painted red, which they purchased in trade stores run by Chinese entrepreneurs. Boxes of this same kind became the focus of ritual activity in the local clan territories. Similarly, the idea of the ancestors travelling down to the capital city was derived from the actual pattern of people flying down to the capital for employment or to visit their kin employed there and, while there, solicit money and goods from them. All of this imagery, then, both reflects and calls upon the power of movement to realize hoped-for aims. The home place, Hagen, and its clan territories are seen as both peripheral to the new centre, Port Moresby, and at the same time central to the adherents' ritual activity. Red boxes come from far away, but are placed as central containers locally. A local woman is reconfigured as a Queen, adopting a persona from yet another faraway centre to which Papua New Guinea is linked through its early colonial history. Adherents lacking in access to wealth expect, or hope, to gain that access by establishing links with such centres, pulling the resources of the centre back into their local world. Even the movement's failure is registered in terms of a new substance: pieces of industrial metal from vehicles and mechanical equipment used to move things around on the introduced roads. Such an appropriation of images constitutes in micro an attempt by peoples newly peripheralized to gain access to resources in centres of power far beyond their own community boundaries. In embryo this pattern is the beginning of the scenario of the cosmopolitanism of the dispossessed.

Parallels to this narrative from Hagen in the 1960s can readily be found in the other areas of the Highlands (see, for example, Stewart and Strathern 2000b). A pervasive feature is the attempt to link indigenous mythology with introduced Christian narratives and theological schemes, and also thereby to create a sense of kinship with the incomers. This attempt most often takes the form of an assertion that the origins of humanity lie in the people's own local area. The 'whites', then, are said to descend from a brother of the original local founding ancestors, who migrated away from the area owing to some quarrel or disagreement with his siblings. A classic case of this syndrome is given in Lorenzo Brutti's account of changing notions of origin among the Oksapmin people (Brutti 2000).

According to Brutti, elders among the Oksapmin developed a new myth of origin in response to the arrival of the 'whites' and their possession of wealth and power in the late 1930s onward. The Oksapmin ancestress and culture creatrix Afek was now said to have had a youngest son, who was white, unlike her other sons, and it was unclear who his father was, so she placed him inside the great Sepik River and gave him many wealth goods as a compensation for his removal from the area. Since the white people were said to have declared that they came from the land of the Queen, a female figure, this Queen was now said to have been none other than Afek. And, when Christian missionaries came and said that the local people were their 'brothers and sisters', this impression of a historical kinship was further reinforced. Maybe, it was thought by some, the father of the 'whites' was God himself and perhaps Jesus was Afek's son (Brutti 2000: 101–11). These attempts at stitching together Christian and indigenous narratives of origin can all be seen as efforts to bridge or overcome social distance and to recreate a moral world of relationships. Since the 'whites' were kin, they should also share their wealth with the Oksapmin. The attempts were thus also attempts to annul new centre/periphery perceptions and to recentre the world on the Oksapmin themselves: once again, a kind of localized cosmopolitanism, turning the exogenous cosmopolitanism on its head.

Such efforts to incorporate the outside into the inside, coupled with fears of outside powers and influences, are also found in Christopher Ballard's discussion of Huli ideas about the Apocalypse around the year 2000. Ballard (2000: 218) reports how Seventh Day Adventists from the Tari Valley painted flat river pebbles placed in the earth mound of a grave site with references to historical disasters in European history along with citations of plagues and famines from the Bible, the Gulf War of 1992, and the possible unification of the Anglican and Catholic churches, as well as the unification of Europe in the European Union. The latter two prognostications were seen as signs of world unification and the impending return of Jesus, and were dampened down only by the failure of ecumenical efforts between Catholics and Anglicans and the rejection by the Danish people of the Maastricht Treaty with its proposals for further steps towards unification. Here we see, not a reaching out and appropriation, but a fear of the outside, a rejection of its cosmopolitanism and universalism and a desire to maintain local integrity.

In effect, these two types of response or reaction to knowledge of the outside represent two opposite poles of the same phenomenon, the sense of vulnerability created by the realization that the community is not autonomous. In one response, people reach out, but only in order to grasp what they can to suit their own purposes. In the other they attempt to reject unfavourable influences, while recognizing that these influences belong to a globalizing world in which their own fate is bound up with complexities far beyond their control. Following the failure of the red box money cult in Hagen, people generally turned to cash cropping and political competition as their means of dealing with the outside world. But, by the turn of the millennium and shortly thereafter, the vagaries in price of the main cash crop, coffee, the increase in local instabilities caused by inter-group fighting, the turbulences and volatilities of urban life and the growing awareness of corruption at the national government level drove many people into a new version of ritual activity: the adoption of charismatic forms of Protestant Christianity, with their dramatic promises of salvation both in this world and in the next (Strathern and Stewart 1997; Stewart and Strathern 2000a, 2001).

The Baha'i in Northern New Ireland: Claiming Connections with 'the Centre'

Graeme Were's study of the Baha'i presence in northern New Ireland in Papua New Guinea shows another specialized attempt to deal with the decentring effects of change by creating an idea of connections with a new place seen as central in the order of the world. The starting point of Were's analysis is one that has resonances beyond his particular ethnography: the ability of people to 'transform images in order to create new understandings' (Were 2005: 659). This approach can be paralleled from the Hagen red box movement, which we have discussed above (Strathern 1979–80; Stewart and Strathern 2000a). In the red box movement one vital image transformation took place that pertained to the ancestors: these, instead of being seen as local and fixed to their clan places, were now envisaged as trans-local and mobile, connecting the clan areas to the capital, Port Moresby, and moving on the wind as aeroplanes appeared to do. Another transformation in this red box money cult had to do with leadership. Instead of a plurality of competing local male figures, a single female figure described as the Queen was created, an exogenous image appropriated by the female leader of the movement for the development of her own endogenous power.[1]

Were argues that Baha'i adherents in New Ireland have been able to produce new images as vehicles for their thoughts and aspirations in ways comparable to the production of images in customary activities derived from the past (Were 2005: 662). Baha'is is a centrist faith, he notes, advocating a 'one world' philosophy (ibid.) based on the teachings of Baha'u'llah, a nineteenth-century Persian nobleman, whose writings are seen by his followers as providing 'new truths for the modern world' (ibid.). The Nalik people of New Ireland, with whom Were worked, saw the Baha'is faith as a way forward for themselves, because Christian teachings were experienced by them as hostile to traditional customs of funerary practice, whereas the Baha'is encouraged them to continue such customs 'as a form of worship' (Were 2005: 663). These customs centred on the production of *malanggan* carvings, representations of the dead that were used in complex ways to deal with memories of them and to reorder social relations.

The Nalik people with whom Were worked claimed that the prophet Baha'u'llah had drawn an arrow on a map of the world pointing at one of their own villages as the focus of the emergence of the Baha'i. This village happens to carry the name Madina, which the Nalik adherents of Baha'i declared to be the same as the name of the resting place of the prophet Muhammad (Were 2005: 664). The movement for Baha'i began when school-educated Naliks joined forces with two outside Baha'i missionaries, against the fierce opposition of the local Christian missions. It has continued with the creation of a ritual centre, a building that combines Arabic, Christian and local motifs, these last exemplified in painted roof designs that are similar in form or colour to those of *malanggan* carvings (ibid.: 667). The designs are in the shape of stars, and stars happen to be prominent both in Nalik funerary carvings and in the nine-pointed star of the Baha'i faith (ibid.: 667). Baha'i prayer books are covered with diamond patterns that are also found on *malanggan* (ibid.: 668).

The Baha'i holy day of Naw-Ruz (21 March) celebrates the arrival of a new calendar year for its adherents, and the Nalik people correlate this with the beginning of their dry season and the arrival of new freshwater springs on the reef, which they also call 'rus' (a chance linguistic analogy revealing the serendipity of conjunctures here). At Naw-Ruz, Baha'i adherents in effect perform their traditional mortuary feasts in commemoration of those who have died in the previous period of ritual time, staging the event at the Baha'i Centre in Madina (Were 2005: 669). In the local Baha'i system of hybridization, also, the Christian God is equated with the Nalik creation god Nakmai (ibid.: 670). These are all symbolic acts of assimilation and unification, which constitute the Nalik version of combining 'localism' and 'cosmopolitanism', we may say.

Were himself argues that, by encouraging *malanggan* practices, the Baha'is created an idea that their faith could also 'harness the ancestral realm' (Were 2005: 671). He suggests, too, that the Baha'is see both customary rituals and cash crop production as ways of creating pathways to the afterlife (ibid.). All this seems strongly tied to local contexts. What makes this case history particularly relevant for our own theme in this chapter, however, is Were's next observation, that in the year 2000 many of the Nalik Baha'is donated money to something called the Ark Fund, 'so that their names would be placed in a purpose-built temple in Haifa, Israel, the spiritual centre of the Baha'i faith' (Were 2005: 671). Further, in doing this the Nalik thought that through these donations they would unite 'with the dead of all races' and so would contribute to the ultimate 'unification of the world under the leadership of the Baha'is' (ibid.).

This last, very telling, detail illustrates one of our themes, i.e. the blending together of intense localism and intense trans-localism or yearning for unification with a new centre on the part of those who, from other points of view, may see themselves as dispossessed of their own centrality in the world. Here the dilemma of the dispossessed is solved by the assertion, through distinctly local and customary means, of a tie to a new and powerful centre of influence in the world.

Comparing this case with our earlier case from our work in Mount Hagen, we note in both cases a transformation of ideas about ancestors: ancestors were made mobile in Hagen, carried on the wind to the capital, Port Moresby, and more mobile still among the Nalik, where ancestral connections are made universal and centred outside Papua New Guinea altogether, in Israel.[2] These shifting contexts of ancestrality are emblematic of the processes of rupture and re-inscription of identities that take place when the local and the global become mixed together: processes in which local things are made global, and global things are made local, in ways similar to the theme found widely in folk tales around the world of shape-shifting or skin-changing, i.e. things examined in one way appear to be one thing, but when examined in another way they appear very different indeed (see Strathern and Stewart 2000b).

Such a theme of skin-changing itself, in fact, can become incorporated into narratives of adaptation to the outside world, as the work of Ira Bashkow (2006) and Andrew Lattas (1998) has shown for other parts of Papua New Guinea. Stories of how white people are actually the spirits of the Papua New Guinea people's own dead ancestors or recent kinsfolk represent attempts to assimilate the exogenous into the endogenous realm, as we have noted earlier from Lorenzo Brutti's Oksapmin study (e.g. Brutti 2000); and the prominence of these narratives in contexts associated with the millennium indicates exactly why adjusting to processes of change was perceived as so problematic at this time. The millennium represented the irruption of outside cosmological time into people's local lives; and the image of disruption of computers (the so-called Y2K problem, with its implication that global networks would be compromised at this time) was, in the Mount Hagen area at any rate, compounded with a general apocalyptic view of the significance of computers, to the effect that, when computers came to Mount Hagen, it was thought that Jesus would come back to the earth (see Strathern and Stewart 1997; Stewart and Strathern 2000a). Another image, expressed much earlier in a song that was sung by adherents in the red box money movement, also contained an apocalyptic image, that of the World Bank breaking open in the sky and descending to earth in Hagen (Strathern and Stewart 1997).

Images of drastic change in these kinds of movements often draw on technological innovations such as computers. Mobile phones, television, videos and the like may also be invoked. Lattas has discussed the incorporation of technological imagery into narratives of change among the Kaliai of Papua New Guinea (Lattas 2006: 15–31). The dizzying speed of technological changes in the media and communication devices in the metropolitan countries themselves may produce similar problems of disorientation for people in these countries; it is easy to understand how much more confusing, then, these can be in areas outside the centres of change.

Taiwan: Cultural Revival Movements and the Reclaiming of Identities

In the introduction to his collection of myths and folk tales of the Paiwan people, speakers of an Austronesian language who live in the south-eastern part of the island of Taiwan, Fr. Hans Egli[3] notes:

Once the whole island of Taiwan was inhabited by large populations of Austronesian speakers. As a result of colonization from China from the sixteenth century onward many of these tribal groups disappeared, while others were driven out of their original dwelling places. Today only nine tribes are counted as having different languages of their own. (Egli 1989: 11, translated from the German original by the authors of this chapter)

The nine tribes referred to by Fr. Egli here are those that were recognized officially by the Taiwanese government and thus made eligible for various grants and programmes to enable them to revive their cultural identities in the contemporary context. Since this was first done, further 'tribes' have been recognized officially – first the Thao, then in 2002 the Kavalan, then the Taruku people as a separate group from the Atayal group, in 2004; and in January 2007 the Sakilaya of Nantou County in Central Taiwan obtained official recognition. A group called the Kahabu were also seeking this official status for themselves during 2007. We were told that the Atayal were asked by the Kahabu to weave garments for them that would signify their customary identity, since they themselves had lost the traditional knowledge of how to weave. The Atayal were also said to be called upon to teach members of the Kahabu group how to weave again.

The process whereby these groups have been recognized at national level, and have thereby obtained political and cultural rights and privileges they did not have previously within the state structure, has to be understood as a part of a wider set of historical changes in Taiwan. The registered people in the indigenous groups comprise only a small percentage of the general population of Taiwan. But their political significance goes far beyond their numbers, since they have become a focus for statements regarding the cultural differences between Taiwan and China, and their identity thus enters into the wider, and highly polarized, conflicts about the historical and current status of Taiwan vis-à-vis the People's Republic of China. They themselves recognize their historically decentred and minority status, and their customary ways have been impacted successively by colonizers from Fujian in China's south-east from the sixteenth century onward, colonial control by the Japanese from 1895 to 1945, and the incursion of mainland Chinese troops under Chiang Kai-shek fleeing from the Communist advance in China in 1949. Particularly under the control of the Kuomintang (KMT) government of Chiang Kai-shek, the indigenous groups were indoctrinated into learning to speak Mandarin, and over the centuries of contact with successive waves of outsiders the use of their own indigenous languages has become diminished. In the latest phase of revival, however, emphasis is being placed on the renewal of these Austronesian languages, on cultural festivals and rituals and on opportunities for economic development (see Stewart and Strathern 2005; Strathern and Stewart 2005b).

Christian churches have, in one way and another, been involved in the construction or reconstruction of identities among these indigenous groups. We are most familiar with activities among the speakers of Paiwan, one of the officially recognized tribal groups within Taiwan (mentioned above). In one village on the south-east coast of Taiwan, some forty minutes by car out from the small city of Taitung, where we have made field investigations, the pastor of the local Presbyterian church and his wife are both prominent in community organization and in sponsoring cultural activities coordinated through or with the support of the church. We have seen activities in this village go through a number of phases since our first visit to it in 2004. We went there originally as part of a group of academics who were participating in an event called the Austronesian Forum, sponsored by the National Prehistory Museum in Taitung. The visit was hosted by the Presbyterian pastor, and was marked by a special festive meal served to us by a volunteer group of village women and consisting of a variety of foods said to be collected from the local environment of gardens and forest land. The pastor said a prayer in the Paiwan language before the meal, and after it there were local dancing and singing, in which guests were asked to participate. We have since found this participatory mode to be standard in other events of this sort that we have been present at.

The visit was also marked by an introduction to aspects of Paiwan culture via a visit to a reconstructed communal men's house containing trophies, guns, insignia and carvings. The pastor gave an illustrated lecture on the occasion, accompanied by his close kinsman, who is known as a writer and has published books in Mandarin, including materials on Paiwan cultural topics and history. The men's house and the feast were thus the focus of activities at this time, and the pastor told us that his aim was to mobilize people to make use of their own local resources rather than depending on work outside the village. One project was to revive the traditional cultivation of millet, which had been important for ritual practices in the past, and had been replaced by rice as a result of prolonged influence from the Han and Japanese peoples.

The next year, 2005, the focus of our visit was different. We were interested to follow up issues to do with conversion to Christianity and the relationship of Christian practice to indigenous custom. Clearly, the point of the performance for the academics in 2004 had been to stress that the church and local culture can get along together. The assertion was thus that exogenous, or global, Christian values need not be seen as inimical to local cultural expressions. The two could coexist, in their separate spheres, or even perhaps support each other in certain ways. During our June 2005 research visit, meetings were arranged for us in two separate Presbyterian churches, at which discussions took place regarding the issue of Christianity and Paiwan culture. Individual pastors who attended these occasions differed quite widely in terms of how they saw this issue. Some clearly stated that, in any conflict between Christian 'norms' and local practices or 'traditions', the Christian rules must prevail. Others, however, thought that mutual accommodation was needed in order to give local culture a space in which to flourish. The pastor of the main village in which we have worked had a creative take on the whole matter, which he had clearly developed out of his experience in running community projects of the kind that had brought us to his village in the first place: the church should provide the crucial moral and community basis on which worthwhile activities, both those revived from the past and those belonging to contemporary economic development, could be successfully mounted. Indeed, the pastor pointed out that, given the historical decline in the effective powers and standing of hereditary chiefly lines in parts of the Paiwan area, the church, in his opinion, had now taken the place of chiefship in the social structure of the village.

On our next visit to this village in January 2007, we found some remarkable further changes. First, it became evident to us that the pastor and his wife were working together as an energetic team to promote village and regional enterprises. The pastor's millet-growing scheme had now grown to be more significant than before. Previously, he said, participation in this had been voluntary. Now all his parishioners were encouraged to take part. On one of the days we were there, a party of academics and legal experts visited the village to learn about the millet planting and to give advice on how this could be provided with a commercial dimension. Later we learned that the visitors were actually part of an NGO, said to be called the 'Millet Foundation', aimed at helping with the revival of millet growing among the indigenous groups, especially in those areas of the Paiwan and their neighbours, the Rukai, where millet grows well. The pastor and his wife showed us examples of bunches of millet that had been harvested from the crop last time, remarking that a thousand of such bundles had been harvested and one-tenth of these (as a kind of tithe, although this, the pastor said, was not foregrounded as a reason for the presentation) had been given to the church. This point confirmed the idea that the church was replacing the chiefship in the village structure, because offerings of millet from the junior lines in the village were traditionally made to the senior, chiefly line in notional return for seed millet given out at the planting season. Indeed, the chiefly line was known as the *vusam*, 'millet seed'.

The pastor also showed us newly designed pottery vessels and cups that could be used for consumption of millet wine, and a jar in which the millet grains were fermenting along with seeds from a locally grown amaranth plant (called *djuli* in the local Paiwan dialect). These vessels were prototypes for items they hoped to have manufactured and to put on sale. It became evident to us that the millet-growing revival had both ritual and commercial purposes. Although the drinking of this wine was a potential source of controversy because of historical church policies stemming from problems of alcoholism in the aboriginal communities, the pastor noted that this was not a stumbling block for their project as long as discretion was exercised in referring to it.

An upper room in the church had also been partially turned into a computer and research arena. Here kinsfolk of the pastor were preparing the church's new website. One of them, at his request, was attempting to download software for Google Earth,[4] so that they could get a better look at a map of Papua New Guinea, about which we had spoken with them, as well as of their own land area, which they were keen to have surveyed in support of their claims to it. They have been mapping on to the land their oral historical record of migration into the current area and also the significant places along this route in the memory of the people. This mapping of history on to the local landscape imbues the land with local meaning by identifying the areas with local Paiwan names in place of the Mandarin ones. The use of GIS (geographic information system) technology to mark claims on indigenous land in these ways is something that many of the tribal groups in the area that we have contacted are currently hoping to work on so as to present to the government and the outside world a 'picture' of claims grounded in oral history.

This busy scene was an indication of the active reaching out by the pastor and his family to a wider world of consciousness via the Internet and its resources. We also found that they were constantly on their mobile phones, during meals, while driving, while drinking tea or while working at computers. This mimetic appropriation of customs linking them to the world in communication networks was substantially new since our previous visit in 2005. It should be taken as yet another index of their brand of cosmopolitanism, adapted for their own local purposes. It should further be noted that the pastor or people within his network had been to places like the Philippines and the USA, pursuing connections with indigenous peoples and their movements for self-advancement. In places in the Pacific like Papua New Guinea, magical ideas have sometimes grown up around new items of technology. In this Paiwan village the items appeared to be used in very practical ways. They may also, however, have carried symbolic significance beyond their immediate usefulness.

We visited the Centre of which the pastor's wife is the director, in Taitung City. This is the Aboriginal Community Development Centre, which has two sections, one dealing with social services, the other with the production of arts and crafts for sale in outlets both in Taitung and in the capital city, Taipei.[5] Here, we were shown examples of beadwork and observed its manufacture on the spot. We were told that they were making three categories of art: 'traditional', 'cultural' and 'contemporary'. 'Traditional' meant according to traditional patterns or designs that were used previously on objects by the group; 'cultural' meant developed out of traditional patterns and signified some specific aspect of local cultural import; and 'contemporary' referred to a further range of experimental variations of design that incorporated into itself motifs from outside of Paiwan 'traditional imagery'. The Centre was prepared to send out items internationally and to accept orders for items by the Internet. They had an Internet-based blog that could be used for these commercial purposes, and which the director told us was more convenient for people to use than email.

Beads are an important cultural item for the Paiwan people. They were part of the wealth belonging to a chiefly house. Various colours and designs have specific meanings, and some of these were explained to us on the spot. One item for sale mimicked the action of items hung up to shake in the wind and frighten off birds from the millet crops. Other items represented millet bunches. They represented a line of products centred around the 'millet theme'. Other foci for representation were being considered for future product lines that could be marketed later and that could also be artistic representations for the group, which could be used in competition with other groups across Taiwan at the national level through arts and crafts programmes.[6] The objects presented were of a multitude of bead designs, of varying prices. A favourite bead motif was called 'the green bug', stylistically representing a kind of insect that comes to eat the millet when the crop is plentiful and itself becomes large and fat from the crop. The Centre's staff were prepared to send out bead necklaces internationally and receive payment by return. As with the village-based enterprises, the craftwork was also related to the church context: providing employment and harnessing creativity was seen as a part of the outreach work of the local Presbyterian church.

Both with respect to the church itself and in the activities of the Centre we see a typical blending of the intensely local, drawing on the cultural wealth of the Paiwan, and the extensively trans-local, drawing on the resources of the Internet to seek marketing outlets for products and to obtain information on a great range of topics. At a Sunday church service one of the elders presiding over the service gave instructions on how people should apply to the Council of Indigenous Peoples, a governmental body within Taiwan, for grants and access to training courses that could enhance their skills and earning capacities.

Given the overall level of economic development in Taiwan and the centuries-old history of contacts between the indigenous Austronesians and the Han populations, it is not surprising that we do not find here quite the same feeling of 'the dispossessed' as is encountered in parts of Papua New Guinea (see Strathern and Stewart-Strathern 2000 on the Papua New Guinea context). Nevertheless, the 'cosmopolitanism' that the Austronesians of Taiwan have created is the cosmopolitanism of the peripheral, if not of the dispossessed. Their emergence into political favour is very recent, since they suffered in one way or another both during the Japanese times and following the arrival of the KMT after the Second World War. The language situation among them reveals an unusual pattern: by and large, owing to the recent historical imposition of Mandarin by the KMT and the people's longer historical acquaintance with Fujian-derived dialects or language forms that have become recognized as 'Taiwanese', the indigenes of all the tribes speak Mandarin as a mode of communication. The indigenous television channel in Taiwan, which was recently set up, features newscasters and commentators all speaking in Mandarin, with special segments that have indigenous peoples speaking in their own indigenous languages during parts of specific local programmes. Songs and ritual speech may be recorded in a local vernacular. Younger people are now being encouraged to learn their own language.

Mandarin is in itself a kind of cosmopolitan artefact as well as a nationally recognized language; the Austronesian languages have to struggle to make their comeback against it, or to achieve a symbiosis with it. Another factor is, of course, that English is a language that younger people and children are being heavily encouraged to learn. Thus, the number of languages that any child can realistically spend time learning becomes somewhat problematic. Local issues are often articulated in a non-local language within Taiwanese indigenous communities. The situation is comparable to the use of written English in Papua New Guinea to promote local cultural concerns and awareness. But in Papua New Guinea, while language loss has occurred, there is a strong residue of knowledge of indigenous languages as regular spoken forms of communication (see, for example, Stewart and Strathern 2002). In the Paiwan village context where we have worked, the pastor told us that he was brought up without much knowledge of the Paiwan language, and began to learn it only in adulthood, with help from an older generation of people. How, then, did he learn the language? We asked him this question, and he smiled and replied, 'Maybe God taught me.' Here again, then, a universal figure (God) is harnessed into a very particular local project.

A number of Christian churches are at work in Taiwan, including Presbyterians, Catholics, Methodists and Seventh-Day Adventists.

Presbyterians do not stress material iconography as much as Catholics, relying rather on verbal rhetoric and imagery. In one village of the Paiwan that we visited, Tjuabar, where there is a Catholic church, there has been a deliberate attempt to harness local Paiwan imagery to the service of a universal religion; or, perhaps, to localize the Christian religion through the use of local symbolism. We were first told about this church by Fr. Egli, who had worked in Tjuabar. He explained that the wish here was to bring together Christian and Paiwan concepts of cosmological significance. To express the idea of the Holy Trinity, the image that was used incorporated the importance of the human head to the Paiwan people and thus had a design of three heads with eyes shared between them. We visited this Catholic church at Tjuabar and found this particular design executed on the inside of the church above its entrance door (source: interview with Fr. Hans Egli, 6 January 2007, in Taitung; visit to Tjuabar, 7 January 2007).

An account of this church and its decorations has been given in much greater detail by Chang-kwo Tan (Tan 2001: 192–217).[7] Tan points out the crucial role played by the female research worker and catechist Tjinuai in the design and execution of the carvings at Tjuabar; and he also notes the distinction between the top-down concept of inculturation promoted by the Catholic church after Vatican II in the 1960s and the bottom-up popular syncretistic appropriation of Christian symbols. He notes, too, how older Paiwan Catholics appreciated the carvings with a sense of nostalgia, and younger ones with an excitement of discovery, whereas middle-aged converts, used to the rejection of 'traditional' culture, were challenged by this innovation and some left to join Protestant churches (Tan 2001: 198). This pattern of generational difference is found widely in the area.

These various methods of self-expression can be interpreted as ways of reclaiming identities that had been submerged by successive waves of colonial influence. We have picked out elements akin to 'cosmopolitanism' in these acts of reclaiming, while also noting that this is a cosmopolitanism strongly geared to local interests. The difference between this phenomenon and the usual way in which cosmopolitanism is represented is that here the emphasis is on drawing things into the locality by reaching out across boundaries, whereas, in the more usual way of viewing things, the emphasis is on supposed universal values and the obliteration of local values. But in both cases people are essentially making claims to a place in a wider world and seeking advantages by doing so. The fundamental processes are akin to those that have happened many times in history, involving border-crossings and the redefinition of social boundaries.

We turn now briefly to a third, and concluding, context to pursue this point, making a shift from the Pacific and the Far East to two other parts of the world where we have conducted research for many years, Scotland and Ireland (see Strathern and Stewart 2001, 2006).

Scotland and Ireland: Border-crossings, Diasporas, and Ambivalent Cosmopolitanisms

A striking and significant feature of the novels of Sir Walter Scott, whose life spanned the eighteenth and nineteenth centuries (he lived from 1771 to 1832), is the emphasis in the narratives on crossings between different geographical, political and personal locations, and the ways in which people handle these crossings. Border-crossings entail an opening out of people's lives, exposing them to risks, giving them opportunities.

This theme of border-crossings has been noted by Claire Lamont in her Editor's Introduction to the Penguin Books edition of Walter Scott's *Chronicles of the Canongate* (2000). The *Chronicles* is a collection of three long stories, each of which tells of the engagement of Scottish persons who depart from Scotland in an effort to improve their wealth and social standing in outside contexts strongly influenced by the imperial history of England. In two of the stories the venues are specifically parts of the Empire: America and India. In the other story, the scene is the familiar one of the border between Scotland and England, so bitterly contested over the centuries. A Scottish Highlands cattle drover, Robin Oig, plans to set out to drive his cattle down to England and sell them. His aunt, who has the gift of 'second sight', warns him that if he goes there will be 'Saxon blood' on his dirk, and says 'Go not this day to England!' To prevent this disaster from happening Robin gives his dirk to a Lowland companion so that he cannot use it, and goes to England in spite of the warning. He has a friend there, Harry Wakefield, but he gets into a quarrel of honour with him, and takes back his dirk and kills this friend after being knocked over and initially refusing to fight him with his fists – something a Highlander would not recognize as an acceptable way of fighting. Robin is taken to an English court in Carlisle and is duly tried and condemned to death for murder.

In the other two stories, the main characters also get into trouble with the law, in highly complex contexts of personal adventure, romance, intrigue and the grand events of imperial history. The message of these stories is ambivalent. The Empire provides a venue for advantages, but it also causes disasters for many individuals embroiled in its affairs. Cultural conflicts loom large in Scott's narratives, both in *Chronicles of the Canongate* and in others of the Waverley novels. Often the conflicts are between the Highlands and the Lowlands of Scotland itself, conflicts that are also mediated by interpersonal ties of friendship, kinship or love (for example, in Scott's works *Rob Roy* and *The Fair Maid of Perth*). Or they may be between Scotland and England, and between Jacobite and Whig factions in history (as in Scott's works *Waverley* and *Redgauntlet*, for example). These novels all describe complex interplays of emotion and social position, with revelations of hidden identities, that result from border-crossings. As Lamont remarks, such crossings raise the question of whether the boundaries in question *should* be crossed or not (Lamont 2000: xxvi). What we know historically is that they *have* been crossed, with complex results. Such complexities have issued in what we might call 'frustrated cosmopolitanisms', fuelled by the desire to reach out and the experience of pain and setbacks in doing so.

The counter-impulse to cosmopolitanism, which nevertheless may lead to a kind of cosmopolitanism of its own sort, is the impulse of diaspora populations to trace their identities back to the places their ancestors migrated from. A diaspora consciousness functions as a kind of nativism, in so far as it ties people back to an idea of their essential origins. At the same time it can link geographically disparate people together on a transnational basis, through reference to these essential origins. The Scots diaspora to the USA, Canada, Australia and New Zealand can stand as an example here. A particularly strong instance of how this works from the side of the places of origin themselves is found in the case of the Ulster-Scots in Northern Ireland and the Republic of Ireland (Strathern and Stewart 2005a). These people have narratives facing two ways: one back to Scotland, the other outwards to countries Ulster-Scots migrated to later from the Ulster region of Ireland. Because of their interstitial position in Ireland generally, these people have been particularly concerned to assert ties both with ancestral origin places and with places their predecessors migrated to. Their claims of links with the diaspora and their vigorous efforts to remake and reassert those links by visits and cultural collaborations, inside and outside Ireland, indicate this variety of what we might call 'ethnic cosmopolitanism' – a combination of inclusiveness and exclusiveness that is thoroughly transnational but certainly not 'universal'. (For a more detailed review of aspects of Ulster-Scots history and identity, see Strathern and Stewart 2005a.)

Conclusion: Varieties of 'Cosmopolitanism'

In this chapter we have been engaged in two related exercises. One has been to show that in the social movements of peoples who perceive themselves and/or are perceived as being, in peripheralized power positions we can discern an outward movement of thought and action tending towards universalism of identification with peoples in parallel positions to themselves around the world. This identification is not just notional. It is seen as a way of learning from others how to gain advantages from the wider world. Our second aim has been to show that this same outward movement may often take the form of the kind of combination of cosmopolitanism and nativism that Cairns Craig has found exemplified in the work of certain contemporary Scottish writers (Craig 1996). Ancillary to this observation, we added a section on the problematics of historical boundary-crossings for populations such as the Scots, whose outward-seeking movements led them into the difficulties of inserting themselves into multiple cultural contexts.

The Scottish diaspora, however, like other diasporas, also led to the creation of yet another kind of cosmopolitiansim: the making and remaking of networks of sociality between those who share diasporic identities. Perhaps it is stretching 'cosmopolitanism' to use it to refer to all of these contexts. Our larger aim has been to show that outward-looking transnational movements do not all necessarily take one political or cultural form of the kind labelled ideologically as 'cosmopolitanism', in the sense of denying or transcending local or ethnic identities. The peoples we have been discussing have rather sought to combine their outward seeking with inner self-definitions, to be both cosmopolitans and nativists. The vision involved is rather different from that articulated by Kwame Anthony Appiah (2006), for example, who sets up a conceptual opposition between individualism and transnational linkages on the one hand and collective and localized interests on the other. That is why we have identified the objects of our interest here as 'alternative cosmopolitanisms'.

Popular usage in relation to the term 'cosmopolitanism' continues to take as its model the image of people of different places coexisting in cities or of particular persons who are able to move with ease between different social contexts: the 'citizen of the world' concept, in short. In our treatment of the topic here, we have taken a number of turns that depart from this popular usage, while still recognizing it as a background scenario. Situating our discussion in a discursive space between nativism and cosmopolitianism, we have concentrated on indigenous people's efforts to assert their identities and interests both in opposition to and in a sought-after alliance with centres of power. Opposition can take the form of claiming a centrality of their own; alliance takes the form of a linkage with power aimed at drawing a share of that power to themselves. In either case, people construct a new constellation of elements that they appropriate for their identity. And these elements constitute what we have called the varieties of alternative cosmopolitanisms. In this way our Paiwan village leaders in Southern Taiwan, so-called cargo cultists in the Highlands of Papua New Guinea and the Nalik followers of Bahai'i can all be seen as pursuing agendas of countering inequality and reaching beyond the confines of their local group in order to expand their strategic identities towards the cosmopolitan configuration. The difference between these various alternative ways of recreating life and movement and the standard cosmopolitan image is that very often the agents involved are rural rather than urban-based, and that their aim is to root themselves more firmly rather than becoming rootless. Their stances thus counter globalization as well as riding on it; and they aim also to capture and adapt neoliberal ideologies for their own ends rather than becoming hostages to the ends of others. In other words, their actions are experiments designed to deal with their own discontents through their own creative energies.

Of course, all such efforts are fraught with difficulties. In highlighting the theme of border-crossings, which is implicit in the idea of people reaching out to the world, we used our examples from Scottish history and its involvement in English colonialism to stress the point that efforts to reach into a cosmopolitan world may easily be frustrated in conditions of inequality. This is most poignantly so when we consider cases of people as individuals. Where diaspora collectivities come into play, stronger possibilities arise, as with the Ulster-Scots in Ireland (both the Republic and Northern Ireland), who have been able to assert transnational connections of diaspora that amount to yet another combination of the local and the far-flung, edging towards a cosmopolitanism of their own sort (which we have called here 'ethnic cosmopolitanism' further running against the grain of conventional usage). In the end, though, we are less concerned to subsume many things under the one label cosmopolitanism and more concerned to see the processes of tense and intense human effort in indigenous peripheries that aim to shift centrality back to themselves.

Notes

Substantial parts of this chapter were composed while we were Visiting Research Fellows at the Institute of Ethnology, Academia Sinica, Taipei, Taiwan (December 2006 to March 2007). We thank the Director of the Institute, Prof. Huang Shu-min, for the renewal of our Visiting positions, which we have also held during periods of time in 2002, 2003, 2004 and 2005. We thank others of our colleagues in the Institute of Ethnology for their hospitality and conversations, particularly Dr. Guo Pei-yi, for her help with the provision of an office during the time of our stay and in general. We also wish to thank the government of Papua New Guinea for various research permissions over the years, and we thank our numerous colleagues, collaborators and helpers within Papua New Guinea, Ireland, Taiwan and Scotland (where we are affiliated as Research Fellows at the Research Institute of Irish and Scottish Studies, University of Aberdeen). Particular thanks go to Mr Yang Shyh-wei for research assistance in Taitung in 2005 and 2007; to Mr Tom-

Kapi for assistance in Papua New Guinea; and to numerous families in Scotland and Ireland for their continuing friendship and interest in our work, as well as to the pastor and his family in the Paiwan area we have discussed in this chapter.

1. Incidentally, this image creation and appropriation by the Nalik was decidedly based on a conflation of 'Western' and 'indigenous' models, as opposed to the idea that somehow images are peculiar to 'Melanesia', while written forms are alone considered to be fully valid in 'the West'. The symbolism of 'the Queen' in Hagen was also undoubtedly based on the rich iconic imagery that helps to constitute the idea of the British monarchy in Britain itself, in addition to any 'written communications' about it. Hageners would have had the opportunity to see pictures of the Queen and to hear about her by this time.
2. The theme of Israel and its significance in world history has been impressed on Papua New Guineans through their acquaintance with missionary teachings as well as their readings of contemporary news. Among the Duna people, we found that the adherents of one local church stressed that the origins of their church went back to Israel.
3. We were fortunate to be able to meet Fr. Egli in Taitung on the evening of 6 January 2007 and to interview him on his life's work with the Paiwan people and their language and culture. Our thanks to Wang Lin for facilitating this meeting.
4. Google Earth, which provides Internet maps and satellite images for particular geographical searches, has become a potential resource of significance to the indigenous groups in Taiwan because they hope to use information derived from it to map and thus validate their land claims.
5. Taitung is some five hours by train journey south-east of Taipei on the eastern coast of Taiwan.
6. One scheme, known as the 'one village, one product' project, is in fact linked internationally to the Asia Pacific Economic Forum, where it was proposed by Taiwan's then President Chen Shui-bian at a meeting in South Korea in 2005. See Chung (2006: 36).
7. We thank Dr. Chang-kwo Tan for presenting us with a copy of his dissertation.

References

Appiah, K.A. 2006. Toward a New Cosmopolitanism. *New York Times Magazine*, 1 January, Section 6, 30–37, 52.

Ballard, C. 2000. The Fire Next Time: The Conversion of the Huli Apocalypse. In P.J. Stewart and A. Strathern (eds) Millennial Countdown in New Guinea. *Ethnohistory*, 47 (1), 205–25. Also in book form, Durham, NC: Duke University Press.

Bashkow, I. 2006. *The Meaning of Whitemen. Race and Modernity in the Orokaiva Cultural World*. Chicago and London: University of Chicago Press.

Berndt, R.M. 1952. A Cargo Movement in the Eastern Central Highlands of New Guinea. *Oceania*, 23, 40–65.

Brutti, L. 2000. Afek's Last Son: Integrating Change in a Papua New Guinean Cosmology. In P.J. Stewart and A. Strathern (eds) Millennial Countdown in New Guinea, *Ethnohistory*, 47 (1), 101–11. Also in book form, Durham, NC: Duke University Press.

Chung, O. 2006. A Gateway to the World. Taiwan is Making its Strength Felt in APEC, But it Always Needs to Do More. *Taiwan Review*, November, 32–37.

Craig, C. 1996. *Out of History*. Edinburgh: Polygon.

Egli, H. 1989. *Mirimiringan. Die Mythen und Märchen der Paiwan*. Zurich: Die Waage.

Lamont, C. 2000. Editor's Introduction. In W. Scott, *Chronicles of the Canongate*. London: Penguin Books, pp. xi–xxix.

Lattas, A. 1998. *Cultures of Secrecy: Reinventing Race in Bush Kaliai Cargo Cults*. Madison: University of Wisconsin Press.

—— 2006. Technologies of Visibility: The Utopian Politics of Cameras, Televisions, Videos and Dramas in New Britain. *Australian Journal of Anthropology*, 17 (1), 15–31.

Rapport, N. 2006. Diaspora, Cosmopolis, Global Refuge: Three Voices of the Supranational City. In S. Coleman and P. Collins (eds) *Locating the Field. Space, Place and Context in Anthropology*. Oxford: Berg, pp. 179–97.

Stewart, P.J. and A. Strathern. 2000a. Introduction: Latencies and Realizations in Millennial Practices. In P.J. Stewart and A. Strathern (eds) Millennial Countdown in New Guinea, special issue of *Ethnohistory*, 47 (1), 3–27. Also in book form, Durham, NC: Duke University Press.

—— (eds). 2000b. Millennnial Countdown in New Guinea. *Ethnohistory*, 47 (1). Also in book form, Durham, NC: Duke University Press.

—— 2001. The Great Exchange: Moka With God. In J. Robbins, P.J. Stewart and A. Strathern (eds) Pentecostal and Charismatic Christianity in Oceania, special issue of *Journal of Ritual Studies*, 15 (2), 91–104.

—— 2002. *Remaking the World: Myth, Mining and Ritual Change among the Duna of Papua New Guinea*. Smithsonian Series in Ethnographic Inquiry. Washington, DC: Smithsonian Institution Press.

—— 2005. Introduction: Ritual Practices, 'Cultural Revival' Movements, and Historical Change. In P.J. Stewart and A. Strathern (eds) *Asian Ritual Systems: Syncretisms and Ruptures*, special issue of *Journal of Ritual Studies*, 19 (1), i–xiv. Also in book form in the Ritual Studies Monograph Series, Durham, NC: Carolina Academic Press, 2007.

Strathern, A. 1979–80. The Red-Box Money Cult in Mount Hagen, 1968–71. *Oceania*, 50, 88–102, 161–75.

Strathern, A. and P.J. Stewart. 1997. Introduction: Millennial Markers in the Pacific. In P.J. Stewart and A. Strathern (eds) *Millennial Markers*. Townsville, Queensland: JCU, Centre for Pacific Studies, pp. 1–17. (Reprinted, 2 May 1999, *World Anthropology, the AnthroGlobe Journal*, electronic journal).

—— 2000a. *Arrow Talk: Transaction, Transition, and Contradiction in New Guinea Highlands History*. Kent, OH: The Kent State University Press.

—— 2000b. *The Python's Back: Pathways of Comparison between Indonesia and Melanesia*. Westport, CT: Bergin and Garvey, Greenwood Publishing.

—— 2001. *Minorities and Memories: Survivals and Extinctions in Scotland and Western Europe*. Durham, NC: Carolina Academic Press.

—— 2004. *Empowering the Past, Confronting the Future, The Duna People of Papua New Guinea*. Contemporary Anthropology of Religion Series. New York: Palgrave Macmillan.

—— 2005a. 'The Ulster-Scots': A Cross-Border and Trans-national Concept and its Ritual Performance. *Journal of Ritual Studies,* 19 (2), 1–16.

—— 2005b. Introduction. In P.J. Stewart and A. Strathern (eds) *Expressive Genres and Historical Change: Indonesia, Papua New Guinea and Taiwan*. London: Ashgate, pp. 1–39.

—— 2006. Narratives of Violence and Perils of Peace-Making in North-South Cross-Border Contexts, Ireland. In A. Strathern, P.J. Stewart and N. Whitehead (eds) *Terror and Violence: Imagination and the Unimaginable*. London: Pluto Press, pp. 142–70.

—— 2009. Introduction. In P.J. Stewart and A. Strathern (eds) *Religious and Ritual Change: Cosmologies and Histories*. Carolina Academic Press.

Strathern, A. and P.J. Stewart-Strathern. 2000. Custom, Modernity and Contradiction: Local and National Identities in Papua New Guinea. *The New Pacific Review,* 1 (1), 118–26.

Tan, Chang-kwo. 2001. Mediated Devotion: Tradition and Christianity among the Paiwan of Taiwan. PhD Dissertation, University College London.

Toulmin, S. 1990. *Cosmopolis: The Hidden Agenda of Modernity*. Chicago, IL: University of Chicago Press.

Werbner, P. 2006. Understanding Vernacular Cosmopolitanism. *Anthropology News,* 47 (5), 7, 11.

Were, G. 2005. Thinking Through Images: *Kastom* and the Coming of the Baha'is to Northern New Ireland, Papua New Guinea. *Journal of the Royal Anthropological Institute,* 11, 659–76.

Whelan, C. 2006. Cosmopolitans, Transprovincials and Being Digital. *Anthropology News,* 47 (5), May, 8.

Chapter 3

SABILI AND INDONESIAN MUSLIM RESISTANCE TO COSMOPOLITANISM

C.W. Watson

Most anthropologists would agree that one of the most depressing features of media coverage of global conflict is the way in which journalistic simplification leads to black and white characterizations of other cultures and a consequent bias against understanding in relation to all those issues – ethnicity, religious belief, nationalism, communal identity, not to mention 'culture' in its various manifestations – that we have been so painstakingly describing, analysing and defining for over fifty years. It is as though we had never written. This despair of ours is nowhere more apparent than in relation to controversies over the clash of civilizations and especially, in the present political climate, in the depiction of Muslim societies.

In a briefing to the government officials in 2001 just prior to the Bali bombing, it was useless for me to say, on the basis of not only my own thirty years' experience of Indonesia but also that of other Indonesia specialists, that the wearing of Osama bin Laden T-shirts did not betoken a violent Muslim society about to explode in anti-Western fury. There were terrorists in Indonesia, I said, but they were few and were not representative of the Muslim population at large. Quizzical eyebrows were raised at the time, and of course it did not help my case that a few days later the Bali bombs went off, causing such carnage, and that those responsible claimed to be inspired by their religion. Nonetheless, I would still argue that, contrary to these appearances and to further bombing incidents and the outbreak of internal conflict in Indonesia, the observance of Islam in the country should not give cause for anxiety. That there is in many sections of the population anti-Americanism and anti-Western feeling no one can doubt, but, equally, it needs to be acknowledged that there is also considerable pro-Western feeling in the country. In other words Indonesian Muslims may be united in their discontent with the current world order, but that discontent takes many forms, varies in intensity and is coupled with an admiration for Western achievements.

One of the most stimulating intellectual developments of recent years has indeed been that recognition on the part of some political scientists (Chabal and Daloz 2006) that this complexity in the diversity of meaning underlying shared political expression is something they need to grapple with, and that the old paradigms of a comparative political science, which for so long held sway and which continue in some quarters to do so in the reductionist descriptions of cultures and civilizations, need to be replaced. With the search for a more nuanced approach, one that eschews easy generalizations, glib comparisons and vacuous dichotomies, the hallmarks of the earlier flawed approach, has come a concomitant openness towards contemporary anthropology, with its stress on interpretation and translation. Some of the new understanding arises from an appreciation that the older approaches, which emphasized themes and institutions and cultural traits and which relied so heavily on surveys, questionnaires and electoral results, paid insufficient attention to other areas in which political cultures found expression. As Chabal and Daloz (2006: 185) say, it may be that a study of 'grey literature' is more revealing than an approach based on extensive questionnaires.

This is certainly the premise of my own recent work on Muslim communities in Indonesia, where, rather than allowing myself to be caught up in the rapidly evolving configurations of Muslim party politics, fascinating as they are and well researched as they have been (Hefner 2000; Effendy 2003; Jamhari and Jajang 2003), I have preferred to look closely at the readers and audiences of widely available Muslim texts and Muslim preaching. I looked first in a general way at Muslim publishing (Watson 2005a) and then I examined the significance and influence of one individual, Aa Gymnastiar, who has an extraordinarily large constituency of readers, listeners and viewers (Watson 2005b). With Gym the emphasis is on the everyday practicality of observing Islamic ideals and showing how effective daily routines in the workplace and in the family predicated on Islamic guidelines can enhance the quality of one's life. His message is essentially non-political: he has no party affiliations and will not be drawn into politics. Closely observing the relationship between him, what he preaches and the audience he appeals to gives us immediate insight, then, into Indonesian Muslim social behaviour. However, although sociologically this one point of entry in terms of size alone is highly significant, it remains one of several, and we need to look at other comparable and apparently contrasting phenomena if we wish to explore further collective Muslim communal experiences in Indonesia.

One curiously under-researched area that any observer of Muslim everyday behaviour knows of, but which until now has escaped any sustained academic attention, is popular religious literature in the form of novels and short stories abundantly visible in special sections in all major bookshops and much read in serial form in journals and magazines as well as in book format. Within this popular genre, the most strikingly successful novel by far, having sold hundreds of thousands of copies, is *Ayat-Ayat Cinta* (Verses of Love) (2004) by Habiburrahman El Shirazy. Recently (March 2008) turned into a film, it has broken all Indonesian box-office records, and the President himself, accompanied by cabinet members, has given it a strong endorsement through a widely publicized viewing of the film. (One might instructively compare the popularity of the film and the book to with that of the American book and film *Love Story* in terms of readership, audience and influence.)

A study of the significance of these exceptionally popular fictional representations of everyday social situations, in which the no-nonsense application of an Islamic code of ethical behaviour provides instant solutions for fraught scenarios, would potentially reveal much about widespread attitudes among Indonesians to globalization and cosmopolitanism – which would here, of course, imply a stance in relation not only to Western but also to Middle Eastern lifestyles and political configurations. In future work I hope to engage in such research, but for present purposes here I want to confine my attention to another, but related, domain, a weekly or fortnightly magazine of social and political commentary. A reading of one such magazine, *Sabili*, has much to tell us about Muslim attitudes, but I shall be arguing that we need to read the journal very closely. What appears at first sight to be confirmation of one's worst fears, of hardening animosity and worrying polarization, hides a more complex outlook, and it is only through employing an anthropological lens, engaging in what we do best, interpreting what lies below the surface, that we can offer a more nuanced and more helpful explanation of what is happening. The starting point for any respectable anthropological approach of this kind must be to stress contextualization: placing the objects of scrutiny – in this case a representative Indonesian Muslim organ – within a historical and discursive framework, taking the longer view of the formation of current ideological positions and recognizing the influences of local contingencies.

Context

The first thing to note in relation to Indonesia is that anti-Americanism per se is not something new: it was strikingly in evidence during the cold war when Indonesia chose to be non-aligned and consequently drew down the wrath of the US and found itself in the early 1960s becoming increasingly dependent on the USSR. Sukarno, the President of the time, was vilified and demonized in terms similar to later denunciations of Saddam Hussein, and like the latter he responded by whipping up anti-Western feeling among the populace at large. They were encouraged to protest and loudly proclaim in terms which still raise a smile among the older generation *Amerika kita setrika, Inggris kita linggis* (we will burn the Americans with our flat irons and we will pulverize the English with our crowbars). At the same time as these slogans were being chanted in the streets, however, a sizeable section of the intellectual elite was shaking its collective head in irritation at the simple-mindedness of it all, and was happily reading the issues of the journals they were sent courtesy of the Congress of Cultural Freedom, *Encounter* and *Quest* in particular. And, just to emphasize the apparent inconsistencies, the same youth shouting the loudest were also those who, when they had the opportunity, listened to the Beatles and Elvis Presley.

Lest that anti-Americanism, with its banning of decadent music, be considered a simple aberration of a Soviet-style regime, we need to note that other more pro-Western regimes in South-East Asia have also taken measures in the past, and in fact continue to do so, against what is regarded as pernicious Western influence. Singapore and Malaysia, for example, still prohibit the import of *Playboy* into their countries; and it was not so long ago that Singapore would not allow men with long hair to enter the country. The unwillingness of the Singaporean government to countenance behaviour and practices acceptable and common elsewhere was always the object of amused comment in the Western press, but it has never, unlike the treatment afforded to similar phenomena in Indonesia, been subject to strong condemnation. This was equally the position with respect to matters that might be considered to strike more closely at the heart of Western democratic principles. When Sukarno spoke out against Western democracy as the tyranny of 50 per cent plus one, he was ridiculed; when Lee Kuan Yew stated that Asian principles made Western democracy an unsuitable vehicle for the conduct of governance, the argument was taken seriously (Nussbaum 1997: 139). I mention these examples simply to locate the debates about contemporary Muslim resistance to Western forms of cultural and political lifestyles within a context of closely comparable situations, from the perspective of which contemporary circumstances appear less strange and inexplicable than they might otherwise seem.

After the fall of Sukarno and the reorientation of Indonesia towards the West, there was, as might have been anticipated, an opening of the doors to the culture and capital of the West. This did not happen all at once, and there were still direct and indirect constraints on what could and could not be imported. However, by the mid-1980s, Jakarta, at least, was a cosmopolitan capital city with opportunities for wealthy elites to enjoy all the amenities, though perhaps not the same level of service, offered by international hotel and retail chains. On only one matter, however, was the regime unwilling to compromise: like its neighbour Singapore, and indeed perhaps influenced by it, Indonesia saw a great danger in allowing the full play of democratic institutions and argued that paternalistic authoritarianism exercised by a single state party was what was most appropriate and most desired by the population. Under these circumstances, the response of the several Muslim communities within Indonesia was predictable: some were prepared to work with the regime, some disengaged from politics and some – a relatively small but vocal group – went into opposition. This latter group, it should be noted, since it is allegedly from this source that the anti-Western terrorism of later years emerged, had little to say about the emerging consumer society, and welcomed the new opportunities: what they seemed to object to – and 'seemed' is the right word since the evidence of their being manipulated by intelligence provocateurs is well established – was the totalitarian nature of the regime and its secularist policies.

It was, however, from among the ranks of those who had disengaged from realpolitik that the first signs of a new orientation to what might be labelled life-style debates began to emerge (Hasbullah 2000). Not that there was homogeneity even here. Many representatives of what had now become the new Muslim middle-class were not persuaded of any need to alter their religious practice and everyday routines. There was, however, a growing movement among students, inspired by what was happening elsewhere in the Muslim world, not just in the Middle East but also in neighbouring Malaysia where the new orthodoxy had come into force some years earlier, to reflect and act upon the application of Islamic principles as they bore on the new life-styles. It was from this period, the early 80s, that one saw significant numbers of women students deciding to wear the head scarf, something which had simply not existed a decade earlier (Hasbullah 2000: 16–19).

Contemporaneously, public debates were initiated with increasing frequency over such issues as the ritual purity of food, whether or not it was halal, whether or not one should shake hands with members of the opposite sex, whether smoking should be prohibited or not, how to promote a better knowledge of sacred texts, whether it was permissible to wish Christians 'Merry Xmas', how to realize the ideals of Muslim charity by voluntary work among the poor, and how one should react to international political affairs that had a religious dimension. All these became matters of intense concern to the students and their mentors, in what was perceived as a *tarbiyah* (education) movement with a strong emphasis on apologetics and textual exegesis (see Kraince 2000 for a useful summary). In tandem with this *dakwah* (preaching) movement, groups within universities consolidated their corporate identity by learning organizational skills: how to manage a budget, how to run a campaign, how to recruit new members. Outside campus surroundings, this relatively small group had very little visible influence: for one thing, because the largest Muslim organizations with their own student organisations held aloof from them and regarded them as essentially ignorant enthusiasts, born-again Muslims who mistook the letter of the religious texts for their spirit; for another, because the regime kept a tight rein on the expression of any ideas that might undermine its stability.

When the Suharto regime fell in 1998 the middle-class trend towards a stricter interpretation of how Islamic principles should be followed in dress codes and eating habits became more pronounced. This was partly a consequence of the student Muslim groups of the 1980s now having moved into the professional middle classes, partly a consequence of what I am tempted to call Muslim chic – it became fashionable visibly to demonstrate one's religiosity through dress, through joining religious instruction groups and through going on the haj – and, finally, in part this movement can be seen as the continuation of an elite drive spearheaded by Suharto himself in his final years in office to promote Muslim culture (Hasbullah 2000: 19–28). All the while, this new middle-class Muslim community found no inconsistency between their new-found piety and their adoption of a comfortable consumer life style.

But, if after 1998 there was continuity in the behavioural trend towards a greater public visibility of Muslim mores, as far as politics was concerned liberalization brought about far-reaching structural changes in the dynamics of party political configurations. Although it is sometimes argued that to some degree these changes from the Suharto period superficially bore traces of linkage with pre-Suharto politics, they in fact heralded a new strategic awareness of potential Muslim political engagement in properly functioning democratic processes and were certainly a radical break with the passive acquiescence of the recent past. Whereas previously many committed Muslims had eschewed politics for the reasons given above, in the new political climate there was a mushrooming of new religious political parties, all eager to contest the national elections to be held in 1999.

Besides this renewed engagement in party politics, there were in addition more disturbing trends emerging outside the standard political frameworks, which were quickly picked up by the international media. I can do little beyond listing them here, but it is important to bear them in mind as part of an overall context for understanding current seemingly anti-Western and anti-cosmopolitan trends among sections of the

Indonesian population today. The most deeply alarming development of the first post-Suharto years was the sudden eruption of violent conflict between Christian and Muslim communities in eastern Indonesia. The proximate and distal causes of this conflict are still insufficiently clear: an argument has been made that it was deliberately provoked by aggrieved factions of the ousted Suharto regime (Kingsbury 2003: 105–7), though the latent possibility of such conflict in earlier times has perhaps not been given proper recognition. Whatever the case, the outcome of months of violence, with killings and burnings of houses on both sides, created within Indonesia at large a much greater distrust between communities of different religions than ever before. Christian missionaries had always been subject to critical commentary from some concerned Muslim scholars from the early twentieth century, but now this anti-Christian sentiment grew stronger, and, consequently, Christian communities felt even more vulnerable and uneasy in areas where they were a minority.

An illustrative example at another level of how perceptions of mutual suspicion have grown, while at the same time the urgency of more interfaith dialogue is recognized, can be seen in the promulgation of new education laws in 2004 and the considerable controversy that ensued with respect to the provision of religious education. The new law stipulated that all pupils in whatever type of school, state or private, denominational or secular, had a right to receive religious instruction in the religion that they professed. This law was considered by representatives of various Christian denominations as an attack against their practice in the many Christian schools they administer throughout the country, which recruit non-Christian students. Henceforward these schools are compelled to employ Muslim teachers to teach Islam to their Muslim students, something they regarded as unacceptable in the pluralist society they claim the constitution implicitly affirms. Muslims, long concerned by the presence of Muslim students in Christian educational establishments, felt that Christian protests confirmed that these schools were intended as vehicles for covert proselytization (*Sabili,* 10 April 2003). A long exchange of polemics ensued in the press.

One last example of a seemingly alarming development: in the aftermath of Suharto's replacement by his deputy Habibie, there sprang up in the major cities in Java a movement calling itself the FPI – Front Pembela Islam (Front for the Defence of Islam) – which campaigned to rid the cities of places that were regarded as dens of iniquity: nightclubs, gambling halls, brothels. There were raids on premises, smashed windows, general destruction of property and dire warnings – never carried out as far as I am aware – about people who were to be 'swept away' in these raids. Who precisely was funding these FPI attacks and the recruitment and training of their members was never clear but the rationale and the ideology, that allegedly informed their actions relied on reference to strong Muslim moral traditions and a crusade against *maksiat* – vice.

These sensational attention-grabbing events of the final years of the twentieth century, egregiously disastrous and deeply disturbing as they were, especially in relation to the inter-religious conflict, do not exhaust the contextual background to the issues we are trying to explain. To probe further, we need to return to those groups who made the decision to re-enter the world of realpolitik.

PKS

When the second general election following the fall of Suharto took place in 2004, the number of Muslim parties had been streamlined down to five. Significantly, the Muslim party to make the greatest gains, especially in the cities of west Java was the PKS, Partai Keadilan Sejahtera (Welfare and Justice Party, where name seems to have been directly inspired by the Turkish party of a similar name), the party associated most closely with the *tarbiyah* movement, which, having put down roots on university campuses, had now spread to the larger urban populations. I want to say more about this party and its supporters here, since it is from this constituency that *Sabili* first emerged in the late 1980s (Damanik 2002: 158–60) and continues to draw most of its readership. A profile of the PKS allows one to interpret the significance and influence of *Sabili* in greater depth than a simple analysis of the journal's contents. It also suggests that the picture often presented of Muslim mobs besieging embassies in Jakarta needs to be radically qualified for any understanding of the nature of political culture in Indonesia.

A report in the British daily newspaper *The Independent* on the demonstrations outside the Danish Embassy in Jakarta following the publication of the cartoons in the Danish press caricaturing the Prophet Mohammad noted the size and anger of the mob, but then went on to say, with an air of bemused puzzlement, that after the demonstrations had ended the demonstrators then proceeded to pick up all the litter in the streets and then disperse quietly. There is, then, this hint of paradox: a baying mob one moment, and the next an orderly controlled group, carefully stewarded and conscious of civic responsibility. But, to any observer of PKS politics over the past decade there is no paradox at all. The party and its student branches, in particular, went out of their way during that time to stress that their principal mission is to show by example that a commitment to Islam means, first and foremost, contributing in as tangible a way as possible to the promotion of social welfare and responding to the pressing needs of those who are socially excluded (Kraince 2000). To the public at large, the most visible evidence of the expression of this principle lies in the ways in which the PKS organizes immediate relief programmes in areas where there have been natural disasters – flooding, landslides, earthquakes. Their relief teams are always the first on the spot with emergency supplies, doing what they can to alleviate suffering and distress. And in crowded urban areas, of which there are many in Jakarta various campaigns are conducted to clean streets and promote hygiene. At a less visible level, PKS supporters also seek sponsorship for the payment of school fees for needy children, assist local orphanages and fund-raise for local charities. All these grass-roots initiatives cannot help but win the sympathies of the urban lower classes, who have responded by giving significant electoral support to the party in the general elections.

Despite these strategic philanthropic contributions to the urban poor, the PKS is not by any stretch of the imagination a workers' party, nor is it in any ideological way socialist. It is a middle-class Muslim party, organized largely by professionals, who, although they recognize a sense of moral responsibility to the poor, do not see that responsibility as incompatible with an acceptance of the present constitution of the political structures of the country or with great discrepancies of wealth in the nation at large. If the issue of endemic corruption could be solved, the implication seems to be, then all could be set right. Although one should be wary of far-fetched comparisons, in this case it might be useful to see them as latter-day equivalents of the Christian socialists of nineteenth-century England with their brand of so-called muscular Christianity and their emphasis on philanthropy, moral improvement and social justice and their preaching on temperance and self-help. There the comparison ceases, because contingent circumstances in early twenty-first-century Indonesia have been affected by endogenous and exogenous factors quite foreign to the English situation. Furthermore, the different evolutionary paths of Christianity and Islam have led to Christianity having abandoned centuries previously any institutional claims to political power and government, whereas many Muslims – not all, since there is a vocal global Muslim intellectual elite well represented in Indonesia, that rejects the idea – recognize no partibility between Caesar and God.

For the PKS, then, the ultimate goal is the establishment of a Muslim state, that is, one predicated on the implementation of *syariah* law. It is here that they and the electorate who support them part company. While very happy to be the beneficiaries of social philanthropy and fully supporting the initiatives of the former leader of the party, Hidayat Nur Wahid, now the speaker of the upper house, in his anti-corruption campaigns and his exemplary modest lifestyle (*Sabili*, 14 January 2005), for a variety of reasons they find the idea of a Muslim state unacceptable.

Recognizing this, the PKS – and *Sabili* (20 September 2007) – have, much to the chagrin of more insistent groups, such as Hizbut Tahrir, decided not to press for the implementation of *syariah* but instead to press on even harder with their *tarbiyah* campaigns within an accepted democratic framework. Continuing in the footsteps of the student groups in the late 1970s, this campaigning has notably meant a strident insistence on taking literally the prescriptions and prohibitions of Islamic texts in relation to daily life and correcting long-established social practice that they regard as un-Islamic.

As a short aside, one should note a major difference here between current *tarbiyah* campaigns and those that divided 'traditionalists' and 'modernists' among the *ummah*, the Muslim faithful, throughout most of the twentieth century. The latter disagreements centred largely upon the proper observance of prescribed ritual, the form of the daily prayers, the ceremonies around the burial of the dead, reverence of Muslim scholars and saints and mystical forms of religious behaviour. While the PKS does still concern itself with many of these matters, the main thrust of its campaigns (*dakwah*) relates to behaviour in non-ritual environments: the separation of men and women in the public sphere, the obligation on women to wear headscarves and modest apparel, the strict necessity of avoiding anything possibly contaminated by alcohol or pork fat, smoking as unacceptable in Islam, the perniciousness of Western influence, all issues that prior to 1975 had very little resonance in Indonesia.

Other noticeable features of what might be called a PKS lifestyle are a strong awareness of the linkages at a regional and global level among Muslim communities. The students of the PKS and their academic mentors are above all exceedingly proficient in the use of IT and this allows them to make immediate and effective link-ups with sources of information and widespread networks which in turn help facilitate the dissemination of their own messages. Furthermore, either because of a feeling of still being an embattled minority within mainstream Indonesian Islam, or simply because of the psychological support that the solidarity gives them, dedicated PKS supporters tend to confine their social life to like-minded members of their own groups. This is especially noticeable in the way in which marriages are arranged: endogamy among the party faithful is not simply encouraged, it is actively promoted by a straightforward scheme of arranged marriages. Coupled with this emphasis on marriage within the group, there is also a promotion of openness towards polygamy – an institution previously frowned upon by all the educated Indonesian elite – and a rejection of the idea of family planning.

The exclusivity and the self-righteousness of the PKS insistence on literalist interpretations of the *syariah* bring it into confrontation with other devout Muslim groups within Indonesia, roughly speaking the old opponents in the former traditionalist and modernist debates mentioned above, who now join forces in university campuses and elsewhere to engage the PKS in public debate. In the eyes of these latter groups, PKS representatives are relatively ignorant of true Islamic scholarship. Underlying their perceptible scorn is the observation that those middle-class educated professionals and students who are most strenuous in support of the PKS do not have a religious educational background. They have come to Islamic scholarship late usually in their university years, and their grasp of Arabic in many cases is poor; they are zealots with all the passion but none of the understanding. Though opponents make exceptions for individuals like Hidayat Nur Wahid, who does have the requisite credentials of scholarship, as well as other individuals who have conscientiously enrolled in a Saudi-funded Jakarta-based Arab school (Damanik 2002: 206–7), they regard most rank-and-file PKS members, however sincere they may be, as having only superficial understanding of how to conduct theological debates and follow the established rules of logical inference from the statements of the texts.

Sabili

The frequent campus debates that pit opponents against each other are now a common feature of Indonesian university life, and, depending on the affiliations of the particular group of students that organizes the events – as a rough guide, PKS supporters and like-minded students are in the majority in secular universities, while their opponents cluster in Muslim tertiary educational institutions – the meetings support one argument over the other. These are, on the whole, occasions for preaching to the converted. Other forums for debates are the daily newspapers, which regularly carry religious columns and lively exchanges in readers' correspondence sections. The most respected Indonesian daily is in fact the Catholic–owned newspaper *Kompas* but its columns are regularly thrown open to Muslim intellectuals, especially those propounding a 'liberal' doctrine. The major Muslim newspaper, *Republika*, seemingly without any concern for the apparent inconsistency, carries strongly contrasting views even within the same issue of the newspaper, and there appears to be no overall editorial line.

Among the more noticeable arenas in which public debate is conducted, however, are the fortnightly and monthly journals available in the towns and cities of Indonesia, especially of Java. Numerous journals circulate, pitched at different categories of the Muslim community – men, women, families, students, old, young – all of which have their special characters. Marketing outlets range from the pavement displays of itinerant hawkers to the special racks of air-conditioned bookshops catering for elites. Among these journals, *Sabili* has a place of its own, and is widely recognized as consistently putting across a 'hard' anti-Western line. It is a journal that PKS supporters regularly read, in addition to their own house journal, *Saksi*, both for confirmation of their own views and for the factual information they need to bolster their arguments. Liberals acknowledge its wide appeal but are scornful of it and are sceptical of its influence. Reading it regularly allows an observer easy access to the way in which political, social and cultural arguments are framed in a Muslim discourse that sees itself as not only uniquely authentic but also necessarily oppositional and uniting the ummah in their collective discontent with non-Muslim global influences on Indonesian society.

Sabili, taking its title from the Arabic word for 'path', is now in its thirteenth year of publication, though it was banned in the Suharto period between 1993 and 1998, and has a circulation of c.120,000 (Damanik 2002: 160). This figure should be multiplied by a factor of, I would say, at least five to get an idea of its circulation, since as a fortnightly journal it frequently lies around on tables in houses and on stalls, where readers will casually pick it up and read one or two items before replacing it. It is professionally marketed and widely distributed and is available in bookshops that cater for all levels of the reading public, from air-conditioned chain stores in elite suburbs to dingy stationers in backstreets. It seems to sell best from the ubiquitous magazine stalls to be found at road junctions in all Indonesian towns, which sell everything from a range of newspapers and news weeklies to celebrity and soft-porn magazines and religious tracts. Currently (January 2008) it retails for 9,400 Indonesian rupiah, about sixty pence. It is half-folio, large paperback, size – 21 cm by 11 cm – and is attractively packaged, with a glossy cover, often, as Meuleman (2006) notes, designed to be startlingly provocative, with cover titles such as Kristenisasi Menyerbu Kampus (Christianization Assaults the Campus) (31 July 2003). Articles are also available electronically (http://www.sabili.co.id). Editions are 112 pages and contain numerous photos and vignettes, several in colour. There is a sprinkling of a few advertisements in the magazines for products and services with a specific Muslim dimension from courses and programmes offered by Islamic institutions of education to tours to the Middle East and Muslim dress for men and women.

The editorial team consists of five or so regulars, and there are in addition several occasional reporters. Some of the reports carried, especially those relating to international events in the Middle East, have been collated from Arab sources. It would take too long to describe in detail the variety of contents making up a typical issue but some indication of its general appearance is called for. In terms of layout, there are several editorial articles, one or two central features, some general columns of advice, a substantial section for teenagers, a section on various corners of the Muslim world, an article or two referring to periods in recent Indonesian history in which Muslim figures played an important role, feature-length interviews with contemporary Muslim personalities in the news, and often a profile of a leading personality. There are also two agony columns, in which general advice is given on personal and family problems. Typical themes explored regularly in its pages include the dangers of Christian missionary activity, with lurid examples drawn from two or three case studies in which witnesses describe to reporters alleged abuses or discuss the provocation arising from the construction of churches in Muslim districts. Zionism is frequently mentioned and condemned. American policies in Iraq are also heavily criticized.

Content

To convey some sense of the tone and style of the journal, let me use the example of the issue of 28 August 2003, which appeared shortly after the bombing at the Marriott hotel in Jakarta. The cover shows a photo in red against a black edging in which an Indonesian task force is shown clearing up the wreckage outside the hotel. The title on the cover has in smallish black letters Bom Marriott and then beneath in large white lettering with red edging 'Islam Mengutuk, Islam Dituduh' (Islam Condemns, Islam is Accused). At the top of the cover is another title in smallish letters 'Mereka Menyerang Syariat Poligami' (They Attack the Syariah Provisions for Polygamy). After the opening page listing the contents of the issue, there is a short introductory editorial piece briefly taking up the title on the front cover and giving some in-house news of weddings of members of staff, a small touch hinting at what appears to a Western scholar as perhaps a quaint sense of *Gemeinschaft*. This is followed by a more detailed commentary on the issue of the new anti-terrorist measures that the government is just about to bring into force and which *Sabili*, along with several other commentators which they quote, fear might herald a renewal of the state repression last seen during Suharto's heyday. The next pages are the correspondence columns containing critical comments from readers about the negative effects of television, as well as two longer commentaries in a separate rubric on matters of the day. This is followed by a short homily of general advice based on Muslim scriptures about how to remain calm despite provocation. Contained within the advice is a further reference to the Marriott bombing, which is said to be unacceptable, and the Prophet is quoted as not only forbidding the murder of women and children even in war but even the destruction of orchards (p. 13).

Immediately following is a two-page editorial piece written to commemorate the anniversary of Indonesian independence on 17 August 1945. Its polemical tone well illustrates the flavour of *Sabili's* hostility to the West and to globalization. Entitled 'Kita Masih Dijajah' (We Are Still Under Colonial Rule), it begins by recalling the winning of independence and the important contribution made by Muslim politicians representing Muslim parties at the time, and tells an amusing anecdote about one of them. It then goes on to make the link with the present situation by saying that today Muslim politicians and Muslim activists are not respected but are arrested and put on trial and the real criminals are allowed to go free. There is then a further link to the penetration into the country of a 'repulsive' culture. Here is an excerpt in my translation:

> With respect to culture our country has been penetrated by a repulsive culture. The style of life of most of us is very far from the values [we hold dear]. It seems we imitate too easily. We swallow whole without shame throwaway goods and culture from outside. In relation to clothes it's as though we didn't have enough material. That's what the Prophet meant when he said, 'wearing clothes but naked'. The 'Abang and None' ceremony in Jakarta [an 'invented' tradition designed to promote a sense of local ethnic pride in being an indigenous Jakartan (*orang Betawi*)], which is allegedly religious because it is adopted from Betawi culture, is nonetheless quite counter to *syariah*. As for the world of entertainment, need we say more; it is very clearly in direct opposition to established morality. Cafes and discotheques become arenas for the transaction of sex and drugs ... Singers, especially the female singers of *dangdut* [a popular form of Indonesian music] display themselves with their erotic actions as though they were inviting their audience to have sex. Television programmes are predominantly vulgar: violence, pornography and superstition ... Our artistic culture has lost its self-respect. It satisfies only the lowest tastes but hides under the [slogan] freedom of expression ... The colonial powers and the destroyers [of our native culture] come together in one network: the group of the devil. Don't allow the political, economic, legal and cultural imperialists to enter our hearts, our thoughts and our behaviour. If we break ranks, we shall merit the anger of God. We certainly won't obtain God's help. (pp. 13–14)

The combination of elements – the reference to respected Muslim figures, the contrast between the way in which the Muslim community is treated and how criminals remain free, the reference to the immorality of foreign cultures and how they have influenced the world of entertainment, the link to sex and drugs and the reference to controversies about the quality of television, the loss of cultural identity, the association of these circumstances with the devil and finally the call to heed religious injunctions and for the *ummah* to stand together against this external tide of political, economic and cultural colonialism – all repeat once again the themes that are to be found in every issue of the magazine and are exceedingly familiar to readers.

Of the remaining articles in this issue, several are taken up with how, as the cover title suggests, Islam in general is blamed for terrorist acts, and in this regard there is a scrutiny with commentary of international media coverage. The 'Muslim World' section addresses the issue of Palestine once again and condemns Israel's actions, in which America is complicit. A theological column expounds the way in which Christian evangelists try to use the Koran to support the doctrine of the Trinity. The last major section of this issue, thirteen pages, is a discussion of the religious law in connection with polygamy, which takes as its starting point the 'Polygamy Awards' instituted by a wealthy Muslim entrepreneur, himself a polygamist, to be given to successful polygamous families.

For the sake of the argument I shall be making below, the repetitiveness of the items forming the staple of *Sabili*'s contents needs to be fully appreciated, so I want to compare briefly the issue of the journal just described with a more recent one. Dated 9 February 2006, the front cover shows a picture of the Playboy Bunny against a black background with the caption 'Teror Akhlak' (Moral Terrorism). The issue is taken up to a large extent with the current debate in Indonesia about permitting the marketing of an Indonesian franchise *Playboy*, something that, as one might have expected, is wholly unacceptable to *Sabili* and its readers. The short comment on the contents page states the issue and the words echo the earlier issue:

'the physical form of colonialism in the past has been replaced by an economic colonialism and a cultural invasion. Not content with that, Western countries continue to slander Muslims with the accusation that they are the perpetrators of terror. Now our morals are being terrorized, by among other things the magazine Playboy' (pp. 3).

The long, extensive discussion in the body of the magazine, playing with the word 'terror', exploiting its overuse in the media and not so subtly subverting it, discusses pornography circulating in Indonesia at the moment, the difficulties in the framing of anti-pornography laws, the comments of feminist activists that pornographic magazines like *Playboy* exploit and degrade women and an interview with a media personality who recommends the production of soaps with a religious content to counter meretricious soft pornography. The 'Muslim World' section looks at Iraq 1,000 days after the invasion. An item on a Muslim figure in the Minangkabau region of west Sumatra describes how he campaigns against the attempts of Christian missionaries, who use all sorts of nefarious methods to achieve their goals, including hypnotism and the use of magic as well as going out with Muslim girls and then getting them pregnant. The story of a victim of childhood sexual abuse seems to repeat a very similar story found in an essay in the 2003 issue. There is also an article stating the dangers of Zionism, this time associating it with freemasonry, which was established in Indonesia during the Dutch colonial period. Of two shorter pieces towards the end of this issue, the first discusses the disappointing fact that Indonesia now has to import rice, and the second piece criticizes the entry into *pesantren* (small religious educational communities) of a supermarket chain owned by Phillip Morris, which is seen to spell the death of small local entrepreneurship. The irony of the situation, as *Sabili* points out, is that the invitation to the *pesantren* that they should welcome the supermarket was made by the Minister of Cooperatives and Small and Medium-sized Businesses. As *Sabili* puts it,

> 'If this is allowed to happened our *pesantren* will be caught in a global capitalist network thanks to our own Minister… The news of the Minister's visit to the *pesantren*, coupled with the Alfamart offer, raises a question, because a Minister is behaving like the marketing agent of a private business' (pp. 106–7).

Conclusions

This description of the contents of two issues of *Sabili* separated by two and a half years – and a perusal of some 2008 issues shows that little has changed over the last two years – should be sufficient to demonstrate both the limited number of themes that the journal recycles, making adventitious use of recent events, and the way in which those themes are framed consistently and coherently in the tones of a strident and pious Muslim discourse that draws constantly on quotations from Islamic scriptures. Transparent as it is, the stylistic signature of all the writing hardly needs elaboration. Criticism relating to moral, political, economic and cultural issues is followed immediately by quotations and references to the scriptures to legitimate the criticism and put the argument beyond refutation. However, simply to dismiss this, as many do within Indonesia, as repetitive and tedious, never going beyond well-established editorial routines, is to fail to perceive how precisely the magazine works and what its intentions are. This is not a magazine designed to win round new readers or convert religious agnostics to a new view of the world. On the contrary, this is a magazine exclusively for those who are already convinced of the correctness of the views expressed there: not consciousness raising so much as consciousness sustaining. Hence each issue is required to repeat in order to confirm and consolidate, to provide security for readers that things have not changed, that the world continues to be a wicked place and that pious Muslims everywhere are beset by the evil machinations of international capitalism, Christianity and Zionism – and more recently (*Sabili*, 20 September 2007) the growing influence of Sai Baba – not to mention being under attack from dangerous secularists at home and foreign governments abroad.

Constant reiteration of a formula, as we know from the analysis of oral literature, cocoons the listener within a familiar cognitive world, in which the pleasure of being able to know in advance, not only the lines of narrative development, but also the literary and linguistic tropes in which it will be played out, and is what the audience seeks out. On this reading, *Sabili*, far from inciting action, can be seen as conservatively maintaining the status quo, a fortnightly ritual of rebellion in which the collective readership shakes its head in despair, heaves a world-weary sigh, mutters a religious quotation or two and then goes about its everyday business in no way changed. The words they read simply echo the sermons of the preachers in their mosques, the texts on the websites they access and the conversations which they have with one another in their professional gatherings, with their regular friends and in family get-togethers. With those who do not share their views they are happy to discuss differences, but they are not open to the possibility of a change of opinion. Perceiving them from the outside, their fellow-Muslims of a liberal outlook either dismiss with a shrug this closing of the mind, which to them resembles the smug satisfaction of lotus-eaters, or they react angrily to the refusal to negotiate a responsible stance towards the world, one that would concede individuals' own responsibility for their conduct without the heavy moral policing *Sabili* and its readers seem to want to impose.

Nonetheless, a blanket condemnation of *Sabili* and all it stands for risks a failure to understand the complexity of the positions taken in many areas where there might be grounds for a common cause. The strident anti-Christian and anti-Jewish messages are, as they stand, absurd and unacceptable, though even here one might find oneself agreeing when the targets are the crass antics of extreme Christian evangelist cults in Muslim heartlands in Indonesia or the brutal treatment of civilian Palestinians by the Israeli armed forces. The criticisms of the Indonesian television industry and its deliberate pandering to a taste for soft porn, violence and gruesome horror are opinions widely shared by discerning viewers of all secular and religious persuasions. So too are the criticisms of the abuse of the political system and the culture of corruption. And the green issues, the rejection of global capitalist franchises, the over-condemnation of the foreign imports and the need to support small businesses, all have widespread support among NGO activists, who would otherwise shudder at the thought that they might be close to a *Sabili* position. Unity in discontent brings together strange bedfellows.

The difficulty of trying to come to any overall evaluation of the significance of *Sabili* and to discuss it in terms of a generic discourse to which it can be reduced lies in just this complex conflation of ideas. There is in fact no homogeneous discourse: *Sabili* therefore is not amenable to those formulaic generalizations; much better to see it in post-structuralist terms as a random collection of themes masquerading under the banner of a unified field. The stylistic impression of coherence and consistency belies the contingency of a set of historical circumstances temporarily, say for a decade or two, crystallized into a set of linked propositions. There is a seeming plausibility in the tightness of structure that an appeal to fundamental Muslim values and the liberal sprinkling of Koranic quotations appear to bestow, but this crystalline structure is always in danger of being dissolved into new solutions as circumstances change. It is because we simply do not have any equivalent journals in any Western countries that we find it so difficult to grasp the character and significance of not just *Sabili* but the thousands of journals like it in other parts of the world. The semi-popular nature of the media in the West has the consequence of narrowing down the range of publications: exclusively, they deal with either politics and economics or lifestyle or religion, and never in any of these cases at a widespread popular level. Only with the weekend newspapers do we perhaps approach some equivalent and in those, of course, there is no religious dimension to speak of. It is, in contrast, the latter element that controls and colours all others in *Sabili* and it is this seeming peculiarity that we find most difficult to interpret.

Wrestling with that difficulty, we sometimes succumb to the easy temptation to declare such a magazine and others like it as the products of mindless fanaticism. Anthropologists should know better than that. The trick is not only to understand the phenomenon in its own terms, tracing the way in which it has been put together, overcoming the resistance to obtaining at least some vicarious experience of 'how natives think', but it is also working with that understanding, preserving it, carrying it back and finally offering it, differently packaged perhaps, but still pristine, as a matter for reflection.

For anthropologists, *Sabili* presents an opportunity to demonstrate their craft. We encounter a magazine designed to convey and confirm a sharp positioning towards the world, one at first sight at least hostile and prickly towards those Enlightenment values championed so robustly in the intellectual environments that anthropologists and their audiences inhabit. Closer inspection, following the well-trodden path of contextualization, within an international political moment, within an evolving national history and within a variety of local discourses, reveals that, even, or perhaps especially, among the discontented, things are not always what they seem. Recognizing the perennial deceptiveness of appearances once again confirms the existential need to be forever pushing our way through the doors of interpretation.

Note

I wish to acknowledge the support of the British Academy for the initial research on which this chapter was based. Two small grants, one in 2003 from the South-East Committee and one from the Small Grants Awards in 2004, allowed me to conduct interviews and collect materials in Indonesia.

References

Damanik, A.S. 2002. *Fenomena Partai Keadilan*. Jakarta: Teraju.

Chabal, P. and J.P. Daloz. 2006. *Culture Troubles: Politics and the Interpretation of Meaning*. London: Hurst.

Effendy, B. 2003. *Islam and the State in Indonesia*. Singapore: Institute of Southeast Asian Studies.

Habiburrahman El Shirazy. 2007. *Ayat-Ayat Cinta*, 20th printing. Jakarta: Basmala and Republika (first edition 2004).

Hasbullah, M. 2000. Cultural Presentation of the Muslim Middle Class in Contemporary Indonesia. *Studia Islamika*, 7 (2),1–58.

Hefner, R. 2000. *Civil Islam*. Princeton: Princeton University Press.

Jamhari and Jajang Jahroni (eds). 2004. *Gerakan Salafi radikal di Indonesia*. Jakarta: PT RajaGrafindo Persada.

Kingsbury, D. 2003. Diversity in Unity. In D. Kingsbury and H. Aveling (eds) *Autonomy and Disintegration in Indonesia*. London: RoutledgeCurzon, pp. 99–114.

Kraince, R.G. 2000. The Role of Islamic Student Groups in the Reformasi Struggle: KAMMI (Kesatuan Aksi Mahasiswa Muslim Indonesia), *Studia Islamika*, 7 (1), 1–50.

Meuleman, J. 2006. *Modern Trends in Islamic Translations* (in press).

Nussbaum, M.C. 1997. *Cultivating Humanity*. London and Cambridge, MA: Harvard University Press.

Watson, C.W. 2005a. Islamic Books and Their Publishers: Notes on the Contemporary Indonesian Scene. *Journal of Islamic Studies*, 16 (2), 177–210.

——— 2005b. A Popular Indonesian Preacher: The Significance of Aa Gymnastiar, *Journal of the Royal Anthropological Institute* (NS), 11 (4), 773–92.

Chapter 4

THE COSMOPOLITAN AND THE NOUMENAL: A CASE STUDY OF ISLAMIC JIHADIST NIGHT DREAMS AS REPORTED SOURCES OF SPIRITUAL AND POLITICAL INSPIRATION

Iain Edgar and David Henig

The convergence of peoples and markets in 'real-world' cosmopolitanism is significantly challenged and indeed fractured in emerging apparent differences as to the ontological status of inner worlds. On the one hand, the Western secular, liberal, post-Christian capitalist ideology and world view 'see' inner worlds, usually, as reflective but not primarily constitutive or generative of outer world dynamics. The Freudian notion of the personal unconscious is emblematic of such a paradigm. The Western psychoanalytical paradigm, however is radically different from that of many societies studied by social anthropologists, notably shamanic cultures. Strongly religious cultures share a differing and variant paradigm as to the nature of the unconscious; the numinous is, or rather can be, the locus of spiritual generativity within the outer world.[1] These abstractions find real-world political, economic and social significance today, particularly, in the ideological world view of the growing militant jihadist variant of Islam.

As well as their critique of Western imperialist aggression and secularism, part of Islamic militant jihadist inspiration is apparently derived from reported experience of true night dreams from Allah, within the Islamic tradition of prophetic revelation through 'true dreams', Al-ru'ya. This chapter presents many such night dream examples from the Al-Qaeda leadership and followers, to the Taliban and ex-Guantanamo Bay inmates. Some examples, particularly the case example of the reported inspirational dreams of Mullah Omar, have been gained through recent fieldwork in the Middle East, particularly Pakistan. We develop anthropological reflections upon the phenomena of the political usage of such reported imaginary data. Following recent debates discussing cosmopolitanism as a mechanism for the transcendence of communitarian, national, local and 'cultural' limits, or as a way of connecting people across particular boundaries (Rapport 2007; Theodossopoulos, this volume), we argue that the partly dream-inspired, militant, Islamic jihadist ideology is a transnational politico-religious movement of discontent and a particular variant of counter-cosmopolitanism (Appiah 2007), rather than Western, hegemonic international cosmopolitanism.

The Dream in Islam

Islam is probably the largest night dream culture in the world today. In Islam, the night dream is thought to offer a way to metaphysical and divinatory knowledge, to be a practical, alternative and potentially accessible source of imaginative inspiration and guidance and to offer ethical clarity concerning action in this world. Islam was both born in and gave birth to spiritual dreamtime. The Prophet Muhammad is said to have received *ru'an* (the plural of *ru'ya*)[2] or 'true dreams' from God for six months before the beginning of the revelation of the Koran. Bukhari (1979: 91), compiler of the best-known Hadith (sayings and actions of the Prophet Muhammad) reports the words of Muhammad's wife, Aisha, that the 'commencement of the divine inspiration was in the form of good righteous [true] dreams in his sleep. He never had a dream but that it came true like bright day of light.' Indeed, there it is said that one-forty-sixth of the Koran was given to Muhammad in dreams (Bukhari 1979: 196).

Sviri sets out the consequences of this for the role of dreaming in medieval Islam: 'While prophecy has ceased, Muhammad being the seal of the Prophets, messages of divine origin can still be communicated through dreams, albeit on a smaller scale than prophecy' (Sviri 1999: 252). The same point is made in a hadith included in Bukhari: 'Nothing is left of prophetism except *Al-Mubashshirat*,' which the Prophet explained as being 'the true good dreams that convey glad tidings' (Bukhari 1979: 99). In mainstream Islam, then, there is no future revelation to come other than through the oneirocratic vehicle of true dreams. This gives such dreams a special charisma, power and authority, and means that – for all Muslims, and particularly for those followers of Islam with a mystical facility – the dream is a potential pathway to the divine. In sleep or in deep contemplation, the mystically attuned have access to the noumenal, not just the surreal.

Three kinds of dreams are recognized, first by the Prophet and then by later dream writers, such as Ibn Sireen (2000), the eight-century dream interpreter from Basra, whose book *Dreams and Interpretations* remains the most popular dream interpretation manual in many Islamic countries today. First come true spiritual dreams, *ru'an*, inspired by God; second come dreams inspired by the devil; third come dreams from the *nafs*, or ego, which are considered unimportant.

True dreams are most likely to be experienced by the pious and the righteous, those who have already stripped away some of the veils of materialism from their hearts. However, from West Africa to the Philippines, the tripartite schematization of dreams explained above is part of the world view of the majority of Muslims, not just the especially pious. Edgar's fieldwork[3] in the UK, Turkey, Northern Cyprus, and Pakistan between 2004 and 2005 confirmed this, using extensive and random, serendipitous, interviewing of people from all walks of life. Ask a Muslim about dreams, and usually you will be told of a significant dream that has influenced their life through focusing their attention on a possibility not previously recognized by their conscious mind. Sufis, followers of the mystical branch of Islam, are especially steeped in the power and extraordinary value of dreaming. Several Sufis in Sheffield, UK, spoke about dreams they had had of their Sheikh, in which they received valuable teachings about their spiritual development or about their core life issues. These Sufis regarded dreams of their Sheikh as true dreams. A Muslim dry-cleaner in the UK told of his mother, who had dreams in which the Prophet advised her about how to pray. A textile seller in Peshawar, Pakistan, told how the Prophet had appeared in a dream and shown him the way to slake the continual thirst he had experienced in his dream, through praying five times a day. Thereafter he had been happy. A fifteen-year-old boy from Birmingham, UK, whom Edgar met in a *madrasah* in Peshawar, told how he had moved to Pakistan to study to become an imam partly through a dream. Muhammad Amanullah (2005) came to similar conclusions after studying twelve staff in the religious studies department of a Malaysian university: the majority reported true dreams, and 50 per cent believed they had seen the Prophet in a dream.

The appearance of the Prophet Muhammad in a dream is of particular importance. The Hadiths say that, if the Prophet appears in a dream, then it is a true dream. Bukhari writes, 'Whoever has seen me in a dream, then no doubt he has seen me, for Satan cannot imitate my shape' (1979: 106). Many people spoke to confirm this. For non-Muslims, the conviction that to dream of the Prophet is to have received a true guidance from God could be seen as opening a Pandora's box, but there are safeguards. The Prophet must be complete in his shape (Bukhari 1979: 104), and no true dream can advocate behaviour contrary to the teachings of the Koran and the Hadiths. An imam in Peshawar gave two examples of this from his own experience. The first involved a lawyer who went to him for help in interpreting a dream of the Prophet rolled up in a carpet. The imam responded by saying 'You are a corrupt lawyer,' presumably because the body and energy of the Prophet were circumscribed. The second example was of a man who had a dream in which the Prophet had said he could drink alcohol. The imam asked him if he was a drinker and the man said, 'Yes,' to which the Imam replied that it was not the Prophet he had seen, but a self-justification for his drinking alcohol.

Dream interpretation in Islam, even given the apparently simple classificatory system, is extremely sophisticated, and takes into account factors that include the piety and spiritual rank of the dreamer, their social position, the time of night of the dream and the time of year. Islamic dream dictionaries, unlike their Western counterparts, may contain many interpretations for the same symbol (Lamoreux 2002). For example, if a poor person dreams of honey, this can be a sign of illness as only then will poor people buy honey, whereas for a rich person to dream of honey is a favourable sign. Religious scholars say that only a prophet can definitively distinguish a true from a false dream; even spiritual leaders such as sheikhs may disagree about interpretations. Anyone, then, may have a true dream, though it is more likely to be experienced by a pious person, or by one who is perhaps going to become more pious on account of the dream. In this sense, Islamic dream theory and practice enshrine the possibility of every believer having true dreams, and indeed in Islamic eschatology all believers will receive true dreams prior to the end time.

Dreams can facilitate conversions, either into Islam or into militant jihadism. An example of the first type of conversion is a Chilean man encountered in Islamabad, who had previously been a TV shop owner in Chile. He said he became a Muslim following a dream in which he saw the first words of the Koran written in the skies. He moved to Pakistan with his family and was studying Islam in a Karachi *madrasah*. His mother had married a Muslim preacher, and his son had trained as a *hafiz* (one who can recite all the Koran). An example of the second type of conversion is the dream of the sister of Abu Mussab al-Zarqawi, the former leader of Al-Qaeda in Iraq, which is said to have been one of two reasons why he converted to jihadism. This dream is discussed later in the chapter.

The Patterns and Analytical Threads Running Through Jihadist Dream Interpretation

Certain patterns inform jihadist dream interpretative narratives. First, jihadists are reported to receive divine inspiration, guidance and divinatory 'news' of future events in this world and the world of the hereafter. Secondly, dream narratives in part legitimate jihadist actions for the dreamers themselves, for their followers and for the Islamic nation, the Ummah. Thirdly, dream visions connect the dreamers with the mythically real past of the revelatory time of the Prophet Mohammed and his companions, the golden age of Islam. As well as this, dreams actually introduce this glorious past into the present: the visionary and revelatory world of Islam is reborn today, as dreamers base their inspired jihad upon the 'glad tidings' that Muhammad said would come through true dreams. Fourthly, there is often a marked reliance on the manifest content of the dream symbolism: sacred figures from the visionary history of Islam (particularly the Prophet, his companions and Hasan and Husain) communicate, usually through the spoken word, directly to the dreamer as in a revelation, announcing and instructing the dreamer. Dreams of heavenly spaces and the glorious reception of the martyrs are reported; dead friends appear with metaphysical information.

As in all dream cultures, jihadists both dream and interpret their dreams within their own culturally specific world view, in this case that of Islam, according to which this material world is not our final destination, but rather a series of lessons and tests and a preparation for the hereafter and the time of judgement at death. The more real world of the hereafter does, however, occasionally intersect with this material world through night dreams, and more rarely through waking visions. Such hyper-lucid experiences can define action and events in this world. This interrelationship between dreams and events positions dreaming as potentially related to the future rather than (as is the case in most Western psychoanalytic theories of dreaming, such as that of Freud) to the past;[4] moreover, it shows how dreaming as a work of imagination is interrelated with social practice. Unlike in the West, in Islam dreams and future events in this world can be clearly related. The Joseph sura in the Koran makes this especially clear as Joseph, through his interpretation of the seven fat and thin cows dream of the Egyptian Pharaoh, enables the Pharaoh to plan ahead for a succession of bad harvests. Specifically, through the prophetic example of Muhammad, dreams can be related to success in warfare. Muhammad dreams before the battle of Badr that the enemy forces are smaller than they actually are, so giving him and his army confidence in victory (Koran 1956: 8.43–8.46).

The Dreams of Al-Qaeda Members

There are many reports of the power and significance of true dreams for many of the best known jihadist commanders and followers, some of which now follow. These accounts come from secondary sources, such as websites and newspaper articles. However, the data concerning Mullah Omar, the Taliban leader, were gathered directly. Overall, it is suggested that – whatever veracity issues there may be concerning particular individual dream narratives – there are definitely thematic patterns, as outlined above, in these dream narratives and in their legitimacy claims which are fully consistent with Islamic night dream teachings and practices.

Osama bin Laden

Osama bin Laden, the well-known leader of Al-Qaeda, seems to relate to night dreams. Following the 11 September attack in New York, many newspapers (e.g. Mirror 14 December 2001) reported a transcript of a video apparently showing bin Laden referring to the anticipatory dreams of some of his followers. These followers apparently did not know of the planned attacks, and bin Laden speaks of his concern that 'the secret [of the attacks] would be revealed if everyone starts seeing it in their dreams.' Early in the video bin Laden says,

> Abu'l-Hassan al-Masri told me a year ago: 'I saw in a dream, we were playing a soccer game against the Americans. When our team showed up in the field, they were all pilots!' He [Al-Masri] didn't know anything about the operation until he heard it on the radio. He said the game went on and we defeated them. That was a good omen for us.

The use of the term 'omen' indicates a belief that dreams are a potential source of divination, especially for pious and spiritually oriented Muslims. Moreover, whilst the military contest is disguised as a football match, the victory over the Americans by the jihadist 'pilots' is made manifest in the dream symbolism. Future victory is clearly symbolized.

Yosri Fouda[5] (2003: 109) wrote about the role of dreaming for the 11 September attackers:

> Dreams and visions and their interpretations are also an integral part of these spiritual beliefs. They mean that the Mujahideen are close to the Prophet, for whatever the Prophet dreams will come true. In a videotape recorded shortly after 11 September, al-Qaeda spokesman Sulaiman Abu

Ghaith is seen and heard speaking in the company of bin Laden, who was playing host to a visitor from Mecca: 'I saw in my dreams that I was sitting in a room with the Sheikh [bin Laden], and all of a sudden there was breaking news on TV. It showed an Egyptian family going about its business and a rotating strap that said: 'In revenge for the sons of Al-Aqsa [that is, the Palestinians], Osama bin Laden executes strikes against the Americans.' That was before the event.

Bin Laden then interprets: 'The Egyptian family symbolises Mohammed Atta, may Allah have mercy on his soul. He was in charge of the group.'

Ramzi Binalshibh would later tell Fouda long stories about the many dreams and visions of the 'brothers' in the run-up to 11 September. He would speak of the Prophet and his close companions as if he had actually met them ... Atta ... also told Ramzi a little anecdote about 'brother' Marwan (al-Shehdi)[6] that he knew would please him. 'Mohammed (Atta) told me that Marwan had a beautiful dream that he was [physically] flying high in the sky surrounded by green birds not from our world, and that he was crashing into things, and that he felt so happy.'

'What things?' Fouda asked.

'Just things,' answered Ramzi.

Green birds are often given significance in these dreams.

Whilst Ramzi is shy about explaining this dream, it would be likely that the 'green birds not from our world' would be interpreted as a heavenly symbol: green is a spiritual colour in Islam, and flying birds are a common symbol of heaven. Marwan reporting that he was flying high in a symbolically constituted heavenly realm and also crashing into things could easily be interpreted as another 'good' omen for the 11 September jihadists. Whilst the rotating strap that speaks is surreal, its message is plain: that the basic political cause fuelling the jihad is the continual oppression of the Palestinian people by Israel, the USA and its allies. Revenge is indeed in the air, and success against the Americans is foretold through the medium of the television, a medium that later presented the 11 September attack so graphically.

By defining the meaning of the dream in relating the Egyptian family image to the person of Atta, bin Laden is taking on part of the traditional spiritually authoritative role of a sheikh, a spiritual master, as an interpreter of dreams. Bin al-Shibh speaks of the Prophet and his companions as if he had actually met them in his visions and dreams, thereby showing his apparent familiarity with and connection to the first days of Islam. His mindset is tuned into an eternally enduring hyper–reality, in which linear temporality is confounded and the glorious Islamist past is evoked with an ongoing intimacy and immediacy. The days of revelation are indeed present today.[7]

Robert Fisk, the Middle East correspondent for the *Independent*, reports (2005: 34) that during one of his three meetings with bin Laden, bin Laden said: 'Mr Robert … one of our brothers had a dream. He dreamt that you came to us one day on a horse, that you had a beard and that you were a spiritual person. You wore a robe like us. This means you are a true Moslem.' This terrifies Fisk, who fears he is meant to 'accept this "dream" as a prophecy and a divine instruction'. Fisk says 'I am not a Moslem, I am a journalist.' Osama replies, 'If you tell the truth, that means you are a good Moslem.' The moment passes.

One view of this could be that bin Laden is using the dream trope as a way of challenging Fisk, or as a device to influence his followers. However, since it is considered wrong to lie about a dream in the Islamic tradition, it is more likely that this provides further evidence that bin Laden considers that dreams are a potentially divinatory form of communication. The beard is a sign of a devout Muslim and the horse is traditionally interpreted in Islamic dream dictionaries as symbolizing a 'person's status, rank, honour, dignity, power and glory' (Sirin 2000: 99). Again, we see bin Laden acting as a spiritual master, defining the meaning of this dream and reframing Fisk's reply to confirm his, bin Laden's, interpretation of the dream. Bin Laden utilizes his companion's dream as a source of spiritual certainty in the prophetic tradition.

Zacarias Moussaoui

Zacarias Moussaoui has often been described as the twentieth member of the 11 September New York attacks. He is a French citizen of Moroccan origins. He was an Al-Qaeda member who had given allegiance to his sheikh, Osama bin Laden, and had attended flight training school in the USA before 11 September. He was tried in the USA in 2006 and was found guilty of conspiring to kill Americans in the 11 September New York attack. He is currently serving a life sentence in the USA. The death sentence was also considered as a verdict. Moussaoui's reported night dream of flying a plane into a tall building was a significant issue in his trial in the USA. There was debate in the trial as to whether such a dream was evidence of schizophrenia or was an aspect of his fundamentalist Islamic belief. Prosecutors argue that 'Mousaoui's fervent belief in his dream is consistent with religious beliefs of Muslims – especially fundamentalist Muslims – and is no more crazy than Christians believing in the resurrection' (USA Today, April 2006).

According to his trial, Moussaoui's night dreams appear to have led him to make his mind up to become a *shahid*, a martyr. Donahue, an anthropology professor who has written a book about Moussaoui, his life and trial (Donahue 2007: 80–81), quotes from the trial transcript, with Moussaoui saying,

> Basically, I had, I had a dream, and I had more later, but I had a dream, and I went to see Sheikh Usama bin Laden, and I told him about my dream. He told me, 'Good.' Maybe, I don't know, a few days later, I have another dream. So I went again, I saw him, and I told him about this. This was after I had declined, I was asked before. Then I had this dream. Then maybe a week, a short time, Sheikh Abu Hafs [Mohammed Atef] came to the guesthouse and asked me again if I wanted to be part of the suicide operation, me and Richard Reid, and this time I said yes.

Later on the same day of the trial, Donahue recounts Moussaoui apparently seeing in one of his dreams a map with the target of the White House on it:

> He went on to describe his reason for wanting to fly a 747:
> ...but if want to say the original reason, okay, what I believe, okay, it is I thought I had a dream where I was into the runway of an airport and I actually took a map out, okay, and I open it and it was the White House with a circle with a cross, like when you do when you do target.
> And next to me, okay, in front of there was the four brother, I couldn't recognize. And next to me there was a 747, the very distinct, you know, like the cockpit, was very distant (tr. 27 March 2006, page 2402, lines 18–250).

Later still the same day, Donahue (Donahue 2007: 80-81) reports how Moussaoui understood dream interpretation in Islam, which was congruent with Islam's traditional teaching on dream interpretation. He says:

> 'So I refer to sheikh Usama bin Laden and some other sheikh there to explain to me the reality, but the dream about the White House, it was very clear to me (tr. March 27, 2006, page 2403, line 24).'

In these trial narratives we see how night dreams were experienced by Moussaoui as decisive in his motivation to become a martyr and, moreover, he reports an accurate dream of an intended target, the White House. Moussaoui is reported as saying, 'he was crazy about those 72 virgins' (Donahue 2007: 99), whether ironically or not, we don't know.

Richard Reid

Richard Reid is the British Al-Qaeda sympathizer sentenced to life imprisonment for attempting to blow up an American Airlines aeroplane flying from France to the USA in December 2001. He was found to be carrying explosives in his shoes. He is reported as divining special meaning about his role as an Islamic militant from his dreams, which he refers to in one of his final three emails (The Times 30 January 2003). I have been unable to obtain a copy of these emails, but the dream is referred to in Moussaoui's 2006 trial. According to the transcript (CNN):

> In the dream, Reid was waiting for a ride, but when the ride (a pick-up truck) came, it was full and Reid could not go. He was upset and had to go later in a smaller car. Reid explained the meaning of the dream as follows: 'I now believe that the pickup that came first was 9/11 as its true that I was upset at not being sent.'

There is little evidence here of how Reid interpreted this dream. However, this narrative does show his perception of its veracity and potential guidance. In Reid's interpretation, there is an interpretative translation from the symbolism of the pickup truck to that of the aeroplane; both are forms of group conveyance. Being upset in the dream connects his dream with his real-world loss of the 11 September attack opportunity.

Mullah Omar

Mullah Muhammad Omar led the Taliban movement in Afghanistan and was effectively Afghanistan's ruler from 1996 to 2001. After the 11 September attacks, there were several media and Internet references to his visionary dreams (Edgar 2004a), referring to his legitimizing the founding of the Taliban by claiming divine guidance and instruction in his dreams. Apparently it was 'common knowledge' in Afghanistan that Mullah Omar had been inspired by a 'holy' dream.[8] In 2005 Edgar interviewed Rahimullah Yusufzai, the BBC correspondent in Peshawar. He was one of very few reporters to have met Omar frequently, and was Omar's main outlet to the Western media.[9] According to Yusufzai, Omar trusted him because:

> the BBC is very powerful in Afghanistan; they (the Taliban) wanted to have good relations with the BBC and I was the first one to reach Kandahar and report about the emerging Taliban. Mullah Omar was grateful to me; that's why he will call me up; I spoke the same language Pashto and I was a Muslim, I was a Pakistani, I was someone he could trust.

Yusufzai described how Omar derived a charismatic authority from his reported dreams:

> The story I was being told everywhere was that because of his courage, because of his very timely decision to fight the Mujahideen that had made him very popular and the Taliban flocked to his banner as they thought he has this vision, this dream, he has challenged the Mujahideen and because he has been instructed to fight the Mujahideen they thought he was going to succeed ... The whole project was maybe built on this dream, he had this task or duty to perform and he must lead his Taliban, his fighters, and he must restore order and peace and enforce Sharia, Islamic law ... I was told by so many Taliban leaders, commanders, fighters: 'Look, you know, Mullah Omar is a holy man and he gets instructions in his dream and he follows them up.' The genesis of the Taliban Islamic movement was this vision, this night dream that Mullah Omar had.

Omar's reputed talent for true dreams was not confined to a single dream. Yusufzai related how such dreams became a source of strategic military action and decision-making: 'I kept hearing these stories, no big military operation can happen unless he gets his instructions in his dreams; he was a big believer in dreams.'

Yusufzai told Edgar that on one occasion Omar had telephoned him and had asked him about a dream that his (Omar's) brother had had:

> [He] asked me if I had been to the White House and I said yes; 'Can you tell me about it?' and I said, yes, and I told him about the White House in Washington (Mullah Omar already knew that Yusufzai had formally visited the White House before as part of an invited group of journalists) and Omar said in Pashto 'White house, white palace, look my younger brother had a dream and he was telling me that a white palace somewhere is on fire ... I have a belief in dreams and this is what my dreams are saying and if you have been there then this description by my brother of a white palace/house means it will catch fire' and this was before 9/11. I am convinced that Mullah Omar was not aware of Osama bin Laden's plans to attack on 9/11.

These reports contain what are now familiar threads: divinatory communication from sacred figures; followers' belief in true dreams as indicating holiness; and the relationship between dreams and events as in Omar's brother's 'white house' dream. Direct guidance as to military action is claimed. Omar is called to implement Shariah law and the true Islamic state.

Pakistani Relations

Dreaming also plays a role in the process of becoming a jihadist in the Pakistani-based movement against the Indian occupation of a large part of Kashmir. Before a young man can go on a martyrdom operation in Indian-held Kashmir, he has to obtain parental permission, which may finally be given following a dream by a mother or maternal uncle (Zahab forthcoming):

> 'In many cases, a few days before the boy "drinks the cup of martyrdom" (*jam-e shahadat nush karna*) mothers and often maternal uncles see him in Paradise, wearing beautiful white clothes, smiling, surrounded by trees and flowers and drinking milk.'

Here, paradisiacal imagery from the Koran justifies martyrdom. The mythical world of Islam is seen, recognized, made present and manifest.

Such dreams are also to be found among radical Muslims in Europe, as in the case of Amir Cheema, a twenty-eight-year-old Pakistani textile-engineering student, who died in 2006 in a German prison while awaiting trial for entering the offices of the German newspaper *Die Welt* with a large knife, intending to kill the editor for reprinting the Danish cartoons of the Prophet Muhammad. Fifty thousand people later attended his funeral in Pakistan. The following dream narrative by Cheema's father was published in the Urdu press and then reprinted in English in the weekly *Friday Times* (30 June–6 July 2006) in Pakistan:

> Fountains of light (noor) had burst forth in all directions as the sacred gathering became visible. It was announced that the companions (of the Prophet) had arrived. Then it was declared that the Prophet PHUB himself was seated in the vicinity but his face could not be seen ... Then the voice of the Prophet PHUB was heard saying Amir Cheema is coming! (Amir aa raha hai). The companions stood up in respect and started looking in one direction. Then the voice of the Prophet PHUB said: 'Hasan and Husain, look who I am sending to you, look after him.'

Hasan and Husain were the sons of Ali and Fatima, and so the grandsons of the Prophet Mohammed. The dream announces the elevated spiritual status of Amir Cheema through the word of the Prophet Mohammed, attended by his companions. We again find the themes of sacred light and of the clear communication of the spiritually elevated status of the martyr.

Guantanamo Bay

Many of the detainees at Guantanamo Bay were from Pakistan. In May 2005 the following dream narrative was published by the *Daily Times* newspaper (23 May 2005) in Pakistan:

> A Guantanamo ex-prisoner named Qari Badruzzaman Badr said in an interview that at Guantanamo many Arabs had dreams in which the Holy Prophet (PBUH) personally gave them news of their freedom and called them the People of Badr.[10] The Prophet said that Christ will soon arrive. One Arab saw Jesus who took his hand and told him that Christians were now misled. Later the other prisoners could smell the sweet smell of Jesus from his hand. His hand was rubbed on all the prisoners.

Again, the dream message is explicit. It is Jesus, a major prophet in Islam, who informs them that the Christian nation, the Crusaders that imprison them, are misled: what a transcendence of their oppression this dream message must have seemed! It is immediately communicated, not only by word of mouth but also by touch, presumably to transfer the *baraka* (blessing) from the dream.[11]

Not only the jihadist leaders but also the foot soldiers in Guantanamo see dreams that they interpret as true though the sacred iconography of their content and the relationship with future events. Jaram al-Harath, a detainee from the UK, reported that he was told in a dream that he would be released in two years – which apparently he was (Mirror, 12 March 2004). Likewise Ibrahim Sen, a Turkish detainee, has written about how inmates experienced dreams of the Prophet Muhammad and the angels that watched over them (Vakit, 10 November 2006).

The Role of Dreaming in Militant Jihadist Action

For Islamic militant jihadists, in Al-Qaeda or not, dreams and visions are a core way of confirming and legitimating to others their ideological world view and the path to becoming a *shahid*, a holy martyr. Whatever the veracity of individual dream narratives reported in this chapter, there is a clear overall pattern of reliance on divinatory dreams for inspiration and guidance on action, within the Islamic dreaming tradition begun by the Prophet Muhammad. The true dream experience is consistently utilized as a powerful legitimating device within the context of the Islamic theological exegesis of the potential, if very occasional, noumenal power and authority of the night dream. The assertions that jihadists are inspired by night dreams and, secondly, legitimate their actions partly on the basis of night dreams constitute the first and second analytical threads of our argument.

While dreams are experienced by the ego, they are not generally generated or controlled by the ego (unless the dreamer is an experienced lucid dreamer or a student of Tibetan dream yoga). Social scientists can, through studies of Islamic dreaming, show how particular dream motifs (such as the Prophet and his companions) are part of a shared visionary world view that can connect present-day believers with the mythically real past, and especially with the imagined early glorious days of Islam, the time of the Prophet himself. Moreover, such true dreams appear to facilitate the re-enactment of this past in the present. This merging of mythical dreamt reality and mundane reality constitutes the third thread of our argument, and this is shown for instance in the quotation from Fouda (2003: 109) concerning Binalshibh, who 'speaks of the Prophet and his close companions as if he had actually met them'. The dreamworld is experienced as more real than this world, and reality becomes more dreamlike, a veil over the sublime glory of hidden paradisiacal worlds. Dreams can be tastes, divinations, of possible welcome futures. Sacred figures are to be emulated and even identified with, and certainly their words are perceived as divine instruction. We see bin Laden clearly interpreting dreams as a spiritual leader.

The fourth thread of our argument is that militant jihadism can apparently be directly authorized by dream content. The classical Freudian distinction between the manifest and latent meanings of a dream is changed. The clearer the manifest communication, the closer to God the dreamer is, as we have seen in many of the dream narratives reported in this chapter. Mullah Omar is given 'instructions' in his dreams as to his military strategy, the US 'white house' burns, bin Laden is said to have 'executed' 11 September to avenge the Palestinians; Moussaoui dreams of flying a plane into a tall building; Abu Cheema is welcomed into paradise and the Prophet is heard speaking clearly; the words of Jesus are heard by a Guantanamo Bay inmate; another is 'told' he will be released in two years.

However, not all the dream narratives are understood solely through reliance on their manifest meaning. Reid's interpretation of the 'full pickup truck' passing him by as referring to his missing the 11 September attack is an interpretation from a manifest to a supposed latent meaning, as is bin Laden's claiming that his soccer team being dressed as 'pilots' and winning against the American team is a good omen, as is bin Laden's interpretation of the 'Egyptian family going about its business' as a reference to Atta.

These narratives clearly show that jihadists understand their dreams within the context of the Islamic world view. Dreamt sacred figures, for example, are not unreal projections of the unconscious, or deeply encoded manifestations of earlier dysfunctional familial experiences, but figures that inhabit the supernaturally real world of Islam and reassert the eternal truths of the Koran and the Hadiths.

The relationship between dreams and events is another analytical thread running through the narratives. Mullah Omar is called to save his country and introduce Shariah law, and for a while the Taliban did achieve extraordinary success (Burke 2003), thereby seeming to confirm to his followers his dreamt inspiration. A final thread – that of the prophetic example of Muhammad's advisory dream before the battle of Badr – is again shown in the dream narratives attributed to Mullah Omar, whose followers appear to have believed that he was strategically guided in warfare by his night dreams. Likewise, bin Laden interprets the successful football match by his 'pilot' team against the Americans as a good omen for his jihadist 'team'.

Dreams, then, can be offered by such charismatic leaders as Mullah Omar as a self-justifying and legitimating device, claiming them to be revelations from beyond this world and containing authorization for radical human action in this world.

Conclusion

We have aimed in this chapter to show through a wide variety of mainly secondary source examples that the experience of the true dream in Islam is a core revelatory narrative that can be understood to legitimate aspects of the contemporary Islamic militant jihadist movement in the Middle East and elsewhere. As such, and in contradistinction to Western psychoanalytical theories of dreaming, perceived, reported and interpreted dreams are a powerful essence of charismatic religious and political leadership, and such dream narratives still contribute today, as they have throughout history, to the generation of existential, political and militant realities. Moreover, the militant Islamic jihadist narratives reported in this chapter evidence a violent and sustained critique of Western foreign policy towards the Islamic nation, and especially the occupation of Palestine. The jihadist rejection of Western liberal democracy, and implicitly the economic and political hegemony of capitalistic cosmopolitanism, and their ambition to create a nation of Islam under the law of Shariah harks back to the golden first age of Islam, and reported dream narratives are a key inspirational trope in this continuing endeavour.

Recent debates have discussed cosmopolitanism as a mechanism for the transcendence of communitarian, national, local and 'cultural' limits; or as a way of connecting people across particular boundaries (Rapport 2007; Theodossopoulos, this volume). In the light of such debates, the dream-inspired militant Islamic jihadist ideology might be seen as a transnational politico-religious movement of discontent, as a particular variant of counter-cosmopolitanism (Appiah 2007), rather than a Western, hegemonic international cosmopolitanism, based on the Enlightenment ideas proposed by Kant (1912). Militant Islamic ideology might be seen as exclusive, thus in profound opposition to the core Western liberal, political and economic values of contemporary ideas of cosmopolitanism.

Jihadist night dreams, as part of the Islamic jihadist ideological rhetoric, publicly presented and interpreted in news media such as CNN, the BBC, Al-Jazeera, the Pakistani *Daily Times* or *Al-Qalam online*, are a persuasive forum with which the message of the Ummah, the nation of Islam, may be constructed and communicated. Through sharing narratives of dream experiences as well as their particular interpretations, ideas about and appeals to the Ummah are spread and strengthened. Following Anderson's (1983) arguments about the importance of the print media for the ability to imagine and belong to a community (in his account to a national one), we can observe, in this case, the continuous spread of communitarian ideas by other means, but with similar effects. This example illustrates the shift, described by Appadurai (1996) and Theodossopoulos (this volume) from 'imagined communities' to 'imagined worlds', sometimes to the particular worlds of discontent(s). As Appadurai argues (1996: 7), through the work of imagination, ideas of neighbourhood and nationhood might be recreated or strengthened. Sharing of the dream experience is a way of mediating a common Islam and strengthening the Ummah:

> '[M]ediation produces and reproduces certain configurations of close-distance, mediated self-understandings that depend on the routing of the personal through the impersonal, the near through the far, and the self through the other' (Mazzarella 2004: 361).

Dreams have been firmly embedded within the rhetoric and practice of Islam and consequently Muslim societies. Sharing and interpreting dreams in particular ways continue to play a vital role for many believers (and non-believers) today. Public use of dream narratives by jihadist leaders (e.g. bin Laden talking about the football/pilot dream) enables the interconnection and 'assemblage' of the listeners from various parts of the globe and unites them in a transnational, counter-cosmopolitan imagined world. To borrow Theodossopoulos's words (this volume), such an imagined community is globalized in its own imagination.

It is paradoxical, however, that the message is not only aimed at the Ummah, or meant to reach *Dar al-Islam* (the house of Islam), but is also a message for *Dar al-Harb* (the house of war), so the message is dialectically powerful. This global reach of the message of the Jihadist ideology is a new or hyper-modern phenomenon, to use Castells's terminology (Castells 1997: 16), in the sense that it is a particular reaction of discontent from the world of Islam (or a part of that world) to the processes of globalization at a time when the (Islamicized) nation states, along with the 'cosmopolitan' organizations (UN, WTO, IMF, etc.), are not able to fulfil all the needs of their inhabitants.

Appadurai (1996: 7, 31) writes about the work of the imagination in the contemporary globalized, cosmopolitanized world saying that its importance lies in the capacity of the imagination to be seen as social practice and, significantly, as a fuel for action. The use of dreams in Islamic jihadist ideological movements might be seen, similarly, as a new way of working with 'traditional materials in the formation of a new godly, communal world, where deprived masses and disaffected intellectuals may reconstruct meaning in a global alternative to the exclusionary global order' (Castells 1997: 20).

Rather than creating links with other anti-globalization movements, Al-Qaeda and its affiliates seek a unity across the Islamic world, from the Philippines to West Africa, leading to a mobilization of the Ummah, the nation of Islam. Islamic dream theory and the reported true dreams of its leaders form a global language and an acceptable, even inspiring, rhetoric of mobilization, legitimization and divine purpose. Moreover, this self-proclaimed divinely inspired jihadist movement uses contemporary globalised technology to communicate such convictions. The dream trope and the prophetically sanctioned accessibility of true dreams to Muslims, generate an inner and imagined unity for its leaders and followers that transcends both time and space. The true dreams reported in this ethnography can then be seen to demonstrate to the pan-Islamic anti-Western masses that divine destiny is on the side of militant jihadism.

Therefore, the Islam employed in the jihadist political enterprise, as a counter-thesis to the Western ideas of cosmopolitanism and as an expression of discontent, provides a rich source of cohesive rituals and emotionally powerful symbols that create and maintain inter-group boundaries and encourage intra-group solidarity and intimacy. In the case we present, dream narratives embedded within ideological rhetoric under the umbrella of Islam offer a persuasive and powerful rhetorical tool that modifies social life and can, at times provide part of the catalyst for events like those that occurred on 11 September 2001.

Notes

We are particularly grateful to Mariam Abou Zahab for facilitating key contacts in Pakistan and for sending us many of the dream narratives quoted in this chapter; also to Dr. Steve Lyon, Anthropology Department, Durham University UK, for facilitating key contacts for Iain Edgar in Turkey and Pakistan, and for his continuous and multifaceted support. Earlier versions of parts of this chapter were published by Iain R. Edgar (2006); they were also published in 2007 by the journal *Nova Religio* 11 (2), in a special edition on 'Islamic Jihadism' under the title 'The Inspirational Night Dream in the Motivation and Justification of Jihad'.

1. We are using the term numinous here in the Kantian sense, as the opposite of phenomenal, i.e. that which is not discernible empirically by the five senses.
2. *Ru'ya* in Arabic can refer to either day visions or true night dreams from God. All my references to *ru'ya* refer to what are considered to be such true night dreams
3. The 2004 fieldwork trip to Turkey, Northern Cyprus and Pakistan (by Iain Edgar) was funded by the British Academy small research grants scheme.
4. The anthropologist Ellen Basso (1987) divided dream cultures into past- and future-oriented interpretative approaches.
5. Yosri Fouda is the *Al-Jazeera* journalist who in 2002 interviewed in Karachi, Pakistan, two of the Al-Qaeda planners of the 11 September attack, Ramzi bin al-Shibh and Khalid Shaykh Muhammad.
6. Marwan (al-Shehdi) was one of the nineteen 11 September suicide bombers.
7. We are very grateful to Marc Applebaum, psychologist and PhD student at Saybrook Graduate School, San Francisco, for his help in developing this idea.
8. Personal communication, Mariam Abou Zahab, a French political scientist (IEP/CERI-INALCO, Paris), who has spent many years conducting research in Pakistan and Afghanistan.
9. Google search.
10. The battle of Badr in AD 622 was a key battle against the Meccan Quraish tribe. The Muslims were victorious.
11. Again, we are grateful to Marc Applebaum for his help in developing this idea.

References

Amanullah, M. 2005. Dreams in Islam: An Analysis of its Truthfulness and Influence. Paper presented at the annual conference of the International Association for the Study of Dreams, Berkeley, 24–28 June.

Anderson, B. 1983. *Imagined Communities: Reflections on the Origin and Spread of Nationalism.* London: Verso.

Appadurai, A. 1996. *Modernity at Large: Cultural Dimensions of Globalization.* Minneapolis: University of Minnesota Press.

Appiah, K.A. 2007. *Cosmopolitanism: Ethics in a World of Strangers*. New York: Norton.

Basso, E. 1987. The Implications of a Progressive Theory of Dreaming. In B. Tedlock (ed.) *Dreaming: An Anthropological and Psychological Interpretations*. Cambridge: Cambridge University Press, pp. 86–104.

Bukhari. 1979. *The Translations of the Meanings of Sahihal-Bukhari*, trans. M.M. Khan. Lahore, Pakistan: Kazi Publications, vol. 9.

Burke, J. 2003. *Al-Qaeda: Casting a Shadow of Terror*. London: I.B. Tauris.

Castells, M. 1997. *The Power of Identity*. Oxford: Blackwell Publishers.

CNN. Shoe bomber denies role in 9/11 attacks, http://www.cnn.com/2006/LAW/04/21/moussaoui.trial (accessed August 11, 2006).

Dawood, N.J. (trans.). 1956. *The Koran*, London: Penguin Books.

Donahue, K. 2007. *Slave of Allah: Zacarias Moussaoui vs. The USA*. London: Pluto Press.

Edgar, I. 2002. Invisible Elites? Authority and the Dream. *Dreaming*, 12 (2), 79–92.

——— 2004a. A War of Dreams? Militant Muslim Dreaming in the Context of Traditional and Contemporary Islamic Dream Theory and Practice. *Dreaming*, 14 (1), 21–29.

——— 2004b. *Guide to Imagework: Imagination-based Research Methods*. London: Routledge.

——— 2006. Analysis of the 'True Dream' in Contemporary Islamic/Jihadist Dreamwork: Case Study of the Dreams of Mullah Omar. *Contemporary South Asia*, 15 (3), 263–72.

Fisk, R. 2005. *The Great War for Civilisation: the Conquest of the Middle East*. London: Fourth Estate.

Fouda, Y. 2003. *Masterminds of Terror: The Truth Behind the Most Devastating Terrorist Attack the World Has Ever Seen*. London: Mainstream Publishing.

Kant, I. 1912. Zum ewigen Frieden. Ein philosophischer Entwurf. In: Gesammelte Schriften VIII. Berlin: Königlich Preussische Akademie der Wissenschaften, pp. 341–86.

Lamoreux, J. 2002. *The Early Muslim Tradition of Dream Interpretation*. New York: State University of New York Press.

Mazzarella, W. 2004. Culture, Globalization, Mediation. *Annual Review of Anthropology* 33, 345–67.

Rapport, N. 2007. An Outline for Cosmopolitan Study. Reclaiming the Human through Introspection. *Current Anthropology*, 48, 257–83.

Sviri, S. 1999. Dreaming Analysed and Recorded: Dreams in the World of Medieval Islam. In D. Shulman and G. Stroumsa (eds) *Dream Culture*. London: Routledge, pp. 252–73.

Sirin, Ibn. 2000. *Dreams and Interpretations*. Karachi: Darul–Ishaat Urdu Bazar.

Zahab, M.A. (forthcoming) 'I shall be waiting for you at the door of Paradise': the Pakistani Martyrs of the Lashkar-e Taiba (Army of the Pure). In A. Rao, M. Böck and M. Bollig (eds) *The Practice of War: The Production, Reproduction and Communication of Armed Violence*. Oxford: Berghahn Books.

Chapter 5

INTIMACIES OF ANTI-GLOBALIZATION: IMAGINING UNHAPPY OTHERS AS ONESELF IN GREECE

Elisabeth Kirtsoglou and Dimitrios Theodossopoulos

This chapter examines an ethnographic paradox. Anti-globalization rhetoric in Greece is predominantly articulated in terms of conspiracy theory, mistrust of other cultures and strong nationalist feelings. The same rhetoric, however, reflects a strong empathy with people and nations that are imagined to be deprived of power, and communicates a global awareness of an imagined community in discontent. In other words, popular anti-globalization in Greece, despite its mistrust of multiculturalism and non-Greek cultural expressions, is paradoxically cosmopolitan with respect to its allegiance to what is perceived to be a community of the non-powerful in the world. To shed some light on this paradox, we look at Greek views of Turks and other ethnic groups as these are negotiated in the critique of globalization and cosmopolitanism. We explore how symbolic enemies (such as the Turks) and other peoples of the Middle East (e.g. the Palestinians) are approached, within the broader context of opposing Western ideological and political authority, with a certain degree of empathy, as fellow victims of the powerful and as disempowered human beings.

Our interest in shared discontent with (and within) an imagined community of unhappy peripheral – with respect to power – individuals is inspired by Herzfeld's (1997) notion of cultural intimacy, the mutual self-recognition of shared familiarity, embarrassment and pride. We argue that anti-globalization ideas in Greece are shared with the implicit understanding that an alternative, culturally intimate audience exists, one that includes other disenfranchised peoples in South-East Europe, in the Middle East and more generally, in the world. This reference to a broader community that resists globalization demonstrates that local anti-globalization rhetoric in Greece is based upon a global – and, in some respects, globalized – consciousness and imagination. It reproduces a global awareness based on the work of local, 'historically situated imaginations' (Appadurai 1996: 33), which are often articulated in daily life in terms of resourceful, but primarily critical, arguments.

In informal contexts and everyday conversation, Western competitive globalization is received in Greece with guardedness, scepticism and reservation. Local commentary is disapproving in its orientation and for the most part is expressed – like other variations of political interpretation (Brown and Theodossopoulos 2000, 2003) – in terms of metaphors, broad comparisons between nations, humour, sarcasm and pointed remarks. Like globalization, multiculturalism is similarly viewed as a new, fashionable idea imported from the West, which has entered Greek contemporary life via the back door, mainly through EU policies and top-down development projects (Yiakoumaki 2007). Cosmopolitanism, a much older concept with the resonance of sophisticated urbanity – for example, in the Ottoman plural society (Ors 2007) – is often conflated with the multicultural orientation of the EU, and treated in local conversation as another by-product of globalization.

In most cases, anti-globalization sentiments in Greece, including reservation towards Western paradigms of cosmopolitanism and multiculturalism, are expressed in local conversation as part of a more general critique of the status quo. In particular, both recent and older examples of Western involvement in the non-Western world are used as evidence of global interference, and fuel, in turn, local arguments against interventionism on a global scale. Cases of Western involvement also provide a handy comparative setting for evaluating and discussing globalization more generally. They form a repository of well-known examples of Western wrongdoing that sets the background and tone in local conversation. Other contemporary topics, such as 11 September and subsequent terrorist attacks, present additional opportunities for assessing global dissatisfaction more generally. In this broad conversational context, the Greeks, and the citizens of other small nations, are juxtaposed against the powerful, those who make decisions of global consequence and shape the face of the world.

In the ethnography that follows, we explore the meaning of locally expressed arguments of this type, in the discourse of working- and middle-class citizens in two medium-sized Greek towns, Patras and Volos, our field sites during previous studies in political anthropology (Brown and Theodossopoulos 2000, 2003; Theodossopoulos 2004, 2007c; Kirtsoglou 2007). Our respondents openly criticize globalization, multiculturalism and cosmopolitanism during informal conversations with ourselves and other fellow citizens in the everyday contexts of social interaction – in shops, cafeterias, while travelling in buses and taxis, but also in private living rooms, kitchens and backyards. Most of them are confident and articulate amateur commentators on wider political processes, who read national newspapers, watch televised political discussions and often have university degrees and/or run private businesses. They have been aware of our interest in their views (and our role as academics working in British universities) since our engagement with them in previous fieldwork, and in many cases they suggested that we should record and take seriously their opinions about the greater political processes that surround them. The following sections demonstrate that we have indeed been attentive to their arguments.

Some Theoretical Predilections

Anti-globalization attitudes – often hastily subsumed under the label of 'nationalism' – represent a complex indigenous reaction to centres of power, and cannot be analysed simply as the opposite of cosmopolitan values. They rather appear to be unfolding as expressions of frustration towards a global realpolitik that creates divisions and inequalities and that is seen as a clear-cut 'Western-inspired' project. To paraphrase an argument that West and Sanders put forward about modernity, globalization is felt by many as a 'fragmented, contradictory and disquieting process that produces untenable situations and unfulfilled desires' (West and Sanders 2003: 16). Thus, globalization and what are seen as its by-products – namely multiculturalism and, to some extent, cosmopolitanism – cannot be perceived as the residual effect of ignorance, nationalism, regionalism and persistence of tradition. Globalization, however, as the nexus of power relations is not felt the same everywhere and therefore is not appreciated equally by everyone.

Following a careful, context-specific approach established by anthropological writing, we do not treat globalization as a single entity. Rather, we feel the need to acknowledge the possibility of multiple globalizations experienced differently in various parts of the world (Comaroff and Comaroff 1993; Fischer 1999: 459). In the same manner, we can talk about multiple anti-globalization attitudes fuelled by diverse kinds of mistrust of those who are seen as the agents of global political power. Trust and mistrust, here, are similarly dependent on contextual considerations, such as local interpretations of history and time contingencies. Concerned with the consequences of modernity, Giddens (1990) has spoken about trust in the sense of confidence towards (or about) the transparent operation of social institutions. Despite the international post-cold war emphasis on transparency, however, a number of authors point out that power does sometimes operate in ambiguous ways, which inspire the development of conspiratorial interpretations (West and Sanders 2003: 2, 12; see also, Bastian 2001; Hellinger 2003; McCarthy Brown 2003).

Our respondents in Greece provide us with very good examples of such conspiratorial interpretations. In informal conversations about international politics, they consistently challenge the idea that the Western powers are moved and mobilized by a humanitarian ethos (or by the values of tolerance and sharing). Some of them perceive cosmopolitanism as a handmaid of globalization, as yet another tool for the establishment of Western cultural and political domination. Such attitudes are not only the result of a felt and lived national history (cf. Sutton 2003; Kirtsoglou 2006, 2007). As Marcus (1999) has discussed in the context of conspiracy theories, the cold war political legacy legitimizes (to a certain extent) people's mistrust of the sincerity of the great powers. The US is indeed seen – not just by the Greeks, but by many others, including academics – as an overtly hegemonic global empire (Stewart-Harawira 2005: 4; see also, Hardt and Negri 2000). Seen in this light, globalization feels to those who exist on the margins of power merely yet another ideology that seeks to legitimize a certain status quo that directly contradicts the ideals of modernity (Kirtsoglou 2006).

Greek arguments against globalization that uncritically encompass other concepts, such as cosmopolitanism and multiculturalism, need therefore to be examined in close relation to warm support for the idea of modernity, as has been well documented in the Greek sociocultural context (cf. Faubion 1993). As has been noted by social anthropologists, Greek subjects are infused with pro-modernity sentiments (cf. Argyrou 2002; Kirtsoglou 2007) and an idiosyncratic desire to be and to be perceived by others as cosmopolitan, tolerant, hospitable and open. The idea that Greece belongs to the West – not only in a geopolitical but also in a cultural and ideological sense – informs a great deal of modern Greek political life (Kirtsoglou 2006, 2007). It is, in fact, the disappointments and inconsistencies of modernity that have led our respondents in Greece to question the sincerity of politico-economic projects like globalization. Unilateralism, the flamboyant exhibition of military power, and the interventionist strategy of the great powers in the political arenas of various countries around the world contradict the ideals of the social contract, consensus, equality and transparency that supposedly characterize the new world order. It is in this context that our respondents speak of the Pax Americana, alluding to the Pax Romana, in order to express their reservations with regard to the democratic values of today's international political strategies and balance. To them, globalization seems like a move 'back to the future': to a new world order that – politically at least – is not new at all, but rather just another imperium.

Our analysis of Greek responses to cosmopolitanism and globalization, then, focuses on this seemingly paradoxical coexistence of openness and closure, pro- and anti-Western feelings and conflicting discourses of empathy and hostility towards various Others. The latter can be viewed as rich rhetorical strategies that situate the actor vis-à-vis wider political processes. Anti-cosmopolitanism is thus a form of discursive and practical empowerment, a critique of the cosmopolitics and a simultaneous, dynamic and decisive engagement with it (Beck and Sznaider 2006: 3, 5). In this sense, discontented cosmopolitanism is not a form of 'cultural fundamentalism' (Stolcke 1995), but perhaps more of an alternative form of 'rooted cosmopolitanism' (Appiah 1998), in so far as the concerns of local actors are indeed global and relate to the problematization of being a citizen of the world. The articulation and expression of discontent in this context constitute in effect a commentary on the workings, transparency and distribution of political power, and not a superficial manifestation of lagging modernization, nationalism, traditionalism or regionalism.

Our Greek respondents situate themselves in the globalized world, and it is from their standpoint as citizens of the world that they comment on the imbalance of power in the international status-quo. It is this particular subjectivity that inspires them to talk about and sympathize with unhappy others who share the same political predicament of powerlessness as themselves. As our ethnography will shortly demonstrate, commenting on the imbalance of power transcends national and nationalistic boundaries and appeals to the idea of a common humanity, as well as the shared positionality of the subaltern. In some ways, our respondents' perceptions of international politics turn the concepts of globalization, cosmopolitanism and multiculturalism on their head, posing serious (and difficult to answer) questions about the legitimacy of power and the authority of the powerful to create and impose politics and also – and perhaps more importantly – ideology and history.

Unhappy Turks and Greeks

In Greek ethno-national classification the Turks constitute an oppositional category, the stereotypical enemy. In everyday conversation and political debate, but also in the Greek national(ist) imagination and historical consciousness, the Turks (generalized, homogenized and frequently mentioned) figure as the 'significant Other' for modern Greeks (Theodossopoulos 2007a). Despite these easily verifiable broad observations, attitudes towards the Turks in Greece are complex and context-specific,[1] more unsympathetic in public, less oppositional in private. In informal settings, most Greeks will differentiate between their critical views towards the state of Turkey (and its official representatives) and their more nuanced views about the ordinary Turkish people. While Turkey, the nation state, is viewed with suspicion (or as a potential threat), the people of Turkey, under certain circumstances and in certain conversations, are favourably compared with the Greeks themselves (Theodossopoulos 2004, 2007c; Kirtsoglou 2007).

A similar distinction in Greek attitudes towards Turks relates to the contrast between the generalized singular notion of the 'Turk' and the more individualized everyday Turks, who can be imagined in intimate terms. The singular, undifferentiated 'Turk' is negatively stereotyped (Theodossopoulos 2004; Spyrou 2007) and rationalized as culturally incompatible, despite many self-evident similarities. He – he is usually male – is a faceless, nameless Turk, a warrior or agent of the Ottoman empire, such as the caricatures that appear in Greek novels and history textbooks (Millas 2007) or the profiles of the so-called 'Kemalists' in contemporary Turkey drawn by Greek journalists of a radical nationalist persuasion (Tsibiridou 2007). In contrast, the more individualized Turks of Greek imagination are depicted in everyday conversation as people like oneself, men and women with familiar everyday worries and aspirations. These are referred to as 'the Turks as people' (*oi Tourkoi san* or, *os anthropoi*) 'the ordinary citizens of Turkey' (*oi anthropoi tis Tourkias*) or the people of Turkey (*o laos tis Tourkias*).

In conversations about the ills of globalization, our respondents in Patras and Volos are more likely to discuss the Turks in terms of their individualized attributes. Everyday Turks, like everyday Greeks, are (and have been in the past) betrayed by their government and politicians, exploited by profiteering business people and subjected to the ruthlessness of penetrating Western capitalism. The people of Turkey, like the people of Greece, have been misled – to some degree or another – by the promises of the West, and now share a comparably disadvantaged position in the global hierarchy. The entry of Turkey into the European Union, for example, represents such a misleading promise and is discussed in comparison to the familiar 'European' experience of the Greeks, who share vivid memories of the painful efforts to meet the entrance requirements and strict conditions set, from the top down, by various EU regulation committees. Notions of affinity between Greeks and Turks rely on perceptions of a shared unofficial orientalism and the conviction that, should both countries wish to 'make any progress', they must 'learn to be good Europeans' (Herzfeld 1995: 134; Kirtsoglou 2007). As a respondent has characteristically stated to us:

'We Orientals (*anatolites*) naively believe that the Others (*alloi*, i.e. Westerners) have *bessa* (*honour*) and that they keep their word, but they don't. If and when Turkey joins the EU, the Turks will finally realize what kind of two-faced bastards the Europeans are. The same way they play with us they will play with them.'

Thus Turkey might be Greece's 'traditional' enemy, but in the global context, our Greek respondents argue, Turkey is nothing more than the puppet of the Americans and the great powers in general (Kirtsoglou 2007). Vis-à-vis the West, Turkey is imagined as powerless as Greece, always at the mercy of Western political interests and caprice. In this respect, Turkey shares the same predicament with Greece; that of being a nation state at the margins of power, always destined – as our respondents vividly describe – 'to dance to somebody else's tune', 'always in a precarious political position', 'another bond servant of the new world order'. As a small independent merchant in Patras pointed out, 'The Turks want to get into Europe, like we did, they want to become "European", but, if they could feel the sweetness (*sic*) of Europe (*tin glyka tis Europis*), they would run away now!'

More often than Europe, the United States of America and its policies – the topic of much animated conversation in Greece – bring Turks and Greeks closer together. Since the collapse of the Soviet Bloc, there has been only one empire, our respondents explain, the 'super power' (*i yperdynami*). This is, of course, an idea that is not only found in lay discourse. Writers such as Held, McGrew, Goldplatt and Perraton (1999: 425) also claim that since the collapse of the Soviet Union the US has become one of the 'world's last imperial structures' (see also Stewart-Harawira 2005: 4). In Greece, this conviction is strengthened by the critical manner in which US international affairs are reported by the Greek media, and further verified by official and unofficial Greek history, which provides many examples of previous Western – and, since the second World War, primarily American – interventions in Greek and Cypriot politics (cf. Sutton 2003; Kirtsoglou 2006). It is this combination of ideas borrowed from local interpretations of history and arguments circulated in the media that led a forty-year-old school-teacher from Patras to claim:

'We talk about our differences, the Greeks and the Turks, and we forget the global superpower. Who makes the small nations fight with each other? Who creates wars here and there? Who makes the people of the world suffer? And who benefits from this?'[2]

The re-familiarization of the abstract Turk in this context is based on the recognition of his or her suffering – a well-recorded empathetic approach in Greece (Dubisch 1995: 213–25). When it comes to Turkey's position in the global political scene, such empathy can be easily documented. 'The Turks are like us,' our respondents often say. 'They have to obey the Americans, otherwise their fate is as sealed as ours.' Following this line of argumentation, the differences between the two nations are presented as having been fabricated by the Western powers, and their responsibility for their own problematic relations is subsequently underplayed (Herzfeld 1992). 'What can the Greeks and the Turks do without the approval of the planet leader?' a thirty-year-old engineer said with rhetorical persuasion. 'What can the simple people do? Everything in globalization is controlled!'[3]

In some other conversations in Greece, Turkey's perceived closeness to the US is criticized. In some of these our respondents portray Turkish political consciousness in terms of cultural notions of trust that are intimate to both nations and foreign to North Americans and Europeans. As a thirty-eight-year-old professional in Volos explained:

> 'the Turks are always trying to be America's favourite child. They believe that their loyalty is guaranteed and should be reciprocated. They don't understand that the American is capable of selling his own mother down the river. The American doesn't have *bessa* (trustworthiness).'

The notion of *bessa*, akin to the concept of *filotimo* (love of honour: see Seremetakis 1991: 237; Dubisch 1995: 202), is believed to be a shared attribute of Greeks and Turks. Our respondents' appeal to it attempts to establish an imaginary community of trust and warn the Turks about the untrustworthiness of the Europeans. The employment of such arguments – which represent examples of union in discontent – are always discussion-specific and appear only in comparisons of the West with the rest. Thus, in discursive contexts that focus on the Balkans and South-East Europe, it is Turkey (and other neighbours of Greece) that is cast as lacking in *bessa* (trustworthiness).

Selective interpretations of this kind appear in several topics of debate. A number of practices that in local-level conversation are disapproved of by our respondents become acceptable (and are considered with a degree of empathy) when discussed in relation to the wider picture of Western-related politics. Suggestive of this is the issue of the headscarf. Most Greek subjects, who readily – and perhaps hegemonically (Argyrou 2002) – embrace modernity and its various expressions, criticize their Muslim neighbours for their support for women wearing headscarves. Women covering themselves are seen by our respondents as a sign of backwardness; 'The Turks are a hundred years behind,' some of them argue. 'Their women are still wearing headscarves.' In discussions about globalization, however, the opinions of our respondents take an unexpected turn. They now admire and defend Turkish determination to adhere to what they see as custom or tradition. 'If they fancy wearing the scarf,' some respondents emphatically argued, 'who are the Europeans and the Americans to dictate to them what to do in their own country? They are right to defend their beliefs.'[4]

Despite the proliferation of arguments that shift around culturally specific beliefs and practices, such as the example of the Muslim scarf, most of our respondents are critical of multiculturalism (in Greek, *poly-politimiskotita*). Many see its introduction as a recent European import intended to undermine the delicate balance of the multi-ethnic regions of Greece and Turkey. In the conversations of our respondents, for example, the Muslim Turkish-speaking minority in Greek Thrace is regularly compared to the Kurdish minority in Turkey. 'The Americans are using Turkey to terrorize us, and the Kurds to terrorize the Turks,' a thirty-five-year-old construction manager stated emphatically. For him and the majority of our respondents in Greece, the minorities themselves do not compose the real problem in the Greco-Turkish relationship. Friction between the two countries is instigated by 'the Americans' or 'the great powers', and minority issues provide the excuse for Western interference in the local affairs of Greece and Turkey. Foreign initiatives, such as EU-led multicultural policies, some of our respondents explain, 'bring more trouble than they are likely to solve'. 'Multiculturalism is a Western idea,' a sixty-year-old accountant underlined. 'We have lived close to the Turks for centuries. Who are they [the West] to teach us [the meaning of] multiculturalism (*poly-politimiskotita*)?'

The problem lies, according to several local critics of globalization, in the uncritical introduction of Western ideas into Greek everyday life. Western versions of multiculturalism or EU cosmopolitanism are introduced in a top-down manner from centres of power abroad. This observation leads some of our respondents, especially (but not exclusively) those of a socialist predisposition, to interpretations that emphasize ideological mystification. Despite the obvious connection, however, and with a few exceptions, our respondents neither quote Marx nor acknowledge his authorship directly; their views are presented as reflecting their own opinion on the nature of politics and some of them insisted that they should be taken as such. Globalization, they argued, is an ideological platform that masks unequal power relations, seeking at the same time to obliterate any possibility of resistance. It is also believed that resistance to this new imperialist status quo is eventually articulated through the richness of local culture, tradition and history, that is, the things that globalization is attempting to undermine. Despite the Marxist overtones of such an approach, it is defended – as we have already said –

by the majority of our Greek respondents and informs most of what is seen as nationalist Greek rhetoric.

In this light, one could argue that academic theories of nationalism do not always explain the full complexity of Greek perceptions on politics. Widely employed nation-building strategies and the documented Greek irredentism notwithstanding, much of what appears to be Greek nationalism at the level of local discourse today is inspired by anti-globalization attitudes. These, in turn, originate in the conviction that the new world order has broken its promises of democracy and equality for all. Globalization, in lay accounts of this type, is reified and personified – in a poetic rather than overtly theoretical manner. Culture, history and tradition acquire new rhetorical overtones as they become the means of celebrating difference and, in the arguments of some respondents, the very loci of the struggle against the invisible forces of homogenization. Hence, what connects the Greeks with the Turks (and eventually a number of other pariahs of the new world order) is a worldwide demand for equality articulated in terms of respect for cultural difference and celebrated in acts of symbolic defiance or resistance. 'Everybody in the world, like monkeys, tries to imitate the West,' a forty-five-year-old housewife in Patras explained, '[but] some peoples, like the Muslims, are resisting. The Turks [resist] more than we do; for this, I give them credit!'[5]

Other Unhappy Others

Greece, Cyprus, Palestine – not a single American left (*Ellada, Kypros, Palaistini, Amerikanos de tha meinei*). (Popular banner used in anti-war demonstrations in Greece).

As with the Turks, conventional Greek nationalism treats the Muslim communities of the Middle East with suspicion and patronizing orientalism, especially with regard to Islamic rules of dress and conduct or attitudes to women, which are generally regarded in Greece as 'backward' and 'repressive'. Despite the fact that our respondents confront Islamic populations near (or indeed inside) the Greek borders with reservation (and in some cases with suspicion and prejudice), Muslims elsewhere in the world, and especially in the Middle East, are portrayed in a rather favourable manner. This attitude is again more clearly apparent in discussions about globalization and worldwide manifestations of power, and represents a further example of parallel, imagined subjectivities of discontent.

The current Greek pro-Middle-Eastern feelings have a historical resonance in the politics promoted by Andreas Papandreou, especially after the fall of the dictatorship in Greece in 1974. As has been argued elsewhere (Kirtsoglou 2007), the US was widely accused in Greece of supporting the 1967 coup and several other cold war political interventions in various countries. The socialist party of Andreas Papandreou employed in its rhetoric a popular – some say populist – anti-American stance, already familiar by that time in the political positions maintained by the Greek Communist Party and smaller leftist groups. Papandreou's anti-Americanism was mostly rhetorical in nature, and when he found himself in a position of power he did not undermine Greece's position in NATO and the European Union. But his anti-American statements, and his close friendship with Arafat, our respondents report, made a significant percentage of the Greek public – at least those of a leftist political predisposition – feel 'pride' for Greece's (safe, and mostly rhetorical) defiance of American hegemony.

Papandreou and the socialist party remained in power throughout the 1980s and most of the 1990s, cultivating warm relationships with anti-American political leaders (not only Arafat, but also Muammar al-Gaddafi). The present Greek pro-Arab stance, however, cannot be entirely explained in terms of the post-dictatorial choices of Andreas Papandreou and the ideological advocacy of a small but always visible Greek communist minority. Until the end of the cold war, the Greek public was separated into two easily identifiable pro- and anti-West ideological orientations—represented by the division between the right wing, on the one hand, and the socialist and left-wing parties, on the other. During the 1990s, however, anti-Americanism reached almost catholic proportions in Greece, and expanded gradually across and beyond the traditional divide of left and right. The NATO interventions in Yugoslavia intensified the growing discontent of the Greek public with the role of the US in international politics (Sutton 1998; Brown and Theodossopoulos 2000, 2003), while subsequent Western involvement in predominantly Muslim countries gave new impetus to the older, cold war rhetoric on American expansionism. Without seeking to lessen the importance of lived post Second World War history, we argue that the current anti-US and anti-globalization attitudes in Greece are the result of an old narrative model that received a new and important stimulus before and after the turn of the millennium.

In this general context of disaffection with the interventionist attitudes of the West, our respondents started presenting a unity with the 'people' of Palestine and later Afghanistan and Iraq. The basis of this unity is feelings of political – though not entirely cultural - empathy. Thus, although Muslim culture and daily life are regarded as 'backward' and 'oppressive', the political predicament of being at the mercy of the great powers is shared and forms a solid platform for the cultivation of feelings of sympathy and solidarity. A graffiti slogan on a wall in Volos, 'The only solution is *intifada*', led a taxi driver to comment last summer: 'They are right. What else is left to the Arabs? What else is left to us? We should raise our heads one day and stop being governed by the Americans.'

The perceived affinity between Greeks, Cypriots and Middle Easterners is explained by our respondents entirely in the context of power, or lack of it, which in modern politics is seen as being directly connected to a nation's general prospects and prosperity. Even when the Western nations are not blamed directly for local events, they are nevertheless perceived as not being capable of understanding the predicament of powerlessness. The following quotation highlights this view; it epitomizes the position of a forty-three-year-old Greek woman from Volos, which eloquently communicates sentiments of bonding at the margins of power:

> 'It is certain that whatever happens at times in the Middle East does not politically activate (*den evesthitopiei*) the Westerners to the degree it mobilizes us and our Cypriot brothers. Such a degree of [political] sensitivity (*evesthisia*) would have been illogical for someone whose everyday security is not at stake. The way we live, our prospects and hopes make us capable of tuning to the messages that come from the troubled Middle East. In fact, we are not completely outside these developments, since centuries of history bind us with this region of the world.'

In 2006, during Condoleezza Rice's (the US Secretary of State) short visit to Greece and Turkey, the owner of an Internet cafe in Patras commented on the latest involvement of the United States and its allies in Middle East. 'Condoleezza', he said, 'is cooking another war, this time in Iran.' He continued:

> 'She will find, remember my words, all the excuses she wants. Excuses for war are made by the powerful (*apo tous dynatous*); take Alexander the Great or the Romans, for example. It is now the Americans… What have the people of this world done to deserve this? The Greeks, the Turks, the people of Iran… We are all victims of the powerful.'

The claim that the local and the global are interconnected and mutually constitutive (West and Sanders 2003: 9) finds its ethnographic expression in local discussions about political developments inside Greece, Greco-Turkish relations, the events in Cyprus, Palestine and Iraq. We began this section with a rather provocative slogan, often heard in various demonstrations in Athens, 'Greece, Cyprus, Palestine – not a single American left', which has recently been transformed into 'Greece, Iraq, Palestine – not a single American left'. During the last three decades, the Israeli–Palestinian conflict has been compared to that in and over Cyprus, and like the Cyprus problem is regarded as an obvious example of political injustice committed by the great powers. The recent crises in Iraq and Palestine offered new opportunities for unofficial commentary of this kind and inspired our respondents to reflect upon the position of the Arab world with familiar metaphors:

> 'It is as if someone comes with a bulldozer and tries to demolish your house. If you can, you will burn that bulldozer to the ground. The Americans know all this and they are doing it on purpose. They divide and rule. It is their way of reigning in the region. Their tactics keep the Israelis as hostages as well. Can Israel ever go against the US? They depend upon them.'

Globalization as an ideological platform of American imperialism represents in the collective Greek imagination a political future where all peoples' fate is at stake and where alliances are never honourable or stable. Bin Laden and, more so, Saddam Hussein are seen by many in Greece as political products of US policy in the Middle East (Kirtsoglou 2006). The fact that the US and NATO turned against those who they themselves invested with power in the past proves to our respondents beyond any doubt that there is nothing trustworthy in the new world order. Power in the globalized world is felt as being deeply repressive, deceitful and suspicious (West and Sanders 2003). The predicament that leads many Greeks to feel a sort of political intimacy with other disenfranchised nations is that of being condemned to serve a profoundly unequal regime that hides behind 'big and nice words' (*oraia kai megala logia*), such as democracy, tolerance, multiculturalism, cosmopolitanism and freedom. A thirty-eight-year-old businessman in Volos expressed this general idea as follows:

> 'The Americans care for no one. They insist on policies that seem innocent and positive on the pretext of multiculturalism, while what they are after is the creation of various thorns inside nations around the world. When the time is right for them, they light a sparkle and the fire of hatred is soon burning strong. Then they intervene to bring peace to a war they had long before prepared.'

Opinions like this fuel discontent with the use of noble ideals, such as freedom, democracy and independence, when these ideals are used to justify what our respondents see as cruel and unilateral interventions. Their sympathy for and empathy with the people of Afghanistan, Iraq and Palestine are expressions of this discontent and of the belief that in the new political order all the powerless are similar and therefore intimate. In this light, the emerging anti-globalization rhetoric is informed by deeply 'global' thoughts communicated by experiences of political inequality in the globalized world. As we have argued in the introduction and conclusion to this volume, anti-globalization presupposes a consciousness of global interconnections.

Seen from this perspective, discontent with globalization can be understood as a feeling that originates not from some stubborn insistence on localism, nationalism, regionalism or 'tradition', but one that stems from a global perception of the world as an interconnected place. In this interconnected world, the supremacy of some is understood as the predicament of others, while power is thought of in a rather holistic fashion. When our respondents speak of power, they do not refer to military or economic power only, but also, and perhaps more importantly, the power to fashion a cosmology according to one's own interests and then hegemonically extend it to the rest of the world as the indisputable, politically correct stance.

In fewer words, our respondents speak of the power to produce history in both its discursive and practical sense. The conviction that history is written by the powerful and the victorious guides local perceptions and misconceptions, conspiracy-driven narratives and composite scenarios that explain and justify – successfully or unsuccessfully, accurately or inaccurately – international political developments. At the heart of such exegeses of historical causality lies the confidence that in world history particular characters (or nations) play the roles that are reserved for them by the most powerful protagonists of international politics. Globalization is then seen as nothing but another chapter, another device, yet another excuse to keep the world divided between powerful and powerless, agents and patients,[6] elites and pariahs.

The Global Awareness of Greek Anti-globalism

Locally shaped perceptions of history inform almost every aspect of contemporary Greek political consciousness. The concept and role of history in this case transcend the notion of a nation-building narrative that seeks to consolidate Andersonian imagined communities. Historical events from the past are constantly reworked in the present, while the present is always evaluated in terms of past historical developments. David Sutton, in *Memories Cast in Stone* has referred to this practice as analogical thinking (1998). Analogical thinking, however, concerns not only events but also processes. Our respondents draw analogies between contexts, strategies, means and ends and ultimately between the distribution and the effects of power diachronically. It is this kind of diachronic, processual, historical, analogical thinking that leads contemporary Greeks to term our era Pax

Americana, alluding to the times of Pax Romana, when the world was politically organized in imperiums.

As has been argued elsewhere (Clogg 1992; Argyrou 2002; Kirtsoglou 2006), the Greek people have collectively (and not bloodlessly) committed themselves to the West and to the project of modernity. Their desire to 'become modern' and to 'develop into Europeans' signalled their ideological commitment to the ideals of democracy, equality, transparency, trust, openness, rationality and fairness that modernity promised to bring to the social and political world. Modernity, however, as West and Sanders argue, produces effectively 'the very opacities of power that it claims to obviate' (2003: 11). As we have argued in this chapter, modernity in this sense also produces disenfranchised subjectivities. Discontent with globalization (among the Greeks or others) can then be analysed in the context of a discussion about power and political subjectivity.

Our respondents speak of the power to produce discourse and to shape history. In their accounts, globalization, cosmopolitanism and multiculturalism are met with reservation at best and frequently with hostility, because they are seen as discourses created and sustained by power and as cosmologies that serve the interests of Western power and ideological authority. In the place of such concepts, most of our Greek respondents pose an alternative understanding of global connectedness, one that is based on the shared political predicament of the powerless. The awareness of global power inequalities leads local-level commentators to empathize with others perceived to be in similar positions and to form with these dispossessed others idiosyncratic and sometimes paradoxical political intimacies.

In order to ethnographically substantiate the aforementioned points, we have first discussed the example of the Turks, the Other of the Greeks par excellence, the traditional enemy so to speak, and the nation with whom modern Greeks have the longest history of military confrontations. When the Turks are discussed vis-à-vis the global political scene, they cease to become enemies, and are seen as equally peripheral and instrumental to the plans of the great powers. In turn, 'the powerful of the West' become further stereotyped as the agents of blame and responsibility. Especially when it comes to Greco-Turkish relations, the West and, sometimes, local politicians who are believed to be acting as its pawns are deemed responsible for the tensions and conflicts of the past. In evaluations of this kind, Greece and Turkey stand closer together in opposition to the West, and the self as commentator readily acknowledges all those intimate aspects of Greek life that the Turks can understand and Westerners cannot (Herzfeld 1997; Theodossopoulos 2007b). In this discursive context, the Greeks and the Turks become united in their mutual discontent.

When the Greeks are prepared to try to understand the Turks – for example, in terms of their more general critique of the West – they resort to the humanizing tactic of familiarizing the unfamiliar (Sutton 1998). They draw upon personal experiences with Turks, reflect upon a shared culture and common predicaments and imagine the unknown Turk as the Greek next door. The empathy that Greeks demonstrate towards Turks – transcending regional politics – extends to other peripheral actors who are perceived as sharing a similarly disempowered position. Thus, while our respondents feel culturally distinct from Palestinians, Iraqis and generally the Muslim people of the Middle East and the Arab world, they simultaneously seek to stand as their political allies. In contrast, when the majority of the Greeks consider the presence of Muslim populations in their Balkan neighbourhood, they feel threatened and at times express resentment towards these geographically closer Muslim groups. Concurrently, however, both at the level of official governmental strategy and at the level of everyday experiences, the Greeks offer their allegiance to the Palestinians and the peoples of Afghanistan and Iraq. They comment upon Middle Eastern politics as being yet another example of the unilateralism of the great powers and the desire of the great powers to intervene in local affairs in order to serve their own interests.

Situated in this ethnographic context, this chapter has explored Greek expressions of anti-globalization and local resistance to cosmopolitanism to the extent that this is connected to globalization and Western authority. The political and cultural implications of the assumption that, although citizenship can remain national in scope, certain values ought to be shared cross-culturally and transnationally (Kymlicka 2001) have some resonances here. In terms of its theorization, cosmopolitanism has been carefully distinguished from universalism (Appadurai 1996; Hannerz 1996). Local actors, however, often fail to make this distinction, not because they are 'unreflexive', but because they are concerned with inequality, power and marginalization (cf. Mehta 2000; Shweder 2000). As Driessen has pointed out recently, apart from the celebration of diversity, cosmopolitanism also entertains a problematic relationship with power, for 'it is mostly embraced by political, economic and cultural elites as part of their cultural domination' (2005: 137).

It could be argued that the sympathy of Greek actors towards the desire of some Turkish people to revive certain kinds of dress code for women is a cosmopolitan sympathy for an idea that is otherwise regarded as backward and unacceptable. Similarly, the allegiance shown to disparate groups such as the Serbs, the Palestinians, the Iraqis and the Afghans is a kind of cosmopolitan allegiance (cf. Levy and Sznaider 2005), an allegiance across cultural difference, which originates in the perception of a shared lived history of being powerless in comparison with the West. It is this kind of idiosyncratic cosmopolitanism that we have called in the present chapter 'political intimacy', inspired by Herzfeld's (1997) notion of cultural intimacy, the mutual self-recognition of shared familiarity, embarrassment and pride. In the context of political intimacy, even traditional or potential enemies are reconsidered with empathy, as fellow victims of the powerful and as dispossessed human beings like oneself.

Our respondents are thus thinking, acting and expressing discontent in an interconnected world (Geertz 1994, quoted in Kearney 1995). Their thoughts, actions and discontent, however, call for a rethinking of how this interconnection takes place and to what purpose, who such processes exclude and what kind of subaltern identities they produce (West and Sanders 2003: 11). Thinking globally and from a cosmopolitan perspective poses no particular difficulty for our Greek interlocutors, whose narratives we sought to analyse in an open-minded fashion, going beyond well-rehearsed exegeses of nationalism, regionalism and tradition. For, in the perceptions and misconceptions of our respondents we have seen their determination to imagine the vast majority of the world as sharing the same humanity, an equal vulnerability, and, as a result, similar anti-Western orientations. In circumstances like these, anti-cosmopolitanism inspires a cosmopolitan imagination of resistance to and discontent with those who – as a well-known Greek expression goes – 'hold both the pie and the knife', thus being capable of 'portioning and sharing the world, just as they like'.

Notes

1. See, for example, the chapters in the volume *When Greeks think about Turks* (Theodossopoulos 2007a), which examine particular cases in diverse social contexts.
2. 'Milame gia tis diafores mas, emeis kai oi Tourkoi kai xehname tin pagosmia yperdynami; pios kanei tous mikrous laous na polemane metaxy tous? Pios skaronei polemous edo kai ekei? Pios kanei tous anthropous na ypoferoun? Kai pios kerdizei apo ayto?'
3. 'Ti mporoun na kanoun Ellines kai Tourkoi horis tin egrisi tou planitarhi? Ti mporoun na kanoun oi aploi anthropoi? Ola stin pagosmiopiisi einai elenhomena!'
4. Ama goustaroune mantila magkia tous. Poioi einai oi Europaio diladi kai o kathe Amerikanos pou tha tous pei ti tha kanoune mesa sti xora tous? Kala kanoune kai yperaspizontai ta pisteuo tous.'
5. Olos o kosmos maimoudizei, prospathei na miasei stin Dysi; orismenoi laoi, san tous Mousoulmanous antistekonte; oi Tourkoi, perissotero apo mas; gi' auto to logo tous paradehomai!
6. The concept of agents and patients belongs to Michael Carrithers and has much more theoretical depth than our expression allows for here.

References

Appadurai, A. 1996. *Modernity at Large; Cultural Dimensions of Globalization.* Minneapolis: University of Minnesota Press.

Appiah, K.A. 1998. Cosmopolitan Patriots. In B. Robbins and P. Cheah (eds) *Cosmopolitics.* Minneapolis. University of Minnesota Press, pp. 98–117.

Argyrou, V. 2002. *Anthropology and the Will to Meaning: A Post-colonial Critique.* London: Pluto.

Bastian, M.L. 2001. Vulture Men, Campus Cultists and Teenaged Witches: Modern Magics in Nigerian Popular Press. In H.L. Moore and T. Sanders (eds) *Magical Interpretations, Material Realities: Modernity, Witchcraft and the Occult in Postcolonial Africa.* London: Routledge, pp. 71–96.

Beck, U. and N. Sznaider. 2006. Unpacking Cosmopolitanism for the Social Sciences: a Research Agenda. *British Journal of Sociology,* 57 (1), 1–23.

Brown, K. and D. Theodossopoulos. 2000. The Performance of Anxiety: Greek Narratives of the War at Kossovo. *Anthropology Today,* 16 (1), 3–8.

——— 2003. Rearranging Solidarity: Conspiracy and World Order in Greek and Macedonian Commentaries of Kossovo. *Journal of Southern Europe and the Balkans,* 4 (3), 315–35.

Clogg, R. 1992. *A Concise History of Greece.* Cambridge: Cambridge University Press.

Comaroff, J. and J. Comaroff. 1993. Introduction. In J. Comaroff and J. Comaroff (eds) *Modernity and its Malcontents: Ritual and Power in Post-colonial Africa.* Chicago: Chicago University Press, pp. xi–xxxvii.

Driessen, H. 2005. Mediterranean Port Cities; Cosmopolitanism Reconsidered. *History and Anthropology,* 16 (1), 129–41.

Dubisch, J. 1995. *In a Different Place: Pilgrimage, Gender, and Politics at a Greek Island.* Princeton: Princeton University Press.

Faubion. J.D. 1993. *Modern Greek Lessons: A Primer in Historical Constructivism.* Princeton: Princeton University Press.

Fischer, M.J. 1999. Emergent Forms of Life: Anthropologies of Late or Postmodernities. *Annual Review of Anthropology,* 28, 455–78.

Giddens, A. 1990. *The Consequences of Modernity.* Stanford: Stanford University Press.

Hannerz, U. 1996. *Transnational Connections; Culture, People, Places.* London: Routledge.

Hardt. M. and A. Negri. 2000. *Empire.* Cambridge, MA: Harvard University Press.

Held, D., A. McGrew, D. Goldplatt and J. Perraton. 1999. *Global Transformations: Politics, Economics and Culture.* Stanford, CA: Stanford University Press.

Hellinger, D. 2003. Paranoia, Conspiracy and Hegemony in American Politics. In H.G. West and T. Sanders (eds) *Transparency and Conspiracy; Ethnographies of Suspicion in the New World Order.* Durham and London: Duke University Press, pp. 204–32.

Herzfeld, M. 1992. *The Social Production of Indifference; Exploring the Symbolic Roots of Western Bureaucracy.* Chicago: University of Chicago Press.

——— 1995. It Takes One to Know One: Collective Resentment and Mutual Recognition among Greeks in Local and Global Contexts. In R. Fardon (ed.) *Counterworks: Managing the Diversity of Knowledge*. Routledge, London, pp. 124–42.

——— 1997. *Cultural Intimacy: Social Poetics in the Nation State*. New York: Routledge.

Kearney, M. 1995. The Local and the Global: The Anthropology of Globalization and Transnationalism. *Annual Review of Anthropology*, 24, 547–65.

Kirtsoglou, E. 2006. Unspeakable Crimes: Athenian Greek Perceptions of Local and International Terrorism. In A. Strathern, P. Stewart and N. Whitehead (eds) *Terror and Violence; Imagination and the Unimaginable*. London: Pluto, pp. 61–88.

——— 2007. Phantom Menace: What Junior Greek Army Officers Have to Say about Turks and Turkey. In D. Theodossopoulos (ed.) *When Greeks Think about Turks: The View from Anthropology*. London: Routledge, pp. 162–76.

Kymlicka, W. 2001. *Politics in the Vernacular: Nationalism, Multiculturalism and Citizenship*. Oxford: Oxford University Press.

Levy, D. and N. Sznaider. 2005. *The Holocaust and Memory in the Global Age*. Philadelphia: Temple University Press.

McCarthy Brown, K. 2003. Making *Wanga*: Reality Constructions and the Magical Manipulation of Power. In H.G. West and T. Sanders (eds) *Transparency and Conspiracy; Ethnographies of Suspicion in the New World Order*. Durham and London: Duke University Press, pp. 1–37.

Mehta, P.B. 2000. Cosmopolitanism and the Circle of Reason. *Political Theory*, 28 (5), 619–39.

Marcus, G.E. 1999. Introduction to the Volume: The Paranoid Style Now. In G. Marcus (ed.) *Paranoia within Reason: A Casebook on Conspiracy as Explanation*. Chicago: Chicago University Press, pp. 1–11

Millas, I. 2007. *Tourkokratia*: History and the Image of Turks in Greek Literature. In D. Theodossopoulos (ed.) *When Greeks Think about Turks: The View from Anthropology*. London: Routledge, pp. 47–60.

Ors, I.R. 2007. Beyond the Greek and Turkish Dichotomy: the *Rum Polites* of Istanbul and Athens. In D. Theodossopoulos (ed.) *When Greeks Think about Turks: The View from Anthropology*. London: Routledge, pp. 79–94.

Seremetakis, N. 1991. *The Last Word: Women, Death and Divination in Inner Mani*. Chicago: University of Chicago Press.

Shweder, R. 2000. Moral Maps, 'First World' Conceits and the New Evangelists. In L.E. Harrison and S. Huntington (eds) *Culture Matters*. New York: Basic Books, pp.158–76.

Spyrou, S. 2007. Constructing 'the Turk' as an Enemy: The Complexity of Stereotypes in Children's Everyday World. In D. Theodossopoulos (ed.) *When Greeks Think about Turks: The View from Anthropology*. London: Routledge, pp. 95–110.

Stewart-Harawira, M. 2005. *The New World Order: Indigenous Responses to Globalization*. London: Zed Books.

Stolcke, V. 1995. Talking Culture: New Boundaries, New Rhetorics of Exclusion in Europe. *Current Anthropology*, 36, 1–13.

Sutton, D. 1998. *Memories Cast in Stone: The Relevance of the Past in Everyday Life*. Oxford: Berg.

—— 2003. Poked by the 'Foreign Finger' in Greece: Conspiracy Theory or the Hermeneutics of Suspicion? In K.S. Brown and Y. Hamilakis (eds) *The Usable Past: Greek Metahistories*. Lanham: Lexington books, pp. 191–210.

Theodossopoulos, D. 2004. The Turks and their Nation in the Worldview of Greeks in Patras. *History and Anthropology*, 15 (1), 29–45.

—— (ed.) 2007a. *When Greeks Think about Turks: The View from Anthropology*. London: Routledge.

—— 2007b. Introduction: The 'Turks' in the Imagination of the 'Greeks'. In D. Theodossopoulos (ed.) *When Greeks Think about Turks: The View from Anthropology*. London: Routledge, pp. 1–32.

—— 2007c. Politics of Friendship, Worldviews of Mistrust: The Greek-Turkish Rapprochement in Local Conversation. In D. Theodossopoulos (ed.) *When Greeks Think about Turks: The View from Anthropology*. London: Routledge, pp. 193–210.

Tsibiridou, F. 2007. Writing about Turks and Powerful Others: Journalistic Heteroglossia in Western Thrace. In D. Theodossopoulos (ed.) *When Greeks Think about Turks: The View from Anthropology*. London: Routledge, pp. 129–44.

West, H.G. and T. Sanders. 2003. Power Revealed and Concealed in the New World Order. In H.G. West and T. Sanders (eds) *Transparency and Conspiracy; Ethnographies of Suspicion in the New World Order*. Durham and London: Duke University Press, pp. 1–37.

Yiakoumaki, V. 2007. Ethnic Turks and 'Muslims' and the Performance of Multiculturalism in Greece: The Case of the *Drómeno* of Thrace. In D. Theodossopoulos (ed.) *When Greeks Think about Turks: The View from Anthropology*. London: Routledge.

Chapter 6

ESCAPING THE 'MODERN' EXCESSES OF JAPANESE LIFE: CRITICAL VOICES ON JAPANESE RURAL COSMOPOLITANISM

Àngels Trias i Valls

This chapter focuses on Japan, in the global economic context vis-à-vis discourses about modernity, nationalism and social exclusion, which have become significant focuses of interest in Japanese ethnographies (Ivy 1995; Robertson 1998; Goldstein-Gidoni 2001). My ethnographic context is a small town in southern Japan, a non-metropolitan location, that in Japanese is called both *machi* (a town) and *furosato* (the native place).[1] My attempt here is to draw special attention to indigenous notions of cosmopolitanism (*sekaijin*), which are loosely connected to ideas such as multiculturalism and globalization and emerge in everyday practice in places that are seemingly non-metropolitan. In doing so, I shall be looking at how ideas of anti-cosmopolitanism emerge in allegedly 'harmonious places' and how these ideas accentuate the kinds of worries and discourses Japanese people have about social inequality, the sharing of environmental resources and national identity.

My discussion has a twofold purpose. First, I wish to examine the interconnections between the local and the global and the ways in which anthropologists may best situate their 'pre-theoretical commitments' within the 'texture' of their ethnographies (Moore 2004). As Hannerz (2004) and Mignolo (2000) have argued, defining cosmopolitanism can be a slippery task. In this respect, I use the term cosmopolitanism in Moore's sense of a concept metaphor, namely, a term that serves as a 'conceptual shorthand', while at the same time it can provide us with the explanatory force necessary in making sense of the interactions involved in both global and centre/periphery relations (Moore 2004: 71). I take this only as a starting point of my analytical interpretations aiming to assess the kinds of discourses that emerge about empathy and global connectedness towards others. Without attempting to conflate globalization with cosmopolitanism, I endorse Moore's questions about the possibility of an ethnography of cosmopolitanism and its potential form and content.

My second concern in this discussion is inspired by an ethnographic realization. During fieldwork, my friends and informants were immersed in a series of national projects of 'town making' (*matchitsukuri*) that aimed to place small rural towns on the 'global map' (Trias i Valls 2001: 230). The tensions of such projects revealed a complex situational process where individuals could make their personal aspirations public (a rare occasion in Japanese social life) (ibid.: 254). In the context of such projects, my informants were also able to express their rejection of cosmopolitanism and their views on 'cosmopolitics' (Cheah and Robbins 1998). Their discourses revolved around the idea of 'escaping' from what they perceived as the excesses of cosmopolitan life in Japan.

This chapter, then, is about a series of views on cosmopolitics and about the tensions of locating different discourses about agency and political power amongst a group of Japanese. I argue, however, that such views cannot be reduced to one-dimensional narratives about a Japanese sense of locality (*furosato*), internationalization (*kokusaika*) and national identity (*nihonjinron*) (Yoshino 1992; Aoyama and Hiroaki 2003; Sasaki 2004). The Japanese case needs to be contextualized within and examined against wider discourses of cosmopolitanism, as part of an 'ethnography of the cosmopolitan'. Namely, it needs to be viewed as part of a project that draws on internal tensions of academic representation (Appadurai 2006: 630), while simultaneously expressing distinctively non-Western understandings of the world (including rejection and new interpretations of those understandings) (cf. Iwabuchi 1994; Robertson 1998; Hendry 2000; Goldstein-Gidoni 2005).

Japan's emergence on the global economic scene in the 1970s generated ambivalence and 'bittersweet' discourses about internationalization and cosmopolitanism, both as a process of emulation and as critical rejection of systems of value (exacerbated in the areas of gender, exchange, global consumerism and environmentalism) within Japan (cf. Goldstein-Gidoni 2001, Atkins 2004). Particular Japanese discourses of repudiating certain 'evils' of internationalization and certain local understandings of globalization and the concomitant inequalities of economic growth (Featherstone 1990) transcend, I claim, 'national identity' and 'group formation' (Arnason 1990: 210, Harden 1994). Japanese reservations complement those of other groups of discontented people who share similar values and demonstrate that cosmopolitanism relates to perceptions of power and can refer –among other things- to a shared ability to recognise processes of incorporation and exclusion of persons and qualities.

New Cosmopolitan Towns: 'Native and Newcomers' and 'Dissonant Others'

The process of 'making the town' (*matchitsukuri*) and that of its predecessor, 'making the village' (*furosato tsukuri*), are political processes related to revival schemes that aim at orchestrating the social and economic viability of Japanese rural localities (Robertson 1991; Knight 1996; Atkins 2004). In Kamikatsu town, these processes started in the early 1950's, with a major 'revival' period in the early 1990s, when all rural 'villages' were, de facto, subsumed under a single type of rural administration, 'the town' (*machi*).

'Making the town' included several operations: the merging of villages under one territorial boundary; the incorporation of non-local families; the introduction of trans-local business; the transformation of local areas into 'national' tourist resources; and the internationalization of learning venues (Trias i Valls 2001: 44, 230).[2] The harsh political transformations of the village boundary and their economic implications were often expressed in a romanticized language of a common sharing of the past and the future (Knight 1996). The opening and reshuffling of villages, however, also meant that foreigners and what I call 'dissonant Others' and 'traditional and new' families would all come together. These political processes created a tension whereby the town became, for a group of families, a place that could be constructed as a rural but cosmopolitan and international place.[3] Several ethnographic episodes below demonstrate this. These will reflect on the different views of cosmopolitanism from within, and on local Japanese answers to what Appiah (2006) has defined as sharing 'a world of strangers'.

For towns like Kamikatsu, the town-making processes meant a larger disruption of the patterns that Robertson (1991) describes so well for 'villages' and village making (*furosatotsukuri*). Unlike Robertson's Kodaira city, Kamikatsu town contained more than just newcomers and native families. Earlier *furosato* identities of the 1950s and 1970s were merged into a new unit, the town, throwing many of the existing social divisions into turmoil. The town in 1995 superseded any previous political unit, and its villagers came together in an enormous effort to obviate differences and merge intentions (Trias i Valls 2001: 235). The town, still decreasing in numbers, was now open to applications by families that, in my informants' perceptions, would traditionally have been 'turned down' in respect of rural processes of inclusion. The local rural authorities were considering, in the name of cosmopolitanism and internationalization, applications from and inclusion of what I call 'dissonant others' (often referred as *chotto henna* – slightly odd). These included single artists, families with no formal means of employment, families with children with special needs, Jet (English) teachers, second-generation Japanese returnees from abroad and Burakumin (a Japanese minority group) citizens. These people formed a distinct category of citizens within the town, and often felt a sense of being 'dispossessed' by virtue of their antagonism to the 'internationalization' processes of town making.

None of these families ever fell into the category of 'newcomer' per se. Other 'newcomers' in the previous decade had already taken that label.[4] They were, of course, *'atarashii machi hito'*, the new people in town. They were, like the broader phenomena of cosmopolitanism and internationalization, new. Like internationalization – which I use as a term that identifies the gradual integration of Japan into global discourses[5] – they were felt to be 'despondent' or 'strange' at times. At the point their applications were accepted it was unclear, if the new residents would settle and/or contribute to the future of the town. As one of the town's officers and the families themselves argued, however, most of these applicants shared the aspiration of returning to a rural way of life as a way of rejecting the concomitant effects of globalization.

For the town administration officers (*yakuba*), concerned with developing the town, these town residents with their 'oddities' and different backgrounds credited the town with a cosmopolitan ethos. The town was made up of many citizens; it even had 'its own JET teacher', a local town officer said. Thus, this period has been characterized by a constant effort by all people involved, nearly two thousand in number, to create a convivial cosmopolitan rurality (Trias i Valls 2001). Spearheaded by key members of the local administration, families and individuals alike found themselves immersed in discussions regarding recycling, new tourist enterprises, HIV and AIDS prevention and Burakumin marriage.

The conversations held in the town were between voices of normative cosmopolitanism and anti-cosmopolitics (Appiah 2006: 14). Pro- and anti-cosmopolitans rarely agreed, not always publicly, as people upheld *tatemae* (public opinion) conventions. However, as Appiah argues so well (ibid.: 57, 85), they were 'united' in achieving the practical means of living with each other whilst maintaining distinctive lifestyles. Indeed, 'social conversation' in town meetings, festivals, gift exchange and every other context of discursive practice created an awareness of the cosmopolitan nature of the people's contemporary lives. Only those individuals and families who failed to 'come together' – placing a high value on the distinctiveness of their/others' identities and lives – found themselves in the position of the peripheral and excluded citizen (Trias i Valls 2001: 288). As such, town making and exchanges between people in the town made up the ethnographic context that frames my discussion about Japanese cosmopolitanism(s) and their discontents. Below I recount several examples that deal with local understandings and rejections of being cosmopolitan.

'We were Modern, too': Being Cosmopolitan in Rural Places

In early August 1996, at the height of 'internationalization' and 'town making', the town of Kamikatsu woke up to the sound of loudspeakers, conveniently located at most intersections, on forest roads and in field terraces. The public announcement referred to a school event that was taking place that same morning. The open day aimed at bringing the town's children (often classed as the future of the town) and the town's elders together. During the day, the children would have the chance to learn from their elders, in particular to listen to the elders' experiences of a pre-war rural childhood. The elders would have the opportunity to pass their experiences on, to be taken into the future. My field entry captures the spirit of the day:

> As I arrived at the school, a class of seven- to nine-year-old children were already sitting at their desks. A group of twenty-nine elderly men and women, between mid- sixties and early nineties, had politely been assigned an area behind the children's desks. We greeted each other in silence as the teacher bowed and thanked everybody present. The teacher explained that we were going to learn about how rural Japanese children used to live in the past, *inaka no kimochi*, and learn the games (now lost) the elders played at school back then. The teacher continued with a brief comment on modernity, proclaiming that currently the children lived modern lives, they had international teachers and they learned English. Japanese children were citizens of the world; their commodities (computer games) and lifestyles (travelling by bus), she indicated, were an index of such belonging. In her talk two ideas, often reproduced in most cultural events in the town, became conflated: The children were citizens of the world because they were also citizens of a (modern) town.

Looking back, one could argue that the children's first experience of cosmopolitan values at school emerged not from the idea of travelling, welcoming strangers, empathizing with others, but from placing themselves in a shared locality. Of course, this alluded to a political fact. Most children and most elders of the town, in fact, lived in five different villages. These villages, connected by roads extending up to a two-hour journey across rivers and forested mountains, had only come together as a political and financial unit during the last twenty years. From a historical point of view, the children and the elders did not share the town as a political space. The elders, in their childhood, had never lived in a town. They lived in separate villages, in villages that often politely antagonized each other, and secluded themselves from other villages through organizing separate Shinto festivals (Trias i Valls 2001). What made the elders modern was that they managed to transcend their small rural localities through participating in the national process of political reconfiguration that brought to these rural localities a strong urban feeling.

The teacher, however, ignored the fact that this 'town' only came into existence in the past twenty years. Her concern was simple. She wanted to emphasize to the pupils that all children were part of the 'town' and, in a sense, to reinvent the political past of their elders by demonstrating a continuous relationship from the past to the present. The town, which had been invented in the years preceding the staged changes in rural administration and land taxation, was now presented as if it had always existed in a continuous fashion: 'we', as people, had always been in a 'larger' (scale-wise) map. In the teacher's account, the group of villages spread out in a remote rural province became a town, an important town, with a place in the province, a place in Japan, a place in the world. Yes, it was a rural town, but even rural towns could have an air of cosmopolitanism and in the 'fad word of the 1990s' (Robertson 1998) an air of 'internationalization':

> The teacher insisted on making her point: the world of rural Japan (*furosato*) had changed, children lived modern lives now, we all lived in a town, Kamikatsu town, and people perceived us as a town and asked about what we had to offer them. The elders remained quiet and attentive. The children looked embarrassed, glancing back and forth to the row of elders at their backs but also making a clear effort to behave politely as the teacher alluded to the elders and how they came down to the school in *geta* (pre-modern shoes).[6] Quietly an elderly man, Nii San, a former council member and a prominent landowner in his late eighties raised his hand and stopped the teacher's story. Politely but firmly he said: 'Thank you, you see, when we were children not all children came to school in *geta* and ragged clothes. We had shoes, and modern clothes, too. Some children were poor, but we, in our villages, were modern (*moden*) too.'

Nii San was rightly alluding to the early 1920s and 1930s period, which was very important for the history of cosmopolitanism in Japan (Martinez 1998). Cosmopolitanism (*sekaijin*) then was not just marked by the introduction of Western clothes. It became a field of discourse about the 'place of Japan' in the political order of the world. It shouldn't come as a surprise that Nii San was able to make this point in 1995, when the financial world order echoed similar concerns regarding the place Japan occupied in neoliberal capitalist markets. Nii San was talking of a sense of cosmopolitan modernity and globalization that was felt throughout Japan, creating waves of discontent, once in every decade from the late 1950s and the late 1970s to the early 1980s and the financial crises in 1995.

Some of the feelings of discontent generated in these periods were reflected in films (such as Musumura's 1958 *Giants and Toys*, which was an attack on post-war corporate society), TV, pop culture and literature. The quest for modernity was an index of Japan's entry into the cosmopolitan world. The discontent that modernity generated was felt intensely as a contradiction in rural areas. Silverberg (1988) argues that the quest for modernity (being *modan*) – a term also used by my informants – often appears in the context of cultural productions, mostly the leisure industry, the bars, fashion shops and coffee places, which are widely identified with the growth of urban cosmopolitanism. Nii San's case represents other, similar voices of individuals in the town who switched between different understandings of cosmopolitanism and modernity, expressing a form of 'mild' discontent. While these elders accepted the process of 'town making', they also found themselves struggling with the over-romanticized discourses on their 'past'. These make their children 'modern' at the expense of making them 'old-fashioned' and thus displaced from modernity, at a time when their lives, prior to town making, had always been felt as 'modern' and cosmopolitan.[7] The processes of romanticizing 'the place of the elders' created a sense of 'dispossession' among elders, who found themselves relegated to 'honourable' positions that had little political power.[8]

Cosmopolitan Modern Homes: Souvenirs, a 'Taste of the World'

Oue San, in her late seventies and a member of the group of elders described above, would often privately comment that she was from a generation of women who struggled to be modern, despite the fact that she followed the traditional pattern of an arranged marriage. In her talks, she called herself modern and a 'citizen of the world' (*sekaijin*). Her understanding of modernity was linked to cosmopolitanism in the only area left to personal choice: her patterns of consumption. Several things made her modern: she bought Western coffee brands, sent her children abroad to study and travelled as a tourist around Japan on visits to *onzens* (hot springs) and other Japanese tourist resorts. It was clear that the index of her 'modernity' was her capacity to appropriate otherness through souvenirs (*omiyage*). The common practice to bring 'souvenir' gifts (mostly food-based) back from a journey made it possible for her family and neighbours to get 'a taste of the world'.

During fieldwork, it became clear that exchanges of souvenir gifts were and still are one of the major channels of communication through which Japanese express ideas about their place in the world. Going abroad, travelling to seemingly cosmopolitan areas, taking pictures and buying a souvenir are almost stereotypical expressions of the Japanese understanding of shared (and imagined) cosmopolitanism. Here, I argue that gifts mediate people's capacity to remove themselves from home, from the immediate community, and to reincorporate themselves back 'home' without becoming 'strangers' (strangers being individuals that have gone too far in assimilating qualities of foreign people, thus losing aspects of the 'Japanese self' – see below for such a case). The souvenir gifts signal the Japanese reincorporation into 'polite society'. The subsequent giving of souvenirs to kin, workmates and neighbours also signals each family's capacity to extend their experience of cosmopolitanism upon returning from their travels. Simultaneously, it also indicates that these travellers (tourists) have not 'gone native' but have retained those imagined cultural qualities that signify them as Japanese.

I shall discuss later how patterns of exchange varied amongst different groups in Kamikatsu town and how, not accidentally, those who expressed the bitterest discontent with cosmopolitan values and with the process of town making rejected conventional types of exchange and opted for barter. In fact, as in much of my work, I shall argue that different types of exchange, in particular, the travelling souvenirs (*omiyage*), were at the centre of people's capacity for dealing with the incorporation and rejection of individuals.

Dissonant Others: Non-normative Views of Cosmopolitanism

After attending the school meeting and talking with my informants, I went home and asked my host family about the events that had taken place there. My host family shared with various fellow citizens a sense of 'dissonance' from other fellow citizens of the town. As a family of a couple and two children, they had been accepted into Kamikatsu ten years earlier. They held strong environmental views and anti-globalization sentiments, often supporting local and international environmental campaigns. They had numerous friends in the capital, where they participated in international art events and attended religious services. A common aspect of this group of families is that they all participated in barter with those who shared a similar interest in 'ecological living'. These were mostly families who made a living from their own small and non-profit-oriented businesses or their own organic gardens.

My host family described the above event as both a school day and a town-making occasion. Indeed, as they critically pointed out, the town council and the school always tried to bring people together in order 'to make a better town' and this was one example of such efforts. My hosts were also quick to point out their disagreement with this type of local politics. As they put it:

> 'We came here to find a place away from the modern Japanese obsession with moneymaking, to return to a more sustainable living. I don't know what to think about 'town making'; it is not what I came here for. I think we must improve the town, and we all work to help. There are lots of events to make the town prettier and attract tourists. But look at how it is done. There are asphalt constructions everywhere, with beds of flowers all around. The flowers are not even autochthonous to this region. I would like to see a town that provides farms with information on how to become organic, how to organize recycling, how to avoid environmental damage, but we are very much alone in this...'

This family, like many other 'new' families, expressed their dissonance even when they tried to help making the town. The paradox in their attitudes and comments is that in fact, they had, like most other new families, moved to this particular rural area after travelling the world. Indeed, they had embraced many ideas about cosmopolitanism, especially a common critique of world poverty and global urban expansion (Featherstone 1990). Unlike others in the town, who only travelled abroad for short tourist or work-related ventures, the couple in my host family had lived abroad. They were, in their view and in that of others, truly cosmopolitan. Upon their return to Japan, however, they had – by virtue of their empathetic understanding of others abroad – found themselves to be marginal strangers. They had become vegetarian, opted for Catholicism and voiced clear critiques of the Japanese educational system (supporting a blend of school and home teaching for their own children). They had their own organic gardens and refused waged work. Living in a rural locality was part and parcel of their decision to repudiate the evils of 'cosmopolitanism'. I recall from my diary:

> My host family had left Japan to see the world, to experience how other people lived. The West, they claimed, was a far more spiritual place than Japan. In our conversation, my hosts argued that they had travelled to India and Nepal, first merely to see the world. However, once abroad, they came to recognize poverty. They felt empathy for others' poverty. They felt angry at the multinational powers that made the Nepalese mountains dirtier (or

those in Japan full of asphalt). The amount of wealth in Japan 'was excessive'. 'If people in Nepal could live with less, so could we, the Japanese.'

Their experience of living abroad, and their empathetic understanding of others made them turn their lives around. They came back to Japan with a 'new conscience' to reject consumerist values, and thus they asked to live in a rural location in order to pursue a more sustainable life. They were cosmopolitan in the sense of sharing empathy with other destitute subjects. At the same time, they were also clearly discontented with their own society and fairly marginal to it. My host family were, furthermore, acutely concerned with the globalizing processes that made Japanese firms like Mitsubishi and local business corporations enter an international context of unfair trade and environmental spoilage. Their awareness of these issues made them (as a part of a semi-national campaign) take a local provincial corporation to court. They hoped to prevent this particular coal company from destroying local ecologies, which would damage future environmental resources in the area. They failed in their attempt to persuade the Tokushima high courts to prevent the coal corporation from continuing to spill their emissions of coal residues over the local river areas. After the trial was over, this group were left expressing their private discontent with the legal and financial processes, which, mirroring other global cases, made these companies and the Japanese legal system too powerful for them to fight against.

The Watanabe family were not alone in their quest. The town was 'bursting' with families and individuals who were carefully crafting their lifestyles in manners very different from previous town dwellers. My hosts had met like-minded people in the town and became friends with them. Such a case was the Shibata family, who had opened an organic bakery. They learned the trade and baked bread for many shops in the prefecture, always struggling to make ends meet. Their customers were also 'new' and young families from the capital who were aiming for sustainable lifestyles, at least to mirror cosmopolitan styles of fairer living. They all took an interest in supporting the Watanabe family in their court case. There were many examples of such 'dissonant Others' around me. Apart from the Watanabe and the Shibata family, there was Kota San, who had started his working life as a 'salaryman' (white-collar worker) and had now become a part-time worker for several farms, living his life in a transient manner, coming and going from different jobs. There were also Diana and her Japanese husband, who lived on bartering their home-made jam and on the leftovers of the affluence around them. The latter were perhaps the ones that suffered most from political tensions in the town. When the Burakumin identity of Diana's husband was revealed, they had to face the decision to 'leave the town' (Trias i Valls 2001:253). Paradoxically, until the moment their identities were revealed, they were successful in attracting the interest of other traditional families, who, in their desire to be cosmopolitan (in the normative sense), welcomed and even exchanged goods with them. A direct diary extract from my fieldnotes states:

> Today I spoke with Suzuki San, who told me that he was going to cease bartering and giving things to Diana. Surprised, but knowing in advance to what he was alluding, I listened: 'We are a good town, we take many different people, but this family, they are, you know … [he pointed at four fingers, indicating in a discriminatory way the imagined non-human origin of the Burakumin people]. Their neighbours in their village think they are not good people, and we cannot be associated with them. It is a sad event, but it is too much for us to keep giving them things like we used to do.'[9]

The new families continued helping the Burakumin family, who nevertheless soon found themselves severely isolated. Of all people in town, this group and a few members of the town office who were aware of the situation were the most accepting and tolerant with 'foreigners'. These families all had something in common. They thought of themselves as rural cosmopolitans precisely because they were capable of rejecting globalization values while embracing ideas of the periphery and the rights of minority peoples.

In a sense, several visions of anti-cosmopolitanism coexisted within the town. There were, of course, many normative views on cosmopolitanism as well. Nearly all families had experienced being 'abroad' and 'foreignness'. They had all experienced urban styles of consumption, directly and through popular entertainment. As Robertson (1988) describes, the arrival of the concept of modernity with transformation of gender roles, the invention of new traditions and the creation of new spaces, like the coffee place, is crucial in understanding how discursive practices are recognized amidst the confluence of cosmopolitan ideas. Furthermore, I would argue, it is through discussions of modernity (what is modern, what is bad about the internationalization of Japan) that people assess not just the conceptual shorthand that cosmopolitanism stands for, but the day-to-day practices of being 'kind to strangers'. I turn next to how this consideration is articulated for many families all over this rural area.

Kindness to Strangers

As a stranger in Japan, I experienced many acts of kindness, and so did every other 'foreigner' (*gaijin*) or 'dissonant' character, including young Japanese women as a new group. In addition to receiving souvenirs, the period of internationalization of the 1990s in Japan meant an effort being made by institutions and households alike to 'offer' to and integrate 'foreigners', young women and 'others' into all sorts of cultural events, from a tea ceremony to carrying Shinto *mikoshi* (portable shrines). One institution, the 'home stay', is perhaps paradigmatic of this processes and one of the most popular ways in which Japanese extended 'kindness to strangers'. Home stays were invitations to foreigners for 'short' (from a few hours to two days) visits to a Japanese home, where they could experience 'Japanese culture' from within. Home stays were meant to construct the Japanese home as a cosmopolitan venue. However, they frequently became the most common context where 'foreigners' and 'others' alike found themselves experiencing exclusion and the limits of cosmopolitanism. Material from my field diaries demonstrates these tensions:

Kamikatsu August 23rd 1995

I have been at Abe's San house for a few weeks now. This is my third home stay (...) I am puzzled by the gifts that I am receiving. These are the kind of gifts you'd find in the tourist shop in town (fans, cakes, postcards). Each home stay has been the same: I am given the chance to live with a family for few days, we exchange information about where I come from and after a few days I start receiving souvenir cards, souvenir cakes, souvenir fans again (...) As I was walking down the street towards the tourist shop, I felt it. Oh, I am a tourist then. I had my short home stay. The souvenirs given to me would be the ones I would be buying if I were planning to leave. In an indirect, polite way my hosts' messages could not be clearer. My time with them was up. I had to go.

The conventional home stay experience, also recounted to me by other 'foreigners' in the region, shows a characteristic of the normative style of cosmopolitan thinking. There is a time limit in accepting strangers, as happens with ancestors at mid-summer time at home and at festivals (Trias i Valls 2001: 179) Like ancestors and passer-by entities, foreigners are invited in, offered drinks and food, and conversation follows. The conversation is often about where you come from, what you eat at home, different food and different social practices abroad. After this, it is 'time to go'.

In short, cosmopolitanism is brought home through souvenirs and inviting strangers to one's home. However, the term foreigner here does not merely imply the outside element in the term *'gaijin'* (alien) but also includes a sense of someone 'passing' through. Indeed, the experience of cosmopolitanism is limited to a short period, after which foreigners must depart again. Much of the ethos of the direct experience of cosmopolitan values within Japan – when Japan itself becomes a 'world of strangers' within and the town is a space shared 'with others' – is based on a temporally framed acceptance of others, for short 'periods' when one has time to learn about otherness. In these short periods of inclusion and subsequent exclusion, gifts mediate the entrance and exit of such individuals.

Cosmopolitanism from within, coping with strangers or becoming a stranger – as a tourist- only exists as a temporal frame of inclusion. When asking my Japanese informants about such decisions, often the answer was (in slightly apologetic embarrassment): 'It is short ... yes ... we are always so busy.' I could not disagree. Most people in town were indeed busy. My host family argued, 'This is the price for being modern and international.' Those 'few days' in a home stay were as much as anyone could give away when combined with already constituted obligations to others. In their exceptionality of rejecting Japanese 'modernity', my hosts expressed their perceived constituted obligation to others, which was to extend the acceptance and inclusion of the poor, the destitute, the transient. They had 'time', meaning they could abandon aspects of themselves to accommodate others with greater ease.

Dramatizing Cosmopolitanism

Fieldwork revealed that kindness to strangers had a variety of meanings. For most people with a strong anti-capitalist and anti-modern ideology (like my host family and their friends), it meant extending kindness into the area of full social inclusion through barter and tolerance for difference (accepting Burakumin citizens, for example). For those who upheld a more normative view of cosmopolitanism, it meant extending kindness only to a point (as in the case of the short home stays described above). Local responses to cosmopolitanism were – like responses to strangers – partial, only for a limited period. Cosmopolitanism in town, as expressed in the different examples in this chapter, meant a tension between idealizing the self as constituted by modern ideas and, at the same time, renouncing an element of the self when meeting foreigners. This element relates, I argue, for rural Japanese, to their existing pre-commitments to their own identity and to national others.

Internationalization and national identity, rootedness and community, mostly expressed by the terms *kokusai* and *furosato*, are, Robertson (1988) claims, the poles of every essentialist discourse in Japanese society. Cosmopolitan analyses (Featherstone 1990; Sasaki 2004; Goldstein-Gidoni 2005) all converge in pointing at the importance of nationalism in contextualizing the tensions within cosmopolitan discourses. The emerging picture is that Japanese identities are predicated on discourses to do with national identity.

However, I would like to extend this point by arguing that the division between 'national' others and 'foreigners' and the insistence upon national identity is not always the most useful one. As a dichotomy, it tends to overdraw our attention to a split between normative cosmopolitanism and anti-cosmopolitanism. Foreigners in the '*gaijin*' sense (foreigners from outside Japan) are not the only category of 'stranger' we find in Japan. The Burakumin is another notable category, although –as I demonstrated- by no means the only one. The categories occupied by some of my informants whom I called 'dissonant others' and 'transient beings' (Ivy 1995; Gill 1999; Kelsky 2001) challenge Japanese normative cosmopolitanism, which cannot be understood separately from local understandings of previous commitments to other people. These commitments to others are not always underpinned by national identity alone. There are commitments that the self incurs with other selves, constituted as subjects (neighbours, kin, work, even the environment) and they circumvent the definition of the 'nation' as the ultimate moral place for individuals.

Robertson (1997) further argues that Japanese discourses about locality are associated with both open borders and protectionism. They exist, she argues, as a refractive process, and they indicate the ambiguity of Japanese national identity and its strenuous relations with cultural identities. In fact, Robertson seems to argue and I would partially agree with her, that there is a tension between being international and being 'from a native place'. However, this tension is the place where Japanese people dramatize cosmopolitanism. It is precisely because cosmopolitanism is a dramatic, performative instance that it tends to highlight national identity over other existing subjective instances of identification with others.

At this point, it is also worth considering Martinez's (1998) argument: what Japanese do with identity in the present is to use it as a centrepiece of their discourses. This 'identity' no longer depends on religion 'but on the wider construct of the imagined citizenship of the imagined national community (which depends on the mass production of mass culture – travelling abroad being one of these productions – capitalistic diversification – touristfying Japan – one identity remains crucial to the construction of the nation-state)' (ibid.: 10).

I think it is important to stress here that understandings of cosmopolitanism in Japan are constructed not only on the experience of travelling and meeting others in tourist contexts -which I see as one of the key instances of the dramatization of cosmopolitanism- but also in imagining the citizenship of these others from within Japan, from encounters that happen within Japan as much as through the experiences of people travelling. In fact, I would suggest that the different visions of cosmopolitanism reflected by my informants come from the same radical positioning vis-à-vis a sense of national identity, one that gets performed and dramatized at each discursive encounter. The other is underpinned in a series of understandings on empathy and renunciation of aspects of the self. The latter appear less visible simply because our attention is not, epistemologically speaking, focused on them.

In my last example I want to turn to the idea of experiencing marginality whilst being cosmopolitan when returning to Japan. Here, my own position during fieldwork illustrates Kahn's discussion on the character of relatedness to the experience of cosmopolitanism (2003: 410).

> When I go back to Japan I meet friends, we sit down with tea; our topics revolve around the same axis, year after year. Their narratives say: 'Oh, you are so cosmopolitan.' They basically mean, I travel, I live abroad, and they inevitably ask me … when are you going to settle down? Or, equally, 'When are you going back?' For my informants and friends I am a paradoxical stranger … being cosmopolitan (*sekaijin*), they make it clear, is not about merely travelling, and being a citizen of the world. And, to some extent, we, in our talks and teas, shared that. However, this view of cosmopolitanism meant, very clearly, that I was not 'living with them'. It was not a matter of just travelling the world and knowing other places and peoples. It was also the fact that I was no longer their neighbour, their coffee buddy, their work colleague, and their home stay.

There was a centrepiece in my talks with my friends and informants. At some point, one friend or another would invariably state that they were less cosmopolitan than I was. They were cosmopolitan, of course, they had pictures of their travels abroad and could openly discuss cultural distinctiveness. Nevertheless, they did not perceive themselves as cosmopolitan as they perceived me, because, while they returned home and continued where they had 'left it', I had not. I was another transient being and it was not surprising to them that I had been associated during fieldwork with various marginal families.

What I find important in the above description is that, for my Japanese informants, it doesn't matter if I am a stranger or not. After all, we all share instances of being tourists. What my friends and informants did with me was the same thing they did with strangers: they imagined an existing relationship being there, having happened and as a kind of precondition. I would say that this is not empathy per se. It is knowledge of shared familiarity. And when the knowledge is not there it can always be imagined. In terms of agency, being kind to strangers also allows people to ignore such processes. In other words, once you have been kind to strangers, you are free to keep or disengage yourself from an imagined connection to them.

It could be argued that the capacity of my friends to make me 'less of a stranger' is a capacity they have and they choose to apply to certain people. If they can imagine certain connections as given, as relational, they can transcend the moment of strangeness, with me or with complete strangers. In a sense this idea of having to negotiate relations back at home, especially in the Japanese case through gift exchange (i.e. souvenir trips), is something that I take with me to the end of this chapter. Therefore I focus, quite intentionally, on the capacities that people have to imagine certain relations with complete strangers. Although these do not cancel estrangement (in fact they emphasize it as dramatic instances), they underpin a relationship of exclusion and inclusion: some people 'return home'; others 'become strangers'; others need to negotiate identities in every context. Furthermore, in the cases of certain people's empathetic experiences with others and their rejection of normative cosmopolitanism, their actions placed them in marginal (odd) positions, not quite 'settled' in the social landscape. Their empathy with others to the point of extended renunciation of the national self, their failure to be continually returning with market souvenirs,[10] signalled them as a new type of dispossessed. The lesson from their dissonance is that we can understand cosmopolitanism better when we disagree with it and when we are removed or cut off from certain dramatizations of it.

Conclusion

Rural locations between the 1990s and 2000s were not an easy place to 'retreat' to from what was perceived as 'cosmopolitan excesses' elsewhere in Japan. Most rural locations had since the early 1970s been involved in one form or another with a political transformation of their constituent political and social units, in the case of both villages (Robertson 1998) and towns (Knight 1998; Trias i Valls 2001). In this sense, relocating to rural areas meant, for most of my informants, facing 'other' families (native and newcomers to the place) who had embraced the goals of rural transformation and the project of aspiring to national politics, which, in fact, were largely about introducing the new 'town' to cosmopolitan values. For some families, moving to a rural area in the early 1990s meant having to confront, sometimes quite bitterly and face to face, the local introduction to the cosmopolitan, internationalizing values that they were aiming to leave behind. These processes also had an effect on residential and 'traditional' families, who – despite their seemingly unproblematic embrace of cosmopolitanism and national politics – often found themselves immersed in a constant re-enactment of 'modernity' through internationalization (school days, home stays) and town-making discourses that made them also feel socially uncomfortable and cut off from political processes.

In short, town-making initiatives, pleasantly done as they were, were not easy for anyone in town. The processes of incorporating others, especially 'dissonant others' were indications of the new cosmopolitan ethos of the town. Their incorporation, however, meant that the new families and those becoming 'new' or wishing to 'escape' national excesses brought with them clear anti-cosmopolitan (anti-global capitalism) opinions.

In the town, several contradictory views on the kinds of relationships to be established with 'others' started taking place. From one angle, any family involved in and accepting the process of town making (regardless of how long these families had been settled in the town) established relations with foreigners in a slightly naive way, one that aimed for an ideal incorporation of 'others' in what they perceived to be a true cosmopolitan sense (citizens of the world). This meant, however, that individuals who were much more radical in their views would often become marginalized and a type of 'alterity' within Japanese society.

The kind of relationships established with 'others' in this type of cosmopolitan context, however, is regarded always as a temporary inclusion of others, whereby the relationship would only last for a short period, after which the 'other' would leave. Focusing on a 'nationalistic' discourse, where the relationship is understood, one of 'us/them' conceals the importance of 'transience'. The confrontation of ideals between families developed, as a result, critical views on modernity and cosmopolitanism based on the idea that relationships with others did not constitute modernity and identity per se, and that cosmopolitanism was only constituted in opposition to it. In any case, a common Japanese understanding of cosmopolitanism, even for the more radical voices, was underpinned by the temporary inclusion of dissonance. However, when meeting foreigners and when dramatizing cosmopolitanism, aspects of the self are renounced for specific periods of time, after which the subject must return to the pre-existing commitments with known, national, others.

For those individuals who rejected these types of dramatization and managed not to engage in such temporary renunciations of the pre-existing commitments to national others, there was a price to pay – that of being associated with the kinds of 'oddities' imagined in 'foreigners'. They remained marginal, destitute, transient and dissonant. In their dissonance, they could clearly criticize the 'cosmopolitan' excesses in Japanese society. The excesses in modern Japan, under the rhetoric of 'internationalization', were many. In fact, the processes described in 'town making' were examples of 'excessive' instances of concessions to national and international demands on the ever-changing meanings of 'modernity'. Critiques of 'town making' became the way through which certain local communities voiced their discontent and their critique of the global discourses that placed Japan in a 'world of strangers' without enough empathy for accommodating these in full, and of the processes that disenfranchised communities 'from within'.

Notes

1. While the term *'machi'* is used to signify a political locality that merges different rural villages into one single administration, a *'furosato'* (the native place) is an expression that denotes 'rootedness' and neatly exemplifies the kind of places that we often associate with the anthropological enterprise of fieldwork (Nakane 1967, Smith 1978, Dore 1978, Robertson 1988, Knight 1996, Hendry 1999). What I propose in this chapter is to revisit the meaning of *furosato* (cf. Robertson 1991) considering what has been essentialized as 'rooted', 'distinctive' and 'local' amongst discourses of internationalization, cosmopolitanism and globalization.

2. In the 1990s period, the three most identifiable processes affecting Japanese ruralities in Tokushima prefecture, where I carried out my fieldwork, were the migration of young families (in their late thirties to mid-forties) to Tokushima's inland rural areas; the reconfiguration and merging of rural localities into 'towns' or larger administrative units in response to economic and depopulation changes, which included large economic transformations of the area and the adaptation of a tourist scheme (Mese and Okuba 1991) and, thirdly, the integration of new towns and villages within national discourses of modernization, internationalization and globalization (cf. Knight 1996; Robertson 1998; Hendry 1999; Atkins 2004, for other parts of Japan).

3. Even in 1997 and later when I returned to the field in 2000, the newcomer–traditional divide was becoming 'problematic'. In addition to its residents, the town was also constituted of non-local very elderly residents in the town's old people's home. The traditional-newcomer divide was further eroded by the very cosmopolitan ethos, which also included several business enterprises from the prefecture (non-local business that used the town for production and distribution), a Burakumin couple (minority citizens whose identity, although known by a few at the local office, was concealed from the social record) and local families that had divorced and de facto became 'new families' (Trias i Valls 2001: 240). As if this were not enough, the many enterprises promoting the internationalization of the town meant a constant

flux of tourists (see also Ashkenazi 1993, Robertson 1998, Hendry 1999, Trias i Valls 2001 on how festivals articulate some of the praxis of social inclusion), seasonal returnees to the town, and a flux of local employees moving outwards into the prefecture and back to the town.

4. I would describe the voices of town making as ones about unity, common sharing of knowledge, often romanticizing a common past with the purpose of reinventing rural localities (cf. Knight 1996). They are discourses that aim to place the town on a national and international map; that aim to present the town as a rural cosmopolitan place, both seemingly exotic, distant but connected to the world, and an example for future generations.

5. The concept of 'internationalization' was the one used by all my informants in the ethnographic present of this work. In Japan, internationalization preceded the term globalization partly due to the particular nationalistic discourses that 'business elites' (Yoshino 1992: 179) generated around this period. Internationalization, in its usage in most parts of Tokushima, identified the complexity of global processes, read as processes of international relations within nations and among international corporate business.

6. In order to clarify her point the teacher thought of an example (one that would include the elders' experience in the classroom): she pointed out at a statue located at the entrance of the school and alluded to a well-known story of Minomiya Sontoku (1787–1856), a Meiji Shintoist intellectual figure, still as a child, dressed in Edo (pre-modern) clothes and travelling to school, seeking knowledge, to be educated in typically Meiji nationalistic and romantic fashion. The teacher continued: 'You all know the story, don't you? He came to school every day, travelling down the mountains on foot, in *geta* (pre-modern footwear). He carried wood on his shoulders and books in his hands. This is how our grandparents came to school when they were little. They came from their *furosato*, in winter and snow, with their *geta* and *kimono* to a school like this one. They didn't have shoes, or school buses like you do, they did not have television or computer games.'

7. Of course, it is not the children who make these claims but the generation 'in between' these two opposing groups. This 'generation in between' constitutes groups of individuals in positions of political seniority, who often work for the local administration. A feature of the 1990s period is that these 'politically senior' individuals were much younger in becoming 'senior' than the previous generation (often being as young as forty-five to fifty years of age). In earlier periods, political seniority would have been achieved in the later sixties and seventies and even the eighties along with landownership and participation in village (not town) politics.

8. In previous generations, especially in the period of village differentiation in the 1950s, the 'elders' would have withheld greater positions of political centrality (specially in 'discourse making') than the1990s elders, who through the process of 'town making' had been politically slightly 'short-changed' (displaced from political centrality whilst being elevated to the category of honourable elders).

9. Discrimination against Burakumin (often by indirect means) was still (and still is in Japan) prevalent, despite the many attempts by the town's administration initiatives to educate their citizens on this issue (especially on marriage discrimination). The few people who were aware of the Burakumin origin of this couple and accepted them in the town, followed non-discriminatory patterns. I could not observe any form of discrimination amongst the 'new' families, in particular the Watanabes, who felt saddened by the events and empathized with this couple.

10. It was common for the Watanabe and other families, for example, when visiting or travelling, to take home-made recipes of Nepalese hot curry or choose home-made, organic products as opposed to conventional souvenirs.

References

Aoyama, Y and J. Hiroaki. 2003. Transmitting the Japanese Story: Toward True Cosmopolitanism, (trans.) D. Robson. (Toshi no katsuryoku o kokka no miryoku e tsunagu) In the Gaiko Forum National Borders Can no Longer be Closed. June, n. 179.

Appadurai, A. 2006. Grassroots Globalization and the Research Imagination. In H. Moore and T. Sanders (eds) *Anthropology in Theory: Issues in Epistemology*. London: Blackwell. Reprint from (2000) *Public Culture*, 12 (1), 1–19.

Appiah, K. 2006. *Cosmopolitanism: Ethics in a World of Strangers*. New York: Norton.

Arnason, J. 1990. Nationalism, Globalization and Modernity. *Theory, Culture and Society*, 7, 207–36

Ashkenazi, M. 1993. *Festivals of a Japanese Town*. Honolulu: Hawaii University Press.

Atkins, T. 2004. Inventing Jazztowns and Internationalizing Local Identities in Japan. In J.E. Hanes and Hidetoshi Yamaji (eds) *Image and Identity: Rethinking Japanese Cultural History*. Kobe: Kobe University, 249–62.

Cheah, P. and B. Robbins. 1998. *Cosmopolitics: Thinking and Feeling beyond the Nation*. Minnesota: University of Minnesota Press.

Dore, R. 1978. *Shinohata: A Portrait of a Japanese Village*. London: Penguin.

Featherstone, M. (ed.). 1990. *Global Culture: Nationalism, Globalization and Modernity*. London: Sage.

Gill, T. 1999. Wage Hunting at the Margins of Urban Japan. In S. Day (ed.) *Consider the Lilies of the Field*. Oxford: Westviews Press.

Goldstein-Gidoni, O. 2001. Hybridity and Distinctions in Japanese Contemporary Commercial Weddings. *Social Science Japan Journal*, 4 (1), 21–28.

——— 2005. The Production and Consumption of 'Japanese Culture' in the Global Cultural Market. *Journal of Consumer Culture*, 5 (2), 155–79.

Hannerz, U. 2004. Cosmopolitanism. In D. Nugent and J. Vincent (eds) *A companion to the Anthropology of Politics*. Oxford: Blackwell, pp. 69–85.

Harden, I. 1994. The Enterprise of Empire: Race, Class, Gender, and Japanese National Identity. *Identities*, 1 (2–3), 173–99.

Hendry, J. 1999. *An Anthropologist in Japan*. London: Routledge.

—— 2000. *The Orient Strikes Back: A Global View of Cultural Display*. Oxford: Berg.

Ivy, M. 1995. *Discourses of the Vanishing: Modernity, Phantasm, Japan*. Chicago: University of Chicago Press.

Iwabuchi, K. 1994. Complicit Exoticism: Japan and its Other. *Australian Journal of Media & Culture*, 8 (2), 49–82.

Kahn, J. 2003. Anthropology as Cosmopolitan Practice? *Anthropological Theory*, 3 (4), 403–15.

Kelsky, K. 2001. *Women on the Verge: Japanese Women, Western Dreams*. Durham, NC: Duke University Press.

Knight, J. 1996. Echoing the Past in Rural Japan. *Japan Forum*, 10 (1), 47–65.

—— 1998. Selling Mother's Love? Mail Order Village Food in Japan. *Journal of Material Culture*, 3 (2), 153–73.

Martinez, D. (ed.). 1998. *The Worlds of Japanese Popular Culture. Gender, Shifting Boundaries and Global Cultures*. Cambridge: Cambridge University Press.

Mese, K. and S. Okuba. (eds). 1991. *Ikkyotoirodorinosato: Kamikatsu*. Tokyo: Obunsha.

Mignolo, W. 2000. The Many Faces of Cosmo-polis: Border Thinking and Critical Cosmopolitanism. *Public Culture*, 12 (3), 721–48.

Moore, H. 2004. Global Anxieties: Concept-metaphors and Pre-theoretical Commitments in Anthropology. *Anthropological Theory*, 4 (1), 71–88.

Nakane, C. 1967. *Kinship and Economic Organisation in Rural Japan*. London: Athlone.

Robertson, J. 1998. It Takes a Village. Internationalization and Nostalgia in Postwar Japan. In S. Vlastos (ed.) *Mirror of Modernity: Invented Traditions of Modern Japan*. California: University of California Press, pp. 112–31.

—— 1991. *Native and Newcomer: Making and Remaking of a Japanese City*. California: University of California Press.

—— 1997. Empire of Nostalgia: Rethinking 'Internationalization' in Japan Today. *Theory, Culture and Society*, 14 (4), 97–122.

Sasaki, M. 2004. Globalization and National Identity in Japan. *International Journal of Japanese Sociology*, 13, 69–87.

Silverberg, M. 1988. The Cafe Waitress Serving Modern Japan. In S. Vlastos (ed.) *Mirror of Modernity: Invented Traditions of Modern Japan*. California: University of California Press, pp. 208–29.

Smith, R. 1978. *Kurusu: The Price of Progress in a Japanese Village 1951–1975*. Folkestone: Dawson.

Trias i Valls, A. 2001. *Wrapped Gifts: Ritual Prestations and Social Obligations in Contemporary Japan*. Kent: CSAC Monographs, University of Kent.

Yoshino, K. 1992. *Cultural Nationalism in Contemporary Japan: A sociological Enquiry*. London and New York: Routledge.

Chapter 7

TWO SIDES OF THE SAME COIN? WORLD CITIZENSHIP AND LOCAL CRISIS IN ARGENTINA

Victoria Goddard

On 24 December 1927, a bomb exploded in the large hall of the Buenos Aires branch of the City Bank of New York. The blast left one man dead and twenty-three people wounded. One of the wounded, a young woman employed by the bank, was to die soon afterwards. The first victim of the blast was a salesman of contraband goods. On that morning, when the banks were due to close early because of the holiday and people were preparing to celebrate Christmas Eve, he found that a number of bank personnel were interested in the French champagne he had to offer. Having completed his business, he began to tidy up his paperwork when the bomb exploded, killing him instantly. The intended victim of the blast was the bank itself but the device had gone off early, with terrible consequences for the bystanders. A few minutes later, a second device broke into flames at the nearby Bank of Boston but failed to detonate.

The bombing of the banks was executed by Di Giovanni, an anarchist born in Chieti, Italy, who was a leading figure in the local protest campaign against all 'rich Yankees' and a mastermind of violent retaliations in response to the execution of two Italian immigrants, Sacco and Vanzetti, in the United States earlier that year.[1] Di Giovanni's attack on the bank was not his first act of aggression against private property.[2] Nor was he the only anarchist to espouse direct action and the use of violence as a political strategy. Durruti, who would later become famous as the leader of the legendary 'Durruti column' in the Spanish civil war, initiated a cycle of bank robberies in order to fund the movement. The campaign started in Spain, moving on to Chile and from there to Argentina. The robbery in Argentina ended tragically with the death of a policeman, which set the Argentinean authorities on his trail. He was finally arrested with his co-conspirers in Paris but the case was shelved after what was essentially a diplomatic charade, played out by the French and the Argentinean authorities. The French were torn between Spanish pressure to extradite Durruti to Argentina (from where he could be extradited to Spain, there being no extradition agreement between France and Spain) and enormous pressure from French public opinion against such a measure. The Argentinean government was half-hearted in its efforts to secure the extradition; on the one hand, it felt the need to pacify its offended police department but, on the other, it was unwilling to follow in the footsteps of the United States, whose image had been severely damaged as a result of the Sacco and Vanzetti affair (Bayer 2003).

Di Giovanni was one of approximately 400,000 Italian nationals who entered Argentina during the 1920s. Since the mid-nineteenth century, the Argentinean state had pursued a policy of development through immigration, with varying degrees of effectiveness. The aim, articulated by nineteenth-century statesmen such as Alberdi and Sarmiento, was to populate what were seen as 'empty' landscapes and to 'improve the stock' of the local population by encouraging migration from Europe. The edict that 'to govern is to populate' was pursued by a series of governments, and by 1914 about 2,400,000 immigrants were permanently settled in the country and 30 per cent of the population was foreign-born (Hale 1996). However, there was a significant distance between the vision and the reality: the 'stock' that found its way to Argentinean cities and, to varying degrees, to the rural areas, was not the kind of population that had been anticipated by the likes of Sarmiento. He had favoured the immigration of Anglo-Saxon yeomen to colonize the expanses of grasslands heretofore (especially until 1879, when the campaign to 'conquer the desert' was deemed to have been successfully completed) occupied by indigenous groups and small and isolated populations of migrants. Instead, poor peasants, workers and craftsmen who originated from Italy, Spain, Russia and the Ottoman Empire were the most prominent amongst the incoming foreigners.

Disappointment at the outcome of this state project was expressed by several national, or indeed nationalist, writers through various expressions of racial pessimism (Hale 1996). For example, Bunge (1903) felt that South American countries were hampered by the Spanish heritage. In an unfavourable comparison with their North American counterparts, he argued that the South Americans were mestizo-ized, Indianized and mulatto-ized Europeans (Hale 1996: 165). Such disapproval of the 'quality' of this mixed population compounded a sense of fear and hostility with regard to 'the masses' (Ramos Mejía 1912). On the other hand, intellectuals like José Ingenieros promoted an optimistic vision. Espousing the ideals of earlier thinkers such as Echeverría,

Sarmiento and Alberdi, he saw the influx of Europeans as a positive measure, contributing to the emergence of a new population, an Argentinean race that would arise from the mixing of different bloods (Ingenieros [1918] 1957).

Nevertheless, xenophobia was a trait of many thinkers and by 1915 immigrants were persistently targeted as culprits responsible for social conflict and degradation (Hale 1996). Immigrant artisans and workers did bring with them ideologies and traditions of struggle, which they (along with non-migrant workers) were soon forced to resort to in response to highly exploitative labour regimes. Ignoring the real causes underlying the social and political unrest, the strikes and protests of the early 1900s were simply attributed to 'foreign agitators'. As the immigrant population came to be seen by some sectors of society as eminently undesirable, the meaning of cosmopolitanism shifted from constituting the virtuous quality of a new, developing country to assuming negative connotations of materialism and political radicalism and, ultimately, to embodying values and orientations that were inherently anti-Argentine.[3] These sentiments were articulated through violent campaigns against workers, perpetrated by organizations such as the Patriotic League, which privileged 'national' values that were strategically linked to concepts of order and submission to capitalist labour regimes.

Prompted by fears regarding immigrant working-class militancy, that were in turn fed by events in Europe and in particular the Russian Revolution, anti-worker organizations emerged between 1916 and 1930 as local expressions of resistance against what were seen as globalized threats to the order of society. For example, the Patriotic League or Liga Patriótica Argentina responded to events at home, including the election of the Radical Party through the first fully democratic elections in 1916 and which introduced the novel possibility of negotiation and dialogue between government and workers. But it was also prompted by anxieties derived from witnessing revolutionary activities in Europe and inspired by counter-revolutionary discourses current in Europe (McGee Deutsch 1993). Local tensions were aggravated by wider economic conditions that prevailed after the First World War. For Argentina, the post-war period signalled a sharp decline in the demand for Argentinean commodities, bringing unemployment, inflation and hardship. This was also a period of intense working-class mobilization and anti-worker and xenophobic reactions; fear of social upheaval was intimately linked to fear of the outsider. Foreigners – and, given a perceived ancestral link with Russia, Jews in particular – were targeted as vehicles for revolutionary sentiment.[4] For the Patriotic League, the answer lay in fomenting sentiments of *argentinidad* which entailed a strong sense of national identity and the acknowledgement of undisputed and unambiguous bonds to the motherland[5] and all the values and cultural forms associated with it.

In contrast to the negative and alarmist notions regarding complex identities and transnational links fomented by the local elites, anarchist organizations identified international solidarity as a core value. Stressing the importance of internationalism, they also articulated a critique of the concept of patriotism, which they saw as susceptible to the manipulative strategies of landowners, factory owners and the state. Thus, one anarchist publication stated that 'the motherland is the instrument used by the politician to make the people believe in him, by the bourgeois so that the people do not realize that they are being exploited, by the military to ensure that they go quietly and calmly to the slaughterhouse' (author's translation, *La Pampa Libre*, 12 January 1924, quoted in Etchenique 2000: 70). Thus, the central pillars of the capitalist state system, and indeed the state itself, were deemed to rely on the concept of patriotism as a source of legitimization and identification. The motherland – or *la patria* – would therefore be inadequate as a framework for a programme of radical change such as that envisaged by the anarchists. Indeed, according to the anarchist Rafael Barret, 'Patriotism is too small a mould for us to forge our future … Patriotism is divisive. We shall not win if we are divided.' Barret, like others, proposed a society without boundaries or nationalities; humanity was a far nobler and superior basis of identity than the motherland. He suggested that it was necessary to 'replace the idea of *patria* for that of humanity and base this on common interest, not on the particularities of class' (in Suriano 2001: 265).

Citibank and the New Global Order

The Buenos Aires branch of Citibank was opened in November 1914. This was Citibank's first step towards internationalization and towards fulfilling the dream of the bank's director, Frank Vanderlip. The moment was opportune: Europe was engaged in war and the pressure of private enterprises in the US encouraged changes in legislation to allow national US banks to operate outside its borders.[6] The bank had already conducted business in Latin America, for example through a large loan (15 million dollars, equivalent to more than half the total costs) to the Bolivian government to finance the construction of the La Paz–Antofagasta railway line. In addition, US companies had important interests in Latin America, such as Dupont's investment in nitrate extraction in Chile. Yet in spite of these established interests, Vanderlip's vision for the future of Citibank faced considerable opposition from within the institution, as the benefits of internationalization were not immediately apparent at the time.

Nevertheless, given strong support from US business interests in the region, his programme of expansion overseas was eventually implemented (Zlotogwiazda and Balaguer 2003).

The choice of Buenos Aires as the first international site for the bank is understandable when placed in the context of Argentina in 1914. The country had shown phenomenal rates of growth from 1880 to the early 1920s and was a major import–export economy; it had the most extensive railway network in Latin America (largely though not exclusively as a result of British investments) and the capital, Buenos Aires, was the eighth largest city in the world. In 1914 it had a population of 1.6 million and was in full process of expansion and modernization; that year saw the opening of the first underground railway in the capital city.

Equally significant is the fact that Argentina was an important recipient of foreign capital, principally British. But times were changing. In 1914, Harrods opened its elegant store in the heart of Buenos Aires. Where the opening of Citibank marked the beginning of the economic supremacy of the United States in the region, the opening of Harrods was to be the swansong of British imperialism (Zlotogwiazda and Balaguer 2003). In fact, starting with the war but continuing after it, British investments stagnated and then declined, and Britain's influence eventually gave way to the greater presence of the United States in the region.[7]

This shift in the distribution of power reflected other changes in the management of overseas interests. Whereas the British project had involved investment in public services and infrastructure such as ports and railways to improve the efficiency of the movement of commodities and trade in general, the new internationalization initiated by Citibank Argentina represented a distinctive shift away from this model of development and, in particular, from investments that favoured the production of exports towards financial services and support for private companies producing goods and services.[8] In fact, the strategy went very well: in 1929 the bank held 32 million dollars' worth of deposits, placing the Argentinean branch in second place in Latin America after Cuba and in fourth place worldwide.[9] The expansion of operations was firmly supported by the growth of US multinational operations in the country and the growing importance of US–Argentinean trade. The bank also attracted a growing sector of local capital, as national enterprises emerged as part of a growing import substitution drive, first promoted by the gap in supplies of commodities caused by the war.

The Citibank example illustrates the range of elements that are central to arguments concerning cosmopolitanism: the movement of capital and the movement of people, issues of identity, of belonging and the fluid boundaries of both profit and solidarity. The example also speaks to a very specific moment in the development of the global system, a moment of crisis and rupture, not only with the decline of British influence in Latin America and the emergence of the United States as the primary economic (and both selectively and increasingly political and military) centre for the region, but also with regard to shifts in the world market. For Argentina, the effects of these shifts were crucial, as demand for the country's traditional export commodities declined and as Britain was superseded as a global power by a country whose export profile actually competed with its own. The trade imbalances that resulted from all these circumstances were to have far-reaching effects.

The period from the 1880s onwards marks the emergence of a centralized Argentinean state, an economy directed towards world markets and aspirations to first-world levels of consumption. Cosmopolitanism was largely a top-down objective, as the state promoted the influx of predominantly European immigrants as a key element of its development and modernization programme. As a result of the state's pro-migration policies, many parts of the country, in particular its coastal cities, came to resemble European cities and reflected a cosmopolitan environment. But the cosmopolitan aspirations of the bourgeoisie, often realized through patterns of conspicuous consumption, including extensive periods of residence in Paris, was one thing. Quite another was the cosmopolitanism of the areas of the city that housed the peasants, the traders and the craftsmen (and, as Guy 1991 points out, very few women).[10] This 'lived cosmopolitanism', constituted through the multiple languages, cultures and experiences of immigrants, encountered in what were all too often conditions of poverty and urban squalor, was a source of anxiety to sectors of the bourgeoisie, who associated the newcomers with social unrest and moral degradation. Yet another form of cosmopolitanism is represented by the extensive networks of solidarity established between political militants inside and outside the country; as we have seen, the anarchists in particular were as committed to defending their comrades in the USA as those who were persecuted or imprisoned in Argentina.

The anti-cosmopolitan position was equally complex and diverse. Some elements of this nationalist anti-cosmopolitanism were perpetuated over time, for example in the populist government of Perón – not only in his anti-American and anti-European rhetoric but in his government's disapproval of the tango (the quintessentially cosmopolitan music and dance) in favour of its equally syncretic but rural (and therefore purportedly 'traditional') equivalent, folkloric dance – and in the ideologies informing the military regimes of the 1960s and 1970s. But another form of anti-cosmopolitanism was evident in the anti-US stance, which rejected the United States' demands for allegiance to a pan-American entity, in favour of an alternative identification with the Iberian or Hispanic American fraternity. This theme was also to emerge at different times and in different political ideologies throughout the twentieth century.

'Patria' or 'Cosmos'?

The diverging views about the relative merits of localized and international values, of *patria* (motherland) versus humanity, reflect enduring tensions and contradictions between national and cosmopolitan identities. As Guibernau (2007) points out, the distinction has its roots in the Stoics' differentiation between *polis* (the city state or boundary-focused political entity, used here by Guibernau to explore the concept of 'nation') and *cosmos* (the world). For the Stoics, the polis drew unwelcome distinctions between insiders and outsiders and fomented boundaries that undermined the potential realization of a shared human condition. Guibernau draws attention to the continuing tensions between national and cosmopolitan identities, pointing to the strength of attachment associated with the first and the ethical potential of the second, and raises the question of whether these two apparently inimical sources of identity might in fact mutually inform and usefully transform each other.

In the current context, the weight and potential of cosmopolitanism and its relationship to patriotism and nationalism have shifted. For Beck, cosmopolitanism today is 'the defining feature of a new era of reflexive modernity, in which national borders and differences are dissolving and must be renegotiated in accordance with the logic of a 'politics of politics' (Beck 2006: 2). The cosmopolitanism he is referring to does not necessarily share the characteristics of solidarity and emphasis on humanity promoted by the anarchists of the early twentieth century. Cosmopolitanism today is more to do with a sense of being in the world, a world perceived in terms of 'boundarylessness': 'An everyday, historically alert, reflexive awareness of ambivalences in a milieu of blurring differentiations and cultural contradictions' (Beck 2006: 3). This makes possible an alternative to identity, replacing the sense of territorially based either/or differentiations with forms of inclusion through both/and relationships. The potential alternatives emerging from this new context do not imply the end of national empathy. Rather, Beck argues that these layers of belonging mutually inform and transform one another, whereby the 'transnational and cosmopolitan should be understood as the summation of the redefinitions of the national and the local' (Beck 2006).

Nevertheless, the quality of boundarylessness and the tensions of local and cosmopolitan identities are located within specific time and space configurations. As such, the very experience of cosmopolitanism needs to be addressed within the context of specific experiences and practices.

Globalization of systems of production and exchange of commodities and services is one of the principal vehicles through which populations are located within a broader reality. Since the 1970s, these systems have increasingly come under the logic of neoliberalism, whereby the specific patterns of movement of goods and people are attributed with 'natural' properties, resulting from the logic of the market. Nevertheless, neoliberalism is frequently understood to be a disciplinary regime, a historically specific combination of material and ideological forces that reflect and perpetuate relations of inequality, both locally and globally.[xi] As Ong points out with regard to Asian politicians and intellectuals, neoliberalism in this region is associated with the deployment of US influence through a strategy of domination based on the market and supported by international organizations such as the International Monetary Fund (Ong 2006). In Argentina, an unprecedented consensus regarding this view of neoliberalism emerged with the economic crisis of 2001. And, as in the early twentieth-century protests of international solidarity, the banks provided a powerful focus for the expression of these views and for a range of protests against the inequities underpinning the global economy.

The conditions of existence within the spaces produced through the 'globalization project of neoliberal capitalism' (Gledhill, this volume) entail particular forms of entanglement, with a range of values, practices, commodities and persons. Part of this entanglement is precisely the sense of awareness of the global condition, which, as Theodossopoulos argues in the introduction to this volume, simultaneously engenders connections and discontent. Indeed, discontent may itself become a source of new imaginings and – through these imaginings – new allegiances and identities, which may span local and global contexts and create the conditions of possibility for the emergence of new understandings of what constitutes lived reality and the 'meaningfulness' of everyday life (Theodossopoulos, this volume).

The 2001 Crisis

The collapse of the Argentinean economy in December 2001 produced a range of verbal and visual imagery that has acquired almost iconic status: armoured vehicles in the deserted, early morning streets of the centre of the capital as they drive away (presumably to the airports, carrying savings out of the country); demonstrators converging on the central square, Plaza de Mayo, banging pots and chanting slogans against the government; images of family groups picking through the rubbish at dusk; angry demonstrators banging against the closed metal shutters of the banks; queues outside embassies, waiting patiently for visas and passports to leave the country and embark on a new life abroad.

The 2001 crisis came as a surprise to those who had grown accustomed to references to Argentina's star pupil status with the International Monetary Fund and the World Bank (Stiglitz 2002). However, there were signs present, for those wishing to read them, of impending disaster, not least the delays, rebuttals and reprimands the government faced in its attempts to reach an agreement with the IMF. In fact, the story of Argentina's success as an IMF pupil is also the story of its eventual crisis. In 1991, the Menem–Cavallo government tackled the hyperinflation that had besieged the economy for much of the democratic period initiated in 1983.[12] This they did through the *Plan de Convertibilidad* or convertibility programme, which aimed to establish a sound currency and involved pegging the Argentinean peso to the US dollar, restricting the production of money. Parity was sustained by the guarantee that the peso could be exchanged for dollars on demand. The policy was effective in relation to its stated aim of curbing inflation, which dropped from 4,000 per cent per annum to single digit percentages in three years. The Central Bank was granted autonomy from government and was unable to produce more money in response to government needs, as had occurred in the 1980s. Furthermore, the Bank was required to hold 100 per cent reserves, a requirement that could be relaxed to 80 per cent of deposits if the government declared an emergency.

The government also privatized state assets (services such as water, telephones and other utilities). The banking sector was transformed since especially after the Tequila crisis in 1994, local banks were taken over by large foreign banks, mainly based in Spain and the United States. After 1995 they were encouraged to arrange foreign lines of credit that could be drawn on in case of a foreign exchange crisis. From the point of view of consumers, foreign banks appeared to offer security, precisely because they were expected to be in a stronger position to honour dollar deposits in the event of a national crisis.

The Argentinean government was able to manoeuvre a way through the Tequila crisis but there were long-term repercussions. The government's response to the crisis was to relax the 100 per cent reserve requirement but also tighten monetary constraints. Interest rates rose well above those of the United States, making the dollar-peso conversion more costly. Another blow was dealt by Brazil's decision to abandon its own exchange rate system, the *Plan Real*, and to devalue its currency. But the long-term problem was to do with the economic system itself. The economy had been in recession since 1995 and unemployment grew, reaching a level of 20 per cent in 2000. A substantive proportion of the unemployed were young, educated people, who faced a labour market that offered them fewer and fewer opportunities. A shrinking economy, the privatization, rationalization and restructuring of public and private enterprises and the reductions in state investments in public services collided with the strategies of generations of international and national migrants, who had embraced investments in the education of their children as a way to achieve social mobility. Since the 1900s, national policy and individual and family goals had largely coincided where education and professionalization as a route to social advancement were concerned. Now, young professionals were forced to abandon their country and, where possible, return to the land of their parents or grandparents.

The Crisis and the Banks

As the crisis loomed, some banks were clearly more vulnerable than others. Perceptions played an important part here, as foreign banks appeared to offer greater security against any possible upheavals within the Argentinean economy. So banks that were identified as largely local, primarily as lacking external credit lines or head offices overseas to back them up in the event of a run on currency, were the first to feel the consequences of the savers' sense of insecurity. Fulfilling these expectations, they were indeed the first to suffer loss of liquidity as savers withdrew their deposits to place them in a safer, 'foreign' bank. Savers were to find out soon enough that the 'foreign' profile of the bank was no guarantee regarding access to their money (Calcagno and Calcagno 2003).

The banking sector as a whole was in a state of disarray. Crucially, the system was depleted: from the beginning of 2001 until the end of 2002, the Central Bank of Argentina lost reserves to the value of 16,687 million US dollars (Calcagno and Calcagno 2003: 33). Citizens' assets abroad increased over the 1990s. Between 1992 and 2000, transfers of assets abroad amounted to 56,467 million US dollars. Property held by Argentineans abroad increased over this period by 46,848 million dollars and in 2001 there was a net exit of capital to the value of 15.686 million dollars, with assets abroad increasing by 12.510 million dollars (www.mecon.gov,ar/cuentas/internacionales, quoted in Calcagno and Calcagno 2003: 33). Cecchini and Zicolillo suggest that the government effectively rescued the banks from an impossible situation when, on 3 December 2001, they declared the *corralito*, freezing and then restricting access to deposits: 'with the country risk index sky high, the intransigence of the international finance organizations with regard to De la Rúa's government and rumours in circulation that for the first time in a decade talked about devaluation, it was only a matter of time before savers ran to their banks to withdraw their money and place it somewhere safe' (Cecchini and Zicolillo 2002: 200). With the declaration of the *corralito*, none of the banks honoured their clients and some overseas head offices refused to support their Argentinean branches.

According to Mariana, a bank employee interviewed in 2002, the banks had made a strategic mistake.

> 'Of course, in any banking system in the world the money isn't there to return deposits. There is no way to stop a bank run anywhere in the world except through building confidence. There had been a run on the banks since March 2001 and the *corralito* was a way to stop it. But the banks should have gone out and talked to the customers. We don't have your money now because that is what banks do ... but we can exchange the value of your deposits for security, etc. None of the big banks did this. A few small banks that did are coming out quite strongly. They were very small so didn't have large deposits and so were fairly liquid and offered clients some kind of package (government bonds plus cash, guarantees). They took a positive approach to their clients. They're very small still, of course, but their behaviour during the crisis might help build them up. You talk to clients, ... sometimes a client will phone you and the more sophisticated client who reads our reports, maybe he's the financial manager of a company ... they, I, would expect to sit down and talk to somebody. But everybody was unavailable. The phones were off the hook. But, by then, what could you say?'

Instead of entering into a dialogue with clients and with society at large, the banks had responded by pulling down their metal shutters because, as Mariana explained, 'basically they were terrified'. The shutters then became the principal sites of protest as angry savers banged noisily against the metal: 'every day they are banging. In some cases there are holes where people have been banging.' The shutters served as platforms to communicate anger, frustration and claims for justice. Interestingly, many of the graffiti were in English, a clear indication that the protest was seen as pertaining to a broader community than the local or national one. It also illustrates the central role of the media and the protesters' perception of their importance, strategically selecting the sites and producing a relevant spectacle. As one informant pointed out:

> 'You mostly see the writings here in the centre, especially along Florida [one of the principal commercial streets] and especially the Bank of Boston, because of the angle [on a corner, on the intersection of a busy avenue and a pedestrian street]. Because if you look at other branches in the suburbs ... [it is almost business as usual].'

Mariana explained that, at the time when the *corralito* was declared, workers in the banks suffered badly from stress, and many suffered from mental health problems: 'They're cursing you all the time.' In particular, the workers who dealt with the public were under enormous pressure and had to put up with insults and, occasionally, violent behaviour. As Mariana explained, an employee whose own money might well be tied up in the *corralito*, and who faced the very real prospect of losing her or his job, was subjected to the insults of angry crowds. But management also felt the pressure. Mariana explained that her boss was mortified because advice he had given clients in good faith had been detrimental to their interests. Many were clients who were known to him personally: he had given his word and he had been trusted. Now he had let them down and was unable to offer any solution. Managers also faced legal problems. With the attempt of savers to seek redress through the courts, bank managers were subpoenaed and arrested. They were legally responsible for the actions of their bank, so even branch-level managers, who had very little power or authority, were liable.

The worst moment had been on the eve of a change in legislation intended to slow down the ability of savers and their lawyers to reclaim their money, which instead precipitated reactions from savers and provoked a wild rush on the banks. As Mariana explains:

> So the banks were closed [because of weekend closure] and since the law was going to come out, the lawyers were desperate to get their *amparos* in and the doors were locked and the lawyers were trying to throw the papers in and our security guards were blocking the doors and sort of pulling us in … and the cameras were filming … The kids in the office were saying 'I wonder what a pothus plant salad tastes like' because we couldn't go out for lunch. We couldn't go out and people couldn't get in. So we pulled in a bag of food with a little rope from the window. It was a very aggressive situation. It was frightening … The people were trying to get back their money and you were trying to not let them in. It was terrible.

The crisis was seen by many sectors of the press, the banking system, the political arena and the protests as a crisis of 'the model'. The collapse of the economy was an indictment of the neoliberal model and its peculiar and extreme application during the Menem–Cavallo years (Calcagno and Calcagno 2003; Azpiazu and Basualdo 2004). But the critique of the 'model' did not have an automatic counterpart in the emergence of an alternative. As Mariana explained, 'the model' had proved to be flawed or, at the very least, it was now obsolete, but there was nothing to put in its place. This meant that everybody – bankers, savers, workers who lost their jobs – continued to think and act in relation to what they knew, what they felt was secure, even though their experience suggested they were in fact confronting a novel set of circumstances.[13] It was therefore not surprising that so many of those interviewed in 2002 expressed concerns about the status of their understanding of current events, about what might constitute appropriate and relevant knowledge and about their own and others' ability to grasp the underlying factors determining the situation, however elusive these might be.

I met Susana for coffee and to chat generally about life. She had spent some very busy days coming and going to the courts to have her case heard. Her savings had got caught up in the *corralito* and she had applied for a *recurso*, a legal demand to have at least some of her money returned. Our long conversation therefore revolved around this situation and the sense of exhaustion and confusion she had been experiencing for months. She described the situation of the country as one where you find yourself in a hall of mirrors, where you cannot trust the image that appears before your very eyes. That image was likely to be no more than the partial reflection of another image, which in turn reflected or refracted yet another one, and so on. The elusiveness of 'reality' was a constant source of anxiety. This acute awareness of the slippery quality of truth, of certainty, of what one might have taken for granted was associated with a sense of powerlessness and was central to her account.

On the other hand, the layers, mirrors and mirages she described were a fairly appropriate representation of the circumstances relating to the crisis. National and international investigators have attempted to discover and uncover the hidden tracks of laundered money through complex routes, involving national enterprises, foreign banks, entrepreneurs and politicians. In 2002 the flight of 27,000 million dollars in a period of three months, from October to December 2001, was investigated. The Central Bank of Argentina had already suffered a massive loss of reserves in the years prior to the crisis. Investigations showed that the reserves had been used to bail out private banks. In this salvage operation, the Bank of Galicia (10 per cent of which is owned by the large Spanish banking consortium BSCH) received 1,120 million. But these funds were not in the Bank of Galicia's deposits – they had been transferred out of the country through an internal loan system within the bank's own circuits but across international borders (to the bank's branches in Uruguay and the Cayman islands). This mechanism had already been explored, and indeed pioneered, by Citibank, whose offshore banking accounts offered a haven for, among others, Argentinean individuals and companies (Zlotogwiazda and Balaguer 2003).

Bank workers and customers were caught up in webs that extended beyond their locality, as savers, pensioners, workers. Clearly, the benefits of the system they found themselves entangled in and the risks inherent in it were not distributed equitably. But the effects of a crisis are not that easy to predict. Some savers had managed to rescue their money in time, some managed to cope with the absence of currency better than others. Many had already embarked on systems of support such as barter clubs, which expanded dramatically during the crisis. Local governments also responded by increasing the scope of applicability of parallel unsupported and local currencies, valid only within specific territorial units (such as the Patacón and the Lecop). Many engaged in the protest movements against the banks, the transnational companies, the government and the IMF. For many of the younger generation, the answer seemed to lie in emigration, often to the homeland of their grandparents.

Five years on from the crisis and three years after the election of President Kirchner, whose brand of Peronism appeared to break drastically with the version promoted by his predecessor Menem, the '*modelo*' had shifted: not away from capitalism or even from neoliberalism, but, necessarily perhaps, from the brand of neoliberalism consolidated during the 1990s (Ong 2006). Rates of growth of the gross domestic product offered relatively encouraging indices of economic recovery. In addition, confidence was increased when in 2005 the government paid off its debt to the IMF – the government had also gone some way towards rescheduling the remaining foreign debt. In this context, banks made a strong recovery, albeit with a reduced body of personnel,[14] 'normalizing' their standard operations, increasing the number of new loans and introducing new products and services. Already in 2002, Mariana pointed out that her bank's clients were returning to their accounts, as fear of crime outweighed their lack of confidence in 'the system'.[15]

In 2006, businessmen and entrepreneurs I spoke to expressed concerns about the long-term stability of the economy. Julián, a successful entrepreneur, pointed out that there was no alternative: inevitably, one is forced to resort to the banks to safeguard one's money, to secure loans and credits and so on. On the other hand, Jaime, whose business crosses the industry/agriculture divide, said that if he had any serious money to spare he would certainly look for ways of taking it out of the country rather than trusting the local banks with it. He added, 'And I would follow it as soon as possible.' After a pause he added wistfully: 'We really are at the end of the world [*el culo del mundo*] here. I still remember when that realization hit me. I was on holiday in Europe, looking for news about Argentina, a newspaper, something. And I found nothing: as though we didn't exist. That's when it hit me: we are the arse of the world.'

Julián, whose factory appeared to be doing well, also indicated that uncertainty was a major obstacle for Argentinean business. A close second was the attitude of the government: 'They put obstacles in your way. Look at Brazil: there the government works to support Brazilian industry.'

Ricardo, having left the corporate world behind to start his own small-scale business venture, summed up the feelings expressed by the other entrepreneurs: a sense of fatigue, born of a never-ending struggle and a sense of the impossibility of achieving anything close to confidence in the future. For these men at least, the global world is tantalizingly uneven, the local difficulties making the 'outside other' both the potential source of the problem and a tempting example of what is achievable under the right circumstances.

To some, the current situation reflects some major underlying changes, similar perhaps to the sea change that took place in the post-war era with the decline of Great Britain and the rise of the United States as the new world power. The strong presence of Spanish interests, ranging from banking to oil and telecommunications, reflects the emergence of Spanish and more generally of European capital and its growing influence in Latin America during the 1990s. On the other hand, the continuities in the processes underpinning globalization and the unequal distribution of wealth worldwide leave little room for illusions about the dawn of a new era. Thwaites Rey (2001) and Cecchini and Zicolillo (2002) describe the far from transparent process through which the privatization of the national airlines was carried out under Menem's government.[16] The case illustrates the overlapping conditions and interconnections of local and global strategies. The Spanish purchase of Aerolíneas Argentinas was central to salvaging the ailing Spanish flagship airline. The acquisition of assets through the purchase of Aerolíneas enabled the restructuring and eventual privatization of the Spanish airline, within the regulatory framework of the European Union (Thwaites Rey 2001).[17] It is tempting to suggest that the prominence of European interests – especially Spanish ones – in Latin America presages the end of US hegemony in the area. But Citibank is still the leading bank in the country. And it was one of the favourite targets of protesters. One protester from a locality on the outskirts of Buenos Aires commented: 'We chose it [a branch of Citibank] because it is the bank that best represents the financial motherland' (Cecchini and Zicolillo 2002: 405).[18]

Intellectuals and militants have grappled with what appeared to be a moment of change, a threshold in the organization of the world economy and the rise of a new, global political domain. The crisis in Argentina is, in part at least, a manifestation of these changes as much as it is a reflection of the shortcomings of 'the model' (Argentinean or global). For some observers and participants in the protests surrounding the crisis, the significance of these struggles is striking, marking a new form of mobilization and a renewal of struggle. For others, they were a temporary upheaval leading to the eventual normalization of a normal capitalism (Petras and Veltmeyer 2004).

Protesters directed their anger principally against the banks, but also against corrupt government and global institutions such as the IMF. These protests overflowed, beyond the banks, to other issues, such as claims for work and social justice. Inevitably, the global dimension informed these protests, given the widespread debates and recognition of the transnational character of the institutions and phenomena that were associated with the causes of the crisis. The engagement with the global was also about making a claim: as members of a global community, perhaps not based on the cosmopolitanism of last century but nevertheless defining a shared sense of entitlement. Like their predecessors in Paris during the 1920s and 1930s, members of the elite who may well express a strong attachment to the *patria* have been known to export their savings to offshore banks. For the non-elite, expressions of disillusionment, shame and rejection of local leaders and of the international entities that are seen to have colluded with the ambitions of Argentinean politicians and entrepreneurs can coexist with the decision to apply for a passport to a country whose language you don't speak or understand but which, through genealogical connections, you can claim as your own.

Shifting Boundaries: The Battle over the River Uruguay

In 2003, a Finnish forestry group acquired the Compañía Forestal Oriental SA from Shell Renewables BV to a level of 60 per cent of the total shares. The remaining shares were owned by UPM-Kymmene Corporation and Finnfund. The purchase involved 48,000 hectares of land in western Uruguay, of which 32,000 hectares were dedicated to eucalyptus plantations. Soon afterwards, the company, Oy Mitsä-Botnia Ab, began investigating the possibilities of pulp production in the area. Botnia SA emerged as the company that would take forward the mill project. The construction of the mill in Fray Bentos, on the Uruguayan coast of the river, was under way when neighbours on the opposite shore of the Uruguay River, in the province of Entre Ríos, Argentina, initiated a cycle of protests that came to include road blocks and regular closures of the international bridge that linked the two countries. In 2006, the Central Court of Justice in The Hague was involved in the dispute and the Spanish King's envoy was in the process of attempting a negotiated agreement between the two countries. In spite of the opposition, the support of the Uruguayan government and the approval of funds by the IMF have encouraged the company to stick to its original plans.[19]

In December 2006, a large demonstration, which had set out in the early hours of the morning from the Argentinean towns at the heart of the dispute, Gualeguaychú and Colón, reached the centre of Buenos Aires. The demonstrators were decidedly upbeat in spite of the distance they had travelled. Many were middle-aged, well-dressed couples, families with children and larger groups of women and children. The demonstrators from the provinces were joined by local groups of *piqueteros*, the unemployed groups who are well known for their road-blocking protests. In addition, smaller groups of environmentalists deployed ingenious constructions intended to draw attention to the pollution of local rivers and environments. A very large Argentinean flag was carried by thirty or forty people through the centre of the wide Avenida de Mayo. There were many Argentinean flags on display and there was a strong sense of 'patriotism' running through the march and the assembly in the centre of the Plaza de Mayo where the marchers congregated. But also evident were other, non-national emblems such as the *wiphala*, the multicoloured transnational flag of the *pueblos originarios* or indigenous populations, and many flags of the province of Entre Ríos. And amongst the crowds of protesters there were also those who had found ways of displaying the Argentinean and the Uruguayan flags together, wrapped around their bodies or sewn one next to the other to form a large banner across the width of the street.

The musical performance, which helped make the searing heat of the afternoon a bit more bearable, had a strong regional flavour, as the accordion, the guitar and the violin exploded time and time again into the lively sounds of the *chamamé*, the music of the North-Eastern province of Corrientes, and couples swirled to the rhythm. The presence on stage of men dressed in the traditional attire of the gauchos of Entre Ríos and Corrientes added to the flavour of localism. In spite of this celebration of local identity, there were few signs of antagonism towards Uruguay. On the contrary, delegates from Uruguay who also opposed the construction of the paper mills on the river were warmly welcomed. The butt of the comments and jokes seemed to be the national entrepreneurs and global business interests, which consistently ignore the long-term interests of local populations.

The range of sentiment displayed in the march was evident in the opinions of residents of Buenos Aires interviewed in November and December of 2006. While some argued that opposition to the paper mills was a patriotic duty, others refused to become subsumed within the powerful embrace of the *patria*. Instead, they pointed out that Argentina's own environmental track record was very poor indeed. Paula pointed out, 'These are the same people who will throw their rubbish in the very same river they are now defending, without thinking twice.' Observers like Paula would often point to Argentina's own paper mills and their unimpressive track record regarding the pollution of rivers. Others went further: surely it was better for such a project to be in the hands of the Uruguayans who were far less likely to mess things up than the Argentineans. And, indeed, some said that the Finns could be counted on to do things properly in a way that Argentinean companies could not.

Carlos, who defined himself as a rebel in thought if not in deed, did not take the *asambleístas* or protesters of Gualeguaychú's environmental credentials seriously. But he posed the question of who had most to gain from this conflict between neighbours. Who would benefit from a rift within Mercosur?[20] He suggested that, at a time when political and social change was sweeping through Latin America, the United States, in particular, had a vested interest in the emergence of divisions within the Latin American political panorama. Silvia, who was equally lukewarm about the demonstrations, echoed this sentiment when I asked her about news regarding the Botnia issue: 'People here are not stupid. They ask themselves who can be behind all of this. The answer is obvious. That country!' (she made it clear through gestures that the country in question was the United States).

Señora Gladys, one of the Mothers of Plaza de Mayo, expressed her deep sadness at the tense situation that prevailed between the governments of the two neighbouring countries. Her view was that these were two countries linked through bonds of brotherhood, two peoples who intermarry, who share a culture. She had been very disappointed by the Uruguayan president who seemed to be acting in response to pressures from abroad rather than following his electoral promises.[21] She pointed out that in Uruguay many people supported the paper mills because they hoped to gain jobs; other Uruguayans opposed them, fearing the long-term effects. But, she pointed out, those who accepted the mills in the hope that they would create jobs failed to realize that once the construction of the mills was completed, there would be a much diminished demand for labour: 'These foreign companies do not come here to solve our problems; they come to make a profit, they come to take from us and it is not a reciprocal relationship.'[22]

Conclusions

The young professionals leave because they have 'no future here'. Are they the true inheritors of the cosmopolitanism of their ancestors, claiming the right to find a better life for yourself wherever that may be? What about the legacy of the anarchists and their commitment to international solidarity? Latin America might well be a site for solidarity and campaigning at one level, but significant differences remain – not least relating precisely to borders and national interests (as in a range of tensions between Mercosur partners). The commonalities between Latin American countries are clearer to most Argentineans today, after the Falklands War and the 2001 crisis, than they were thirty years ago. At the same time, the understanding of these commonalities cannot be framed in terms of a common Hispanic heritage, as proposed by President Yrigoyen in the 1920s. Instead the commonalities are historical and conjunctural, and require that we recognize that local struggles are necessarily also global, given the collusion of local and international interests and institutions and the seamless web of relations that both construct and undermine national boundaries.

In December 2006, the retail sector registered record sales in the run-up to Christmas. Those who were at that point able to participate in the world of goods produced largely through global capital did so with enthusiasm. Their relationship to the globalized world, as in Beck's 'reflexive cosmopolitans', appears to combine distrust with desire. The crisis of 2001 laid bare the effects of neoliberal policies implemented during the 1990s, along with what are seen as their corollaries, political and economic corruption, social polarization and exclusion. But those who can do embrace the global community and the economy; customers have returned to their banks, consumers have returned to the shopping malls.

Boundaries are not dissolving, as suggested by Beck, but they are redrawn and their significance continues to shift, in terms of both meanings and possibilities, identities and antagonisms. The national community perseveres not only because boundaries are more enduring than might have been predicted by the pundits of globalization and the global village. The nation also endures as a source of identity which, as Guibernau explains, is capable of providing a strong attachment and sense of place in the world. In her view, identification with a national community can play an important role in self-fulfilment and self-worth, even (or especially) for those for whom personal success is denied by circumstances or because of their class, gender or race. But, when the national community has not proved itself worthy, other more complex strategies are called for. As Gledhill shows in his chapter (in this volume), these may entail joining a congregation as a fast-track route to cosmopolitan participation. Or they may entail selective privileging of tangible and intangible natural assets and cultural achievements, such as food, dance or even the capacity for protest and solidarity (see Gledhill, this volume). Alternatively, the virtual or material transgression of boundaries may provide opportunities for the disaffected to 'reach out to the world', as described by Theodossopoulos and exemplified by Strathern and Stewart and other contributors to this volume.

Unemployment and enduring poverty in Argentina are a testimony to the failures of the 'model' and are the product of a crisis that spoke not only of global power structures but also, and importantly, of national, local collusions. Being in the world is thus a difficult and challenging affair that requires all sorts of identifications: with the *patria* (motherland), but tempered by the knowledge that this identity has justified all kinds of injustices; as cosmopolitans, enjoying the material and intellectual products of the world market, while recognizing the country's marginal and vulnerable place within it. The 'lived cosmopolitanism' of today is largely expressed through an enduring ambivalence, emerging from an ongoing tension, but also from the synergy between being here, in a specific place and time, and the world at large.

Notes

1. Sacco and Vanzetti were Italian immigrants found guilty of robbing the Braintree enterprise and, in the process of doing so, killing two members of personnel. The case attracted worldwide attention and protests in support of the two men.
2. Di Giovanni was executed in 1931, after the military coup of 1930 against Yrigoyen's Radical government (Bayer 2003).
3. The Law of Residence of 1902 and the Social Defence Law of 1910 were aimed at drastically limiting the rights of foreign-born workers, reflecting the shift in elite understandings of cosmopolitanism, which now came to be associated with materialism and political radicalism.
4. The anti-worker and anti-Semitic reaction culminated in the 'tragic week' or *Semana Trágica* in January 1919, when civilians and police roamed the streets of Buenos Aires and carried out arrests, attacks and acts of vandalism against working-class and Jewish neighbourhoods (see Munck et al. 1987; McGee Deutsch 1993).
5. The concept of *la patria* is a feminine noun and best translated as 'motherland'. The feminine association is clear when Spain is referred to as *la madre patria*, the original or colonial homeland.
6. Woodrow Wilson approved the Federal Reserve Act, which enabled US banks to open branches outside the country, in 1913.
7. The United States companies often moved in on British enclaves such as the production and export of meat products, when Swift established itself in the country in 1907 and rapidly expanded thereafter. The First World War precipitated an economic crisis in Argentina, as European investors removed funds from the country, depleting national reserves to the point that the government was forced to intervene, declaring a banking holiday and restricting exchange rates and movements of capital. The advances of the US in the economic sphere were not translated into political or ideological acceptance. For example, when the US finally joined the war in 1917, it hoped to draw Latin American states in with it. This was opposed strongly by the then President Yrigoyen of the Radical Party, even in the face of German

destruction of three Argentinean merchant ships. Yrigoyen's anti-Americanism reflected a general mood that emerged after the Cuban war in 1898. Yrigoyen rejected the US-promoted Pan-Americanism that claimed allegiances across the continent and instead favoured an attachment to a Latin American heritage that excluded the US. For example he declared 12 October a holiday as the Day of the Race, i.e. the descendants of the Iberian tradition, as opposed to the Anglo-Saxon one (Romero 2002).

8. This was largely due to the similarities in the commodity specialization of the US and Argentina and it had long-term implications with regard to imbalances in trade partnerships.

9. Equal to 20 per cent of regional deposits and 40 per cent of world deposits (Zlotogwiazda and Balaguer 2003).

10. See Donna Guy (1991) regarding the gender imbalances produced by immigration and the anxieties and realities of the 'white slave trade', frequently associated in European circles with the city of Buenos Aires.

11. It is worth noting that contemporary analysts locate the origins of the neoliberal model in Argentina in the economic policies and repressive government of the military regimes of the 1970s (1976–83). One indication of this is the escalation of the foreign debt, which increased from 7,875 million US dollars in 1975 to 45,087 million US dollars in 1983 (Calcagno and Calcagno 2003: 32). The emergence of the 'model' entailed repressive interventions against working class militants, artists and thinkers and initially the gradual and, after the military dictatorships, the radical rollback of the state. The repressive regimes aimed at silencing not only radical and left-wing theorists and activists but more mainstream thinkers and professionals as well. For example, the establishment of think tanks inspired by the Chicago school was an important aspect of the economic strategy, which aimed to displace the influential models of the Economic Commission for Latin America (Calcagno and Calcagno 2003).

12. The democratically elected government of Alfonsín had to contend with uprisings by military personnel, in protest at the attempts to uncover human rights abuses committed during the military dictatorship of 1976–83 and bring the perpetrators to justice. The democratic government also inherited a massive foreign debt. The foreign debt grew at a rate of 46 per cent during the military regime from 1966 to 1972, 62 per cent during the Peronist governments from 1973 to 1976, and 364 per cent from 1976 to 1983 during the military regimes led by Videla, Galtieri and Bignone. Under Alfonsin's government the rate was 44 per cent, increasing to 123 per cent during the 1990s under Menem and Cavallo (Cecchini and Zicolillo 2002).

13. Mariana explained that often those customers who got some of their money back from her bank through a *recurso*, or legal demand, brought the money back to the bank. Others drew out the meagre sums allowed under the *corralito* in order to buy dollars.

14. In 2002, private banks employed 60,318 workers, a figure that fell to 40,928 in 2003 and only rose slightly in 2004 to 41,507 (Annual Report of the Asociación de Bancos de la Argentina 2005). Banks were helped by rescheduling foreign

debt, the return of deposits after the crisis and the fact that following the crisis many banks were capitalized by their head office.

15. Bank deposits have increased significantly since the crisis in 2001. In 1998, deposits amounted to 34,432 million pesos; in 2001 these fell to 18,681 million pesos. In 2005 they had reached the level of 122,604 million pesos, of which 73,791 correspond to the private banking sector (Annual Report ABA 2005). Loans also increased from a low point of 40,458 million pesos in 2003 to 103,450 million in 2004 (Annual Report ABA 2004).

16. There are two crucial factors intervening in the choice of Iberia as the purchaser of the airline. In the first place, there is the objection raised by US airline corporation, that US law prevented them from engaging in the disbursement of 'facilities' to local officials involved in the sale, whereas the Spanish were able to engage in a range of persuasive tactics. Secondly, there are the political influence and strong links between Spanish leaders and the Argentinean government, both the Socialist Felipe Gonzalez government and the Popular Party Aznar government.

17. A more general point is the growing importance of Spanish companies in Latin America, which not only provides a source of revenue but has also supported Spain's position of influence in the European Union (Cecchini and Zicolillo 2002).

18. The term used is *patria financiera* or finance motherland, a term that refers to the unrestricted opening up of the country to financial capital, most notably during the second half of the military regime of the 1970s/early 1980s, under the Ministry of Martinez de Hoz during the military regime.

19. A Spanish company was also involved in the original Fray Bentos project but decided to relocate further down the river. The reason given for this decision was that two large plants in the same location would be impractical and inadvisable.

20. A free trade agreement between Argentina, Brazil, Paraguay and Uruguay.

21. The conflict over the bridges linking Uruguay and Argentina are reminiscent of similar contradictory claims to brotherhood and antagonism in relation to borders, in the context of the bridge over the river Paraná opened in 1990. Political rhetoric envisaged the bridge joining Paraguay and Argentina as a material expression of fraternal links. But the bridge became the site of a number of protests and the elaboration of quite specific nationalist discourses by the press. Interestingly, Grimson (2000) points out that the protest by local businessmen on the Argentinean side, which he refers to as a 'patriotic blockade' was directed at the national government. By blocking the two most important connections across the borders with Paraguay and Brazil, the protesters indicated that 'the problem [relating to taxation of border trade goods] was precisely defined through circulation within the borders of the national state. Marking the boundaries was in their view the best way to make the authorities of that state, located more than 1.000 kilometres away, listen to their demands' (Grimson 2000: 223).

22. This stance of suspicion vis-à-vis foreign companies took other forms, such as the suggestion that the Finns had been obliged to locate their new plant 'in the

South' in response to the strict EU regulations relating to the release of contaminating substances into the environment.

References

Azpiazu, D. and E. Basualdo. 2004. Las privatizaciones en la Argentina. Génesis, desarrollo y los impactos estructurales. In J. Petras and H. Veltmeyer (eds) *Las Privatizaciones y la Desnacionalización de América Latina*. Buenos Aires: Prometeo Libros, pp. 55–112.

Bayer, O. 2003. *Los Anarquistas Expropriadores*. Buenos Aires: Planeta.

Beck, U. 2006. *The Cosmopolitan Vision*. London: Polity Press.

Bunge, C.O. [1903] 1918. *Nuestra América*. Buenos Aires: La Cultura Argentina, Biblioteca Formato Mayor.

Calcagno A.E. and E. Calcagno. 2003. *Argentina. Derrumbe Neoliberal y Proyecto Nacional*. Buenos Aires: Capital Intelectual.

Cecchini, D. and J. Zicolillo. 2002. *Los Nuevos Conquistadores. El Papel de los Gobiernos y las Empresas Españolas en el Vaciamiento de Argentina*. Buenos Aires: Siglo XXI Editores Argentina.

Etchenique, J. 2000. *Pampa Libre. Anarquistas en la Pampa Argentina*. Quilmes: Universidad Nacional de Quilmes, Ediciones Amerindia.

Grimson, A. 2000. El puente que separó dos orillas. Notas para una crítica del esencialismo de la hermandad. In A. Grimson (ed.) *Fronteras, Naciones e Identidades. La Periferia como Centro*. Buenos Aires: Colección Signo, pp. 201–31.

Guibernau, M. 2007. *The Identity of Nations*. Cambridge: Polity Press.

Guy, D. 1991. *Sex and Danger in Buenos Aires: Prostitution, Family and Nation in Argentina*. Lincoln, NE: University of Nebraska Press.

Hale, C. 1996. Political Ideas and Ideologies in Latin America, 1870–1930. In L. Bethell (ed.) *Ideas and Ideologies in 20th Century Latin America*. Cambridge: Cambridge University Press, pp. 133–205.

Ingenieros, J. [1918] 1957. Sociología argentina. In *Obras Completas*, vol. VIII, pp. 214–304.

McGee Deutsch, S. 1993. The Right under Radicalism, 1916–1930. In S. McGee Deutsch and R.H. Dolkart (eds) *The Argentine Right. Its History and Intellectual Origins, 1910 to the Present*. Wilmington, DE: Scholarly Resources Books, pp. 35–63.

Munck, R., R. Falcón and B. Galitelli. 1987. *Argentina from Anarchism to Peronism. Workers, Unions and Politics, 1855–1985*. London: Zed.

Ong, A. 2006. *Neoliberalism as Exception. Mutations in Citizenship and Sovereignty*. Durham and London: Duke University Press.

Petras, J. and H. Veltmeyer (eds). 2004. *Las Privatizaciones y la Desnacionalización de América Latina*. Buenos Aires: Prometeo Libros.

Ramos Mejía, J.M. [1912] 1974. *Las Multitudes Argentinas*. Rosario: Editorial Biblioteca.

Romero, L.A. 2002. *A History of Argentina in the 20th Century*. University Park, PA: Pennsylvania State University.

Stiglitz, J. 2002. *Globalization and its Discontents*. London: Allen Lane.

Suriano, J. 2001. *Anarquistas. Cultura y Política Libertaria en Buenos Aires 1890–1910*. Buenos Aires: Manantial.

Thwaites Rey, M. 2001. *Alas Rotas. La Política de Privatización y Quiebra de Aerolíneas Argentinas*. Buenos Aires: Temas Grupo Editorial.

Zlotogwiazda, M. and S. Balaguer. 2003. *Citibank vs Argentina. Historia de un País en Bancarrota.*, Buenos Aires: Sudamericana.

Chapter 8

HEGEMONIC, SUBALTERN AND ANTHROPOLOGICAL COSMOPOLITICS

John Gledhill

Anthropologists often claim that one of our discipline's virtues is its cosmopolitanism, while at least some of the forms of cosmopolitanism that exist in the world today seem inimical to the sensibilities of most anthropologists. The anthropological dilemma lies, in the first instance, in the way our mainstream disciplinary cosmopolitics (Vincent 1990; Ribeiro 2006), founded on the North Atlantic colonial metropolitan regions, have been critiqued by scholars speaking in the name of the colonial subject. Yet, valid or otherwise, this critique is to some extent yesterday's challenge. Today's lies, first, in the violent reassertion of claims to a global civilizing mission on the part of North Atlantic powers facing declining economic hegemony, and secondly, in new intellectual efforts to provincialize Northern anthropological scholarship within our own global community (Restrepo and Escobar 2005; Ribeiro 2006). Like the post-colonial critiques, this latest debate builds on, and would be unthinkable without, the intellectual values generally (though not necessarily uniquely) associated with the Western Enlightenment. Indeed, it may be even friendlier to fashionable Northern theoretical frameworks, despite its problematization of 'hegemonic anthropologies'. Yet the latest critiques may have different implications from their precursors, since they reflect a movement less dependent on diasporic intellectuals and more focused on South–South linkages.

This chapter is principally about the kinds of cosmopolitics that we find in broader social worlds, now and in the past. Yet exploring these visions may also lead us to ask whether the traditional vantage points of 'progressive' Northern intellectuals (and indeed many of their Southern counterparts) are limiting our understanding of developments in contemporary subaltern cosmopolitics, which may provide unexpected challenges to existing hegemonies.

The Discontents of Neoliberal Globalization

My starting point is the globalization project of neoliberal capitalism, seen from the perspectives of the region in which I live, Europe, and the region in which I work, Latin America. The latter has clearly been part of 'the West' since the sixteenth century and yet 'different' in its trajectory of economic development and placement in global hierarchies of race and ideas about exemplary 'modernity'. The elites that built Latin American nation states in the nineteenth and twentieth centuries increasingly came to see their problem as one of overcoming 'backwardness' relative to North American and European metropoles. It is easy to lose sight, however, of the variety of strategies adopted and the extent to which shifts in the composition of elites were sometimes associated with confident visions of the possibilities of creating sovereign, prosperous and culturally distinctive entities on the world stage that would combine the best that the Old World had achieved with rich and novel contributions grounded in the creative coming together of people of many different origins (cosmopolitanism in the sociological sense).

It is true that racial hierarchies were reproduced in social practice even under regimes that celebrated 'mixing' (*mestizaje/mestiçagem*), revalued African or indigenous culture (within clearly defined limits that were integral to twentieth-century hegemonic projects) and proclaimed their superiority to North Americans in terms of the achievement of a 'racial democracy' that is increasingly questioned today. Early visions of nation building were strongly premised on attracting 'white' immigrants (and biological theories of the genetic suppression of the 'weaker' sectors of the population through miscegenation). As Goddard shows for the case of Argentina in this volume, nation-builders who dreamed of populating 'empty landscapes' with an 'improved stock', based on the mixing of European immigrants with the existing population, were disappointed by the kinds of immigrants that Argentina attracted, which included former subjects of the imploding Ottoman Empire, and tended to descend into 'racial pessimism' about the development potential of the working population as a whole. Their North Atlantic-oriented cosmopolitanism drove them to paint unwelcome newcomers as a threat to 'national values', but, as elites sought to make patriotism a basis for building a capitalist state, they were confronted by counter-movements of immigrant cosmopolitanism that rejected the motherland for the nobler ideal of a common humanity. These were, Goddard notes, quite distinct in their call for solidarity across borders against national identities from the 'boundarylessness' characteristic of a contemporary cosmopolitanism of 'reflexive modernity', which does not imply 'the end of national empathy' (Goddard, this volume).

The passage between historical eras is evident in the changing nature of 'popular struggles'. As Theodossopoulos points out in his introduction to this volume, local expressions of disconformity with the cosmopolitics of neoliberal elites now frame themselves in terms of culturally specific claims and visions and yet also seek to place their struggles within an 'imagined community of the discontented that is paradoxically globalized in its imagination'. Equally ironic is the way that the longer-term recomposition of Latin American elites articulated to the neoliberal cosmopolitical project that ended the economic nationalism of earlier state projects. Not only did many Latin American countries end up with an even greater ethnic pluralism by not excluding Middle Eastern and East Asian immigrants, but some of their descendants, such as Carlos Menem in Argentina and Alberto Fujimori in Peru, became heads of governments driving that transition in the late twentieth century.

Contemporary Latin America has produced strong movements against the rule of transnational corporations and geopolitical subservience to the United States and its allies. At one level, opposition to imperialist violence might be seen as a unifying principle (cross-cutting class and political divisions), although intractable oppositions exist at other levels. Although, as I have argued elsewhere (Gledhill 2005), the techniques and premises of neoliberal governmentality have pervasively penetrated the contemporary 'left' of the party political spectrum, the region is also strong on challenges to visions of 'democracy' that rest simply on the alternation in state power of political machines sustained by electoral marketing techniques. It is also a region where governments that do not simply represent the continuity of an established political class with a modicum of rebranding are now looking to China with optimism rather than dread.

Recent developments suggest that some analysts may have been over-pessimistic to suggest, on the basis of experience in the 1990s, that the era of grass-roots social movement activism had drawn to a close under the remorseless pressures of poverty, increasing dependence on 'informal' economic activity for livelihood, 'NGOization', and the incorporation of many former movement leaders into the now 'democratic' state itself (see, for example, Foweraker 2001). Nevertheless, collective mobilization against neoliberalism is far from the whole of the story in a context where violence and insecurity are towards the top of most citizens' concerns (rich and poor alike). In the case of Bolivia, Goldstein has shown how the successful mobilization against plans to grant Bechtel the contract to manage Cochabamba City's water supplies coincided with an upsurge in lynchings in the poorest neighbourhoods, in which poor indigenous people killed other poor indigenous people (Goldstein 2005: 405). He concludes that people who contest the restructuring of their lives by transnational capital and the neoliberal state simultaneously behave in ways that 'enact' the way that such restructuring has transformed the conditions of everyday life (ibid.: 406). Yet a picture of Latin America focused solely on lynching, drug trafficking and gang violence would be as sociologically blinkered as one that painted a unified 'popular subject' rising up to break the shackles of imperialism on every street. A growing number of citizens combine arduous strategies for gaining a livelihood with going to a church of their choice (as distinct from practising a religion into which they were born). Some of these choices are, as we shall see, another possible way of becoming 'cosmopolitan' and their long-term significance may lie in the (unintentional) tensions that emerge between their subjective effects and the established cosmopolitics of elites, including conservative and liberal forms of multiculturalism designed to contain the social contradictions of past capitalist restructuring and contemporary neoliberal globalization.

Another neglected aspect of the discussion of the global impacts of neoliberal capitalism is the situation of the 'middle classes', and through this I want to make a bridge between analyses of North and South. At one level, Davis (2004) is correct in arguing that, if present tendencies continue, we shall end up with a 'planet of slums' in which the urban shanty town will become the social habitat of the largest segment of humanity. Despite differences in scale and levels of deprivation, the 'brown zones' are advancing even in the former imperial heartlands, and developing some striking similarities in their social consequences (Mollona 2005). Yet the lives of 'middle-class' families are also changing. Neoliberal capitalism has certainly produced 'winners' below the level of corporate CEO and investment bankers, even if the material lifestyles and increased asset values enjoyed by middle-class beneficiaries remain fragile in the bubble economies spawned by global financialization and the global process of redistribution of income between classes has multiplied 'losers' through the process Harvey dubs 'accumulation by dispossession' (Harvey 2005: 161–62). Yet some of these losers have been middle-class.

In some Latin American countries, such as Argentina, there have been massive changes in economic class position (not, however, accompanied by immediate changes in class subjectivities). Hopes for social mobility through improved access to public education – at first sight the success story of the neoliberal era – have been confounded by employer demand for higher credentials to access poorly paid jobs. As jobs and salaries in the public sector have declined, small business and NGO employment has filled part of the gap (in a way that reflects the polarizing impacts of neoliberalism, creating consumer demand at the top and more poor people requiring services and 'empowerment' at the bottom). Yet the gap and the frustrated expectations this engenders remain obvious relative to earlier decades of hope and more frequently satisfied aspiration.

There is still a substantial middle class in countries such as Brazil and Mexico, variegated in terms of income and status, even if changes in the demand for domestic servants reflect the need to make economies some way up this scale. It tends to disappear from view simply because those further below are so much more numerous. Nevertheless, the historical significance of 'intermediate strata' (between elites and masses, capital cities and provinces) is disproportionate to their size in the political histories of most Latin American countries and certainly crucial to understanding recent developments, even in cases such as Venezuela where the mobilisation of a mass base underpins the radical dimensions of the rule of Hugo Chávez (Valencia Ramírez 2005).

Yet it is not simply in Latin America that times are harder for middle-class citizens. In Britain, we can already see changes that will affect the children of middle-class families now entering the labour market. They will still do so from a position of educational privilege, but with higher levels of debt, a need to contribute more of their earnings to the costs of their social security and pensions and with reduced chances of owning their own homes. Living with parents and not having children may be one way of adjusting, but the social and political implications of these changes seem unlikely to be trivial. European countries are reacting in different ways. In the case of France, for example, a still significant labour movement backed the 2006 revolt of secondary school and university students against the CPE (*contrat première embauche*), and some (though probably not enough) of those students managed to make the connection between their problems and those of the mostly immigrant unemployed in the Paris brown zones (*banlieux*). As these transformations intersect in real people's lives and patterns of sociality across class and ethnic boundaries, two distinct tendencies emerge: a strengthening of the kind of cosmopolitics that sees global connections and provokes a desire to empathize with 'others' across domestic and international frontiers, and growing xenophobic fears and loathing. Generally we can see both reactions at work within most national societies, accompanied by political attempts to exploit them.

This 'double movement' reflects the other side of the coin of the process by which the discontented see themselves as united in their disenfranchisement within the current global order, through the 'local critiques' that Theodossopoulos shows in the introduction to this volume are 'facilitated by the flow of ideas and the cosmopolitan ethos that sustains globalization'. White working-class people increasingly invoke the postcolonial trope of 'indigeneity' when they argue that they are becoming an underprivileged minority in 'multicultural' Europe. Violence against migrant workers from neighbouring countries is increasingly common in the global South even in the apparent absence of differences of 'race'. Equally intelligible in terms of this 'double movement' is the way in which 'autonomy', so frequently at the centre of indigenous movements' demands for a new place in the multicultural nation, received a new reading in 2008 during the escalating conflict in Bolivia between the government of Evo Morales and the 'white' (*criollo*) elites of the country's most prosperous states, when the latter mobilized gangs of *mestizos* to commit brutal and explicitly racist assaults on indigenous peasants.

Elite Cosmopolitanisms: Then and Now

Latin America has a long history of elite forms of cosmopolitanism that look to Northern metropoles as centres of international 'high culture'. On closer inspection, however, a strong element of transculturation occurs in the formation of such cosmopolitan social spaces, even when they rest on the most brutal inequalities and local elites appear to hold masses seen as racially distinct in contempt. One of the paradoxes is that metropolitan elite cultures fed off and incorporated elements of 'otherness' for their own diversion and the satisfaction of desire. If we take Brazil as an example, we find French artists and intellectuals flocking to the country in the early 1920s in search of the sensual and exotic to underpin a 'world' avant-garde high culture that also served as a point of reference for some elite groups in Latin America. Blaise Cendrars, a collaborator of Jean Cocteau, came to Rio de Janeiro to meet the *sambista* Donga in the infamous black neighbourhood of Favela Hill. It was here that he also befriended Gilberto Freyre, anthropologist and student of Boas, as well as leading figures in the Brazilian modernist movement in art and literature. Particularly notable among them was Oswald de Andrade, whose 1924 *Brazilwood Manifesto* was to announce the turn of Brazilian modernism away from the importation of all things avant-garde from Europe towards a search for something authentic, distinctive and national (Schwarz 1992; Vianna 1999).

Yet Cendrars hadn't needed to go to Brazil to meet Donga, because Donga had already been to Paris, where he had worked with the composer Milhaud for six months (Vianna 1999: 73). After the dictatorial New State of Getúlio Vargas turned the samba of Rio into Brazil's national music by exploiting the possibilities of the new medium of radio in the 1930s, Donga and other leading musicians went abroad even more frequently, but to play jazz. Elite patronage and transnational movements were long-established processes in the reproduction and transformation of popular musical styles in Brazil. Late eighteenth century musical styles that originated in north-east Brazil were exported to Portugal, where they were made less 'African' and separated from the dancing, because

Europeans thought it too sexy, although it was perfectly normal among aristocratic Bahians (Vianna 1999: 17–18).

Within Bahia itself, the dancing and drumming, which continued to be refreshed by ongoing relations with West Africa, was subject to repeated bouts of repression through the nineteenth century, especially after the Muslim slave rebellion of 1835. Yet liberals defended the right of blacks to practise their revelry 'in a submissive voice' in private space, and, since drumming was incorporated into Catholic processions as well as *candomblé* (which also attracted some whites and *mestiços*), attempts at containment proved futile in the longer term (Reis 2005). In a highly contradictory way, given their continuing anxieties about the slave population and their descendants (Chalhoub 2003), elites found black culture hard to resist, even in the south, where dreams of whitening the country through new immigration were strongest. Yet, in the construction of strongly patriarchal elite cultures of social distinction and participation in global modernity, imports were more extensive than exports, and the fact that popular cultures were also clearly the product of transnational processes created a major dilemma for nationalist intellectuals. They realized, intellectually, that there was no immutable essence of Brazilianness to be discovered in folklore and rural popular culture. Their commitment to nation building led them to repudiate 'imitation' of foreign styles, even if they actually appreciated them artistically, yet in the end everyone had to settle for notions of Brazilianness that acknowledged hybridity in one way or another.

Freyre's 1933 anthropological classic *The Great House and the Slave Quarters* (Freyre 2003a) was a crucial contribution to the revaluation of the African contribution to Brazilian uniqueness, contrasting the 'real Brazil' and its 'luso-tropical' culture, born of the miscegenation between white masters and their slaves, with any image of the country that only emphasized its Europeanness. Yet, when in the sequel, *The Mansions and the Shanties* (Freyre 2003b), he wrote about Afro-descendants in the contemporary urban context, Freyre lamented the way history had loosened the intimate bonds between the poor and the paternalistic masters of the plantations. The aristocracy had not only become more Europeanized culturally, it had increasingly separated itself into a social world apart. The good thing about cities for Freyre was that they had brought the people in the mansions back into closer contact with the poor in their shanties, though he generally shared the conviction of other nationalists that the 'fatal internationalism of urban environments … softens national values' (Vianna 1999: 76). Nevertheless, from the point of view of Freyre's redeeming feature of urbanism, the real irony was that *The Mansions and the Shanties* was published just as the Haussmannization of Rio de Janeiro was increasing the segregation once again as the tenements where black residents and migrants had lived in the centre were demolished and the workers transferred to the *favelas* and northern industrial zone.

Freyre, like other intellectuals and even elite politicians, enjoyed interacting socially with lower-class black musicians. Yet he was an elite cosmopolitan whose nationalist zeal did not inhibit him from the enjoyment of many foreign things of the kind to which only elites had access: he disliked jazz because he saw it both as a product of 'industrial culture' and at the same time as 'barbarous' and even 'animalistic' (Vianna 1999: 61). Furthermore, his anthropology ultimately told a story that elites liked to hear, one that wrote the brutality of class exploitation out of the picture and celebrated racial democracy. His definition of Brazilian *mestiçagem* was exclusionary in relation to the broader cosmopolitanism of the Brazilian population (which included people who identified themselves as the products of 'mixing' between indigenous people and Europeans and by the twentieth century, large numbers of immigrants of Italian and German origin as well as the Middle Eastern and East Asian communities).

Nevertheless, despite its contradictions, in a society that had only abolished slavery a few decades previously, the changing attitudes to African cultural heritage and black religious and secular organizations promoted by the new state's nationalist project were an unambiguous advance. So was the ability to celebrate *mestiçagem*, albeit in a limited way that did not efface racism from social practice, in the light of the extermination that elites had ordained for what they saw as the unacceptable blot on the country's modernizing credentials posed by multicoloured millenarian movements in the backlands behind the coastal cities during the previous century. Furthermore, Vargas's approach to nation building was also adopted by the conservative elite of the now stagnating former colonial centre of Bahia, which sought to rebuild regional identity through its patronage of key black religious and cultural organizations. As their successors pursued a conservative path of attempted capitalist modernization under the military and subsequently the modern Party of the Liberal Front, under the leadership of the regional political strongman Antônio Carlos Magalhães (ACM), an equally conservative but comprehensive 'multiculturalism' centred on African heritage became a dominant motif in Bahian politics (Dantas Neto 2006).

Brazilians have long stopped worrying about cultural imports 'softening national values', but in 2004, on the fiftieth anniversary of the suicide that ended Getúlio Vargas's second period of power (1950–54), people from a variety of social classes to whom I spoke about Vargas often expressed nostalgia for the days when the country still had a 'national project' embodied in a developmentalist state. The fact that under the civilian presidents who succeeded Vargas that project took an increasingly phantasmagorical turn (of a kind similar to the 'magical state' whose history Coronil (1997) charts for Venezuela and which ended in two decades of military rule) has not entirely eliminated the attractions of statism for some technocrats in the Brazilian bureaucracy. Nevertheless, in its first term, the current Workers' Party government of President 'Lula' da Silva did not roll back the neoliberalization policies of Fernando Henrique Cardoso, and its reward for early repayment of debts to the IMF was an injunction to push forward with further privatization and deregulation. Yet it was not just the promise of a better future embodied in what seemed a more autonomous and combative national state that people sensed they had lost in Brazil. For Freyre's worst fears have been realized, and elites have increased their separation from the rest of society in a far stronger way than they did in the period when Vargas shipped off the poor to the *favelas* on the urban periphery.

As Caldeira (2000) has shown in her ethnography of patterns of urban segregation in São Paulo, Brazil's staggering inequalities are accompanied by the withdrawal of the upper echelons of Brazilian society into fortified condominiums whose boundaries are privately policed against intrusions. Within the walls of the high rises, the rich eschew sociability even amongst themselves. Better-off segments of the middle class have adopted the same patterns, but lower middle-class people and working-class people living in neighbourhoods not stigmatized as *favelas* still differ from these groups in their attitudes to sociality. Although their members share upper-class fears of crime, they still value interaction with neighbours in public space, and prefer family homes to condominiums, although they have added fences, walls and bars on the windows (Caldeira 2000: 289–96). The decline in personal security experienced by all social classes has therefore produced strong, though still contested, tendencies towards privatization and fragmentation in the fabric of Brazilian society (ibid.: 258–59).

Caldeira has also shown that a further consequence of these tendencies is the enthusiasm of working-class people for retributive justice to be meted out against their neighbours in the *favelas*. This entails rejection of the kind of cosmopolitics that middle-class activists and academics tend to advocate, in which the principles of universal human rights must be guaranteed even to 'criminals'. As I noted earlier, lynching and vigilantism have become common enough in the 'brown zones' themselves, but the unerstandable irony in the attitudes of lower-class people who see themselves as 'different' from the people of the *favelas* is that they support the extra-legal actions of 'police who kill' despite the fact that they are routinely victimized themselves by the police and official justice system.

Within the 'brown zones', many analysts have argued that local drug-trafficking gangs now substitute for a state whose own ordering power is reduced to sporadic displays of violence. The police are often outgunned and combine violent rituals of 'authority-building' action with accepting pay-offs from the gangs and collaborating with them in the delivery of rough justice to 'anti-social elements' within the community. The local gang offers a degree of protection to its community against invasions from rival gangs (Goldstein 2003: 225). Yet the wider dynamic that produces the rise and fall of community gangs involves complicities between more powerful actors in the 'second economy', civil authorities and politicians. In the last analysis, all this is a consequence of the kind of privatization that neoliberalism has produced, far beyond the more obvious sales of public assets and withdrawal of public services, and it is also the dark side of neoliberal strategies of 'government at a distance' transplanted from the Northern metropoles to different terrain (Rose 1999; Gledhill 2005). In contemporary Rio, the decline of public power is reflected in the recapture of some *favelas* from the *bandidos* by community militias involving former or serving police officers: some of these are serving as springboards for leaders to gain elective office, despite the extra-legal nature of their power.

The 'cosmopolitanism' of the contemporary Brazilian elite (and that of most of Latin America) involves a largely unqualified embrace of the discourse of globalization and the virtues of market society. The vision is transnational, and it is a world of business, lifestyle, education and consumption in which freedom of movement is central, not simply for people but for capital. A desire on the part of Latin American elites to imitate the *gringos* (and form partnerships with them for the exploitation of national resources) is not a historical novelty: indeed, it was the rule rather than the exception before political pressure from other social classes underpinned a phase of economic nationalism. It is also quite possible to be 'cosmopolitan' in this sense of identifying with a global community of business and economic deregulation and still take a certain amount of pride in cultural things that are 'national', from eating beans and liking 'traditional' music to rejecting abortion even for child rape victims in the name of a morally superior Catholic tradition. Indeed, converted into heritage and tourism assets, culture and religion – both *candomblé* (Van De Port 2005) and the sites associated with the once detested 'fanatical' folk religion of the backlands (Pessar 2004) – can prove very good business. Yet while Latin American politicians still need to press the flesh of the poor occasionally in their electoral campaigns despite the increasing predominance of telemarketing in the process, the increasing social segregation of elites means that their construction as people with weak attachments to the nation is all the easier. Faced with the evidence that both national elites and foreign companies seem to be doing rather well out of globalization, the adjective *vendepatrias* (sellers of the motherland) comes up rather frequently in conversation, as less privileged citizens try to relocate their social elites and neoliberal politicians in the global scheme of things.

Yet anyone who browses the news-stand at Brazilian bus terminals will notice that less advantaged citizens seem to be avid consumers of translated, but US-sourced, self-help and personal improvement manuals. It is not simply elites who look northwards in at least a partially admiring way. In considering the Trinidadian preference for 'shiny peanuts', Danny Miller (1997) argues that this as an expression of a popular vision of 'attaining modernity' that is not only unhelpful to West African peanut producers (and therefore to the dreams of South-South economic integration), but also symptomatic of a wider orientation that fuels ever-growing migration to the United States. It is therefore time to look more closely at subaltern cosmopolitics.

Technologies of the Self and Other Globalizations

I develop my analysis around the examples of indigenous autonomy movements in Mexico and two contrasting examples of grass-roots 'cosmopolitanism' that have become significant in Brazil's brown zones, globalized black style culture and neo-Pentecostalism. Both have an ambiguous quality in the sense that, on the one hand, they may ultimately be compatible with neoliberal governmentality projects and the neoliberalization of social life and a means of 'enacting' those processes, and yet, on the other hand, can produce resistance to existing frameworks of hegemony.

Indigenous rights movements in Latin America sometimes pose serious challenges to the resource extraction projects of transnational corporations and have been strengthened by the way indigenous rights have become articulated to the transnational politics of human rights, while the confidence of indigenous militants has been strengthened by a consciousness that local struggles form part of a broader international movement. It is undeniable from the experience of countries such as Mexico that indigenous rights and autonomy demands may take a very un-cosmopolitan direction. For some anthropologists, notably Kuper (2003), the problems with indigenous rights in general are insuperable, whereas for others, such as Hernández Castillo (2005), this kind of position ignores not only more positive cases but the way in which conflict inside indigenous communities gravitates around resolving precisely the problems that critics emphasize. Here I want to take a different tack to this line of debate by pointing to some possibilities of building a broader cosmopolitics out of indigenous rights issues.

The Zapatista movement in Chiapas has achieved cosmopolitical significance through the way it has become iconic for the transnational anti-globalization movement, and its model for grass-roots democracy has been taken up by other local movements in Mexico that have won significant victories against major projects backed by politically connected corporate capital. Two significant examples are the anti-golf course movement in Tepoztlán, Morelos, and the movement of land-reform farmers in Atenco, state of Mexico, which forced cancellation of the construction of Mexico City's new international airport (Stolle-McAllister 2005). Whether or not people in such movements still see themselves as 'indigenous', many can identify with the Zapatista project in terms of broader ideas about local democracy and self-government, which have a long history in Mexico. Ideas like these have been revitalized by both the depredations of transnational capital and a widespread feeling that 'the state' has not simply been reduced to an agent of those transnational corporate capitalist interests, but is the property of a political class that is corrupt, alongside the neoliberalized right across the spectrum of existing political parties, including the supposedly more left-wing Party of the Democratic Revolution. Within the region of Chiapas, which the movement still dominates, the Zapatistas have developed novel forms of supra-municipal regional autonomous government, based on rotation of office holders, very practical arrangements for 'scaling' direct democracy and the inclusion of both non-indigenous *mestizos* and non-Zapatista supporters. While I do not wish to paint an over-idealized picture of the Zapatistas, since they have had to struggle with internal conflicts, divisions over strategy and the practical difficulties of balancing democracy with maintaining ethico-political leadership, their approach is different from conventional criticisms of indigenous rights movements.

The movement has never been ethnically essentialist (its original base was ethnically mixed) and it has always sought to build bridges with *mestizos* that would permit the radical deconstruction of a 'boundary' that is an artefact of nation and state building (Stephen 1997). It might be argued, that in focusing its efforts on maintaining its base in Chiapas, the movement became locked in an impasse, bogged down by vain efforts to obtain radical legislation on indigenous rights from governments determined not to overstep the bounds of neoliberal multiculturalism (Hale 2002). It has also been difficult to satisfy the material aspirations of the movement's supporters by insisting that they reject government social development funds, not a stance adopted by most other indigenous movements. As Viqueira (2002: 87) notes, a significant number of people who once supported the Zapatista project have 'voted with their feet' by migrating, and even young Zapatista activists have quite often abandoned their rural communities with the aim of participating more fully in 'global modernity', a move often facilitated by their links with foreign NGOs.

The movement responded to these dilemmas by taking advantage of the 2006 Presidential elections to launch a new national campaign that sought to build links between the diversity of local movements that have built up around antagonism to neoliberal capitalism and disillusion with state and party politics. Utopian, arguably, and perhaps still too dependent on the individual charisma and media-friendliness of *subcomandante* Marcos, the Zapatistas' new initiative was nevertheless now unambiguously the embodiment of an anti-capitalist, anti-politics-as-usual cosmopolitics. It sought explicitly to build a new, non-electoral, 'left' and to promote the kind of dialogue across ethnic and social boundaries that might deconstruct the bases of a past hegemonic politics of divide and rule. Movements with an indigenous base can clearly insert themselves into broader, pluralistic political projects.

Land- and place-identity-based anti-capitalist autonomy movements do, however, have their limitations. One is that local 'autonomy' may be all too consistent with the reduced public service commitment of neoliberal states and the enthusiasm of multilateral agencies for fiscal decentralization, cost-cutting-targeted anti-poverty programmes and encouragement of 'self-help'. Nevertheless, the experience of Bolivia suggest that impeccably neoliberal decentralization projects may unintentionally open up spaces for challenges to 'politics as usual' at the national as well as regional level. In Chiapas, the stakes in regional autonomy projects are not ultimately the defence of an ecologically and demographically fragile rural idyll, but obtaining control over and benefits from non-agricultural resources (oil, minerals, biodiversity), preventing 'conservation' serving the needs of the ecotourism industry rather than local people, and, most important of all, fighting for alternatives to jobs in the global sweatshop.

Yet a second problem is that many indigenous people are migrants displaced from their 'communities'. In a study of indigenous migrants from the south of Mexico working in Baja California's agribusiness in the north, Martínez Novo (2004) uncovers a series of illuminating paradoxes. State officials running programmes targeted at indigenous migrants often have personal histories of activism in militant movements, but the way they focus on building the 'ethnic consciousness' of the migrants suggests that these commitments have been harnessed in subtle ways to neoliberal ends. The indigenous population of Tijuana city is ignored, and, while strengthening the capacity of indigenous farm workers to defend themselves against human rights abuse and the violation of their labour rights by their employers has its positive side, less positive consequences flow from the fact that the state does not address the employers' treatment of their workers directly. This form of state intervention makes it less likely that the migrants will join autonomous militant movements, while conserving their ethnic identity reproduces the basis through which racial stereotyping has been used to justify lower pay and sub standard living conditions for 'Indians' (Martínez Novo 2004: 364). Although official agencies now accept self-identification as the criterion for ethnic membership, Martínez Novo argues that this attempt to stabilize the indigenous identity of migrants conflicted with the desire of many to achieve social mobility by assimilating socially and culturally with the mestizo majority in the north and thereby 'articulate themselves to the "modern" as they perceive it' (ibid.: 374).

'Technologies of the self' expressed through consumption and lifestyle are central to that alternative cosmopolitical articulation (*norteño* culture is trans-local and transnational), which brings me to another Brazilian example, from the urban brown zones of Salvador, Bahia. In particular, I focus on the peripheral 'suburbs' that extend along the edge of All Saints Bay towards what was once the prosperous agro-export zone called the Recôncavo. They have a past history of industrialization, but today they contain many relatively recent rural migrants lack public services and transport links to the zones of the city where work is available, and available jobs are now casualized and low-paid. They are also zones marked by high levels of drug-related violence. These problems are at the top of the agenda of the residents' association of the district called *Plataforma*, a militant (and periodically repressed) social movement that has also developed a series of cultural politics initiatives centred on young people designed to contest the stigma attached to their place of residence and its people (supported by foreign NGOs and academics from the Federal University).

Some young people do manage to enter higher education despite their disadvantages, again aided by public programmes intended to stem 'delinquency'. Nevertheless, Sansone (2004) has shown that 'unemployment' has now become a positive status for many young black men. Unable to achieve the kinds of jobs that their fathers obtained, they prefer to find ways of participating in a globalized black consumer culture. Kids with low levels of education who try to stay out of trouble dream of working in a fashion store in a shopping mall close to unattainable symbols of global cool (Sansone 2004: 56). But participation in the illegal economy and the gangs offers a way of closing the gap between desire and income (albeit at the likely cost of a short life). The involvement of young and adolescent people in violence has increased dramatically as they desert both school and the labour market in pursuit of greater 'respect' though consumption and style.

Sansone argues that a consequence of these changes is that young black men under twenty-five years of age from the poorest districts of Salvador are less deferential to their white social superiors than their parents, and also less likely to seek solace in Afro-Brazilian religion (ibid.: 57). Nevertheless, from this perspective, no 'oppositional' collective identity in relation to dominant social groups emerges from individuals' everyday struggles for respect and recognition of personhood. Aided by the sartorial conventions of a coastal tropical city, young men strive to mask their actual class status by presenting themselves in public space as co-participants in a global modernity of shared consumer symbols, with the inflection of a transnational black 'style' promoted by a flourishing global tourist industry. There is a form of subaltern cosmopolitanism here, with a subtle and diffuse impact on the hegemonic elite definition of the way 'blackness' should take its place in Brazilianness and Bahianness. Yet it ultimately seems to strengthen rather than threaten the vitality of neoliberal market society.

Yet this is not the only game in town. Although Catholic and Afro-Brazilian religious associations remain important in the lives of many poor families, affiliation to Pentecostal churches is now perhaps the major alternative to the gang as a vehicle for gaining respect, although within the poor neighbourhoods it is a clearly gendered alternative, since women outnumber men by two to one (Goldstein 2003: 219). Particularly striking is the third, neo-Pentecostal wave of churches that have spearheaded a sixfold growth in the number of evangelicals in Brazil over the past twenty-five years (Kremer 2005: 97–98). Prominent to the point of notoriety within this group is the Universal Church of the Kingdom of God (Igreja Universal do Reino de Deus). The Universal Church has enjoyed spectacular transnational expansion, not only to countries like Mexico (where it currently has forty-eight churches) but to North America and Europe, including the UK. The Universal Church differs from older forms of Pentecostalism in multiple ways. Organizationally, it rivals the Catholic Church, leaving behind a culture of small chapels and acceptance of 'marginality', to construct huge cathedrals in prime urban locations adjacent to shopping malls, while using the 'tithes' incessantly demanded of its congregants to finance a powerful TV network (Birman and Lehmann 1999: 148–49).

A transnational religious community with no ideological need for the 'rooted' traditions of Brazil presents a stronger challenge to existing hegemonies (ibid.: 158). It has launched scandalous public attacks on Catholic 'idolatry' and toleration of Afro-Brazilian possession cults: in doing so it attacks that part of the hegemonic strategy of twentieth-century elites which is based on the positive evaluation of syncretism and development of a conservative multicultural politics, discussed earlier (ibid.: 156). In its own practice, the Universal Church focuses on a spectacular enactment of 'spiritual warfare' through public exorcism and a 'prosperity theology' that made it possible to market Pentecostalism to the upwardly mobile and middle classes (Birman and Lehmann 1999: 153; Kremer 2005: 97). Eschewing the traditional logic of patron–client relations and the notion of suffering as virtue leading to a heavenly reward, it tells the individual to transform his or her own life – into one that is not merely more prosperous, but will also be free of drugs and violence, and full of marital happiness and (heterosexual) pleasure (Birman and Lehmann 1999: 160–61).

The officiating bishop or pastor manifests prosperity in his person, a model for the consumer empowerment that comes from practising appropriate technologies of the self (ibid.: 103). It is therefore tempting to see the Universal Church as Christianity fully updated for the neoliberal era, but this is to ignore its possible further consequences. One of these is the effect on poor congregants of feeling that they belong to a powerful, global organization, and the new cosmopolitical vision that this engenders. Its 'war' against mobile spirits that can attack anyone is a war against the everyday evils that assail lives, conducted as grand spectacle in an institution that does not depend on the charisma of a pastor but manifests its global reach through its media apparatus (Kremer 2005: 116). Certainly, those who have no realistic hopes of attaining temporal success can obtain psychological comfort from participating in actions to strike back against the sources of evil, so we might still argue that this is religion acting as an opiate of the masses. Furthermore, many of those who join the Universal Church do not stay in it, but leave out of dissatisfaction with the impersonal treatment they receive within this large-scale institution or from sheer disillusion with its constant demand for money. Nevertheless, they may still leave with transformed subjectivities.

Other neo-Pentecostal churches also seem to run against the grain of hegemonic ideologies that ultimately seek to keep everyone in their place in relations of dependence on patronage and open up new spaces for demands for this worldly equality. John Burdick has shown ethnographically how Pentecostal churches are experienced as self-esteem-enhancing by black people, especially women (Burdick 1999) and how black identity-based organisations have developed within an evangelical setting, linking the latter to the frustrated expectations of upwardly mobile educated blacks and their heightened awareness of glass ceilings even within churches preaching equality (Burdick 2005: 330). It remains true, however, that militant black identity organizations fail to appeal to a majority of potential recruits from the lower classes and are divided amongst themselves by the tendencies of evangelicals to attack *candomblé*, while other militant organizations see Afro-Brazilian religion as crucial to maintaining subaltern cultures of identity and resistance. Both ordinary citizens and many 'progressive' intellectuals remain wary of a potential racialization of politics in a country in which the absence of an actually existing 'racial democracy' does not necessarily undermine its power as an imaginary defining struggles for a better future (Sheriff 2001).

Yet ethnographic research shows that changing popular religious affiliations can participate precisely in the expression of this imaginary as active counter-hegemonic practice. Collins offers a striking example is his research on the transformation, in the 1980s, of Salvador's historical centre, the Pelourinho, from a run-down red-light district inhabited by poor working-class families into a UNESCO World Heritage site and 'pastel-hued mnemonic device designed to showcase the Bahian state's version of national pasts' (Collins 2004: 191). As the redevelopment apparatus set in motion by the political machine of Antônio Carlos Magalhães set about displacing the Pelourinho's unfolkloric existing residents, it tried to defuse their active resistance to dispossession by sending in squads of bureaucrats and bourgeois female supporters of charitable inclination to reaffirm ACM's enthusiasm for *candomblé* as the Afro-Brazilian poor's assumed religion of self-identification. Yet their distribution of the ritual meals known as *carurus*, associated with the Catholic saints Cosmas and Damian and the Yoruba divinity Ibêji, provoked a virulent reaction on the part of many residents, who, whether they were fully committed Pentecostalists or not, used the argument that the elite were trying to seduce their children with 'the Devil's food' as another means of denouncing 'the state's attempt to "folklorize" them and confiscate their homes' (Collins 2004: 203). Religious changes can therefore have significant consequences through which apparently apolitical alternatives feed back into the conditions structuring the political field, since the architects of new religious organizations cannot completely control what those who embrace a faith will actually make of it in the longer term. They may even have contributed to the progressive loosening of ACM's long-lasting grip on Bahia, which culminated in the capture of the state government by the Workers' Party (PT) in the 2006 elections.

Anthropological Cosmopolitics for the Twenty-first Century

It would be unwise to exaggerate the underlying unity of the diverse manifestations of discontent that neoliberal capitalist globalization now faces. The social divides between the actors remain enormous, reinforced by an economic and physical insecurity that reaches a long way up the social ladder. Professional intellectuals and managers are also disciplined by neoliberal regimes of audit and evaluation. Yet my examples suggest that, while emergent subaltern cosmopolitical visions remain entangled in wider fields of power relations, they escape complete determination by those relations. Furthermore, they can recombine in unexpected ways, shattering the boundaries on which elite strategies for containing the social catastrophe of contemporary neoliberal market society depend. In the case of Latin America, a series of diverse and, at first sight, radically incompatible tendencies contribute to an erosion of the ideologies on which the region's hierarchies of class, race and gender have been based, in a way that may reinforce other challenges to transnational capital's alliances with the political classes of the region. Despite this, we must also recognize that racialized ideologies of difference can still be remobilized explosively in the 'double movement' of discontent that may result from political advances for those at the bottom of societies pulverized by neoliberal capitalism.

What does this imply for anthropological cosmopolitics? North Atlantic power clearly did reshape the world, and is still dominant in shaping the way it is thought about academically. It also figures strongly in many subaltern imaginings of attaining 'development and modernity'. Yet, as that power declines, the object of anthropology should be decentred towards the new worlds emerging from the contradictions of the moment. From our present vantage point, which still tends to juxtapose 'the West' and its 'others', it is difficult to see the significance of emerging relations that might become more significant than those between North and South in the near future. We cannot fully exploit our ability to understand subaltern ways of life and cosmopolitics if we cling to increasingly irrelevant models of what 'modern societies' should be like. Transcending the colonial legacy is no longer a matter of seeing colonialism, it is a matter of seeing beyond colonialism, towards what anthropology always could have been (Vincent 1990: 125), a study of the production of social and cultural similarity and difference in a world constantly being reshaped by the uneven development of capitalism and changing global power structures.

References

Birman, P. and D. Lehmann. 1999. Religion and the Media in a Battle for Ideological Hegemony: the Universal Church of the Kingdom of God and TV Globo in Brazil. *Bulletin of Latin American Research*, 18 (2), 145–64.

Burdick, J. 1999. What is the Color of the Holy Spirit? Pentecostalism and Black Identity in Brazil. *Latin American Research Review*, 34 (2), 109–31.

———— 2005. Why is the Black Evangelical Movement Growing in Brazil? *Journal of Latin American Studies*, 37 (2), 311–32.

Caldeira, T.P.R. 2000. *City of Walls: Crime, Segregation, and Citizenship in São Paulo.* Berkeley: University of California Press.

Chalhoub, S. 2003. *Machado de Assis, Historiador*. São Paulo: Companhia de Letras.

Collins, J. 2004. X Marks the Future of Brazil. In A. Shryock (ed.) *Off Stage/On Display: Intimacy and Ethnography in the Age of Public Culture*. Stanford: Stanford University Press, pp. 191–222.

Coronil, F. 1997. *The Magical State: Nature, Money, and Modernity in Venezuela.* Chicago: University of Chicago Press.

Dantas Neto, P.F. 2006. *Tradição, Autocracia e Carisma: A Política de Antonio Carlos Magalhães na Modernizacão da Bahia (1954–1974)*. Belo Horizonte: Universidade Federal de Minas Gerais.

Davis, M. 2004. Planet of Slums: Urban Involution and the Informal Proletariat. *New Left Review (NS)*, 26, 5–34.

Foweraker, J. 2001. Grassroots Movements and Political Activism in Latin America: A Critical Comparison of Chile and Brazil. *Journal of Latin American Studies*, 33 (4), 839–65.

Freyre, G. 2003a. *Casa-Grande e Senzala: Formacão da família brasileira sobre o regime da economia patriarcal*. 47th edn. São Paulo: Global Editora.

———— 2003b. *Sobrados e Mucambos: Decadência do patriarcado rural e desenvolvimiento do urbano*. 14th edn. São Paulo: Global Editora.

Gledhill, J. 2005. Citizenship and the Social Geography of Deep Neoliberalization. *Anthropologica*, 47 (1), 81–100.

Goldstein, D.M. 2003. *Laughter Out of Place: Race, Class, Violence and Sexuality in a Rio Shantytown*. Berkeley: University of California Press.

Goldstein, D.M. 2005. Flexible Justice: Neoliberal Violence and 'Self-Help' Security in Bolivia. *Critique of Anthropology*, 25 (4), 389–411.

Hale, C. 2002. Does Multiculturalism Menace? Governance, Cultural Rights and the Politics of Identity in Guatemala. *Journal of Latin American Studies*, 34(3): 485–524.

Harvey, D. 2005. *A Brief History of Neoliberalism*. Oxford: Oxford University Press.

Hernández Castillo, R.A. 2005. Gender and Differentiated Citizenship in Mexico: Indigenous Women and Men Re-invent Culture and Redefine the Nation. In W. Assies, M.A. Calderón and T. Salman (eds) *Citizenship, Political Culture and State Transformation in Latin America*. Amsterdam: Dutch University Press and El Colegio de Michoacán, pp. 323–40.

Kremer, E.W. 2005. Spectacle and the Staging of Power in Brazilian Neo-Pentecostalism. *Latin American Perspectives*, 32 (1), 95–120.

Kuper, A. 2003. The Return of the Native. *Current Anthropology*, 44 (3), 389–95.

Martínez Novo, C. 2004. We Are Against the Government, Although We Are the Government: State Institutions and Indigenous Migrants in Baja California in the 1990s. *Journal of Latin American Anthropology*, 9 (2), 352–81.

Miller, D. 1997. *Capitalism: An Ethnographic Approach*. Oxford and New York: Berg Publishers.

Mollona, M. 2005. Gifts of Labour: Steel Production and Technological Imagination in an Area of Urban Deprivation, Sheffield, UK. *Critique of Anthropology*, 25 (2), 177–98.

Pessar, P.R. 2004. *From Fanatics to Folk: Brazilian Millenarianism and Popular Culture*. Durham and London: Duke University Press.

Reis, J.J. 2005. Batuque: African Drumming and Dance Between Repression and Concession, Bahia, 1808–1855. *Bulletin of Latin American Research*, 24 (2), 201–14.

Restrepo, E. and A. Escobar. 2005. Other Anthropologies and Anthropology Otherwise: Steps to a World Anthropology Network. *Critique of Anthropology*, 25 (2), 99–128.

Ribeiro, G.L. 2006. World Anthropologies: Cosmopolitics for a New Global Scenario in Anthropology. *Critique of Anthropology*, 26 (4), 363–86.

Rose, N. 1999. *Powers of Freedom: Reframing Political Thought*. London: Cambridge University Press.

Sansone, L. 2004. *Negritude sem Etnicidade*. Salvador and Rio de Janeiro: Edufba/Pallas.

Schwarz, R. 1992. *Misplaced Ideas: Essays on Brazilian Culture*. London: Verso.

Sheriff, R.E. 2001. *Dreaming Equality: Color, Race and Racism in Urban Brazil*. New Brunswick, NJ and London: Rutgers University Press.

Stephen, L. 1997. The Zapatista Opening: The Movement for Indigenous Autonomy and State Discourses on Indigenous Rights in Mexico, 1970–1996. *Journal of Latin American Anthropology*, 2 (2), 2–41.

Stolle-McAllister, J. 2005. What Does Democracy Look Like?: Local Movements Challenge the Mexican Transition. *Latin American Perspectives*, 32 (4), 15–35.

Valencia Ramírez, C. 2005. Venezuela's Bolivarian Revolution: Who are the Chavistas? *Latin American Perspectives*, 32 (3), 79–97.

Van De Port, M. 2005. Candomblé in Pink, Green and Black: Re-scripting the Afro-Brazilian Religious Heritage in the Public Sphere of Salvador, Bahia. *Social Anthropology*, 13 (1), 3–26.

Vianna, H. 1999. *The Mystery of Samba: Popular Music and National Identity in Brazil*. Chapel Hill and London: University of North Carolina Press.

Vincent, J. 1990. *Anthropology and Politics: Visions, Traditions, Trends*. Tucson: University of Arizona Press.

Viqueira, J.P. 2002. *Encrucijadas Chiapanecas: Economía, Religión e Identidades*. Mexico City: El Colegio de México, AC.

Chapter 9

CONCLUSION: UNITED IN DISCONTENT

Elisabeth Kirtsoglou

Globalization and cosmopolitanism are terms with a certain theoretical and analytical attraction. Their appeal – much like the appeal of the term postmodernism in previous decades – relates to a certain extent to their all-encompassing character. To borrow a pertinent notion from Theodossopoulos (2007), all three concepts can be seen as 'hollow categories' in the sense that they can be filled with distinct meanings. They are shifting but catchy idioms because they can signify many different things while saying nothing in particular that is necessarily new. This observation concerns, of course, academics and informants alike. For it seems that we all use these concepts as marks for political commentary, although we inexorably focus our attention to different events and thus we do not automatically refer to the same processes. Globalization and cosmopolitanism have no essential core. They are internally fragmented, multiple, contradictory and semantically vague phenomena. Agreeing precisely upon their content might lead us to reductionism, while tolerating their imprecision imposes – for academics at least – a certain theoretical and analytical vulnerability that is hard to swallow, especially since its consequences tend to hit us when we thought we had produced a really strong argument.

The generalized discontent with the aforementioned concepts that has been documented in social analysis is, of course, correspondingly differentiated. Social actors around the world 'resist', but not essentially to the same events, not necessarily for the same reasons and inevitably not in the same manner. It is then safe to argue that globalization, cosmopolitanism and multiculturalism, as well as the resistance and dissatisfaction they evoke, cannot be seen as homogeneous entities or unwavering processes. The present volume has been concerned with imagined communities of discontent, largely treating both globalization and cosmopolitanism (and the resistance to them) as epiphenomena of more general concerns with power, inequality and political subjectivity. My use of these all-encompassing terms so far in an undifferentiated fashion has by no means the purpose of collapsing them on to each other. They are unquestionably distinct concepts that reflect variant discursive and practical political developments. Their transformation in the perception of our informants, however, into generic categories of blame entices one to discuss them as if they had a common basis.

In some ways, my discussion here starts with a call to provisionally accept an 'as if' assumption: 'as if dissatisfied people around the world were entirely right in their judgement that current political and ideological developments relate closely to an unfavorable distribution of power that excludes far more than it includes'. My call is theoretical, analytical and methodological. It is theoretical to the extent that various academics have observed the close relationship between globalization, cosmopolitanism and power. It is analytical because, even if such an assumption is not entirely valid, it is true in its consequences, and it is methodological because social anthropology – since its inception – has been dedicated to viewing the world from the informants' point of view, to take their concerns seriously and to pay attention to the meaning of local discourse.

Resistance to globalization is a global phenomenon that frequently utilizes the very technologies of globalization in order to express itself. New social movements thus acquired a global character that cut across cultural and national boundaries and transformed identity politics into a public and common quest (Touraine 1988; Melucci 1989). Seen from one perspective the generalized dissatisfaction with globalization relates to its economic dimension and its association with neoliberal capitalism (Appadurai 2001: 4). While Eriksen observes that globalization is perceived as an outcome of neoliberal economics (2003: 4), in this volume Goddard documents local discontent with the economic consequences of globalization and the effects of the failure of neoliberal policies in Argentina. There are cases when indeed, as Turner argues, globalization 'constitutes an essentially unregulated intensification of the capitalist dynamic of competition, accumulation [and] exploitation' (2004: 90). Corporate-managed globalization has been presented to the world as the only option (Thornton 2004: 3), signalling a new era of 'capitalism that presents itself as a gospel of salvation' (Comaroff and Comaroff 2001: 2).

Reflecting upon globalization as the creation of centres of accumulation, Friedman argues that we should adopt a cyclical perspective and treat globalization not as a new phenomenon, but as a phase in history that people have experienced before (2004: 50–52). The undesirable historicism of this approach notwithstanding, if we assume that globalization is related to the creation of centres of accumulation, then we have to accept Friedman's second argument that 'the wealth of any centre depends to a large extent on the formation of a periphery' (ibid.: 69; see also Comaroff and Comaroff 2001: 8; Sassen 1998: xxxiv). Disaffection with globalization, then, is certainly connected to unequal distribution of wealth, which is partly a consequence of the over-accumulation problem (cf. Harvey 1989), as well as of changes in employment relationships (flexible labour, for instance) that come as a result of the deregulation of products and capital markets (Friedman 2004: 59–62; see also Schoppa 2002). Hence the character of the global economy evokes a justifiable discontent in so far as it further marginalizes certain peripheries (Dirlik 1998) creating spaces of social exclusion all around the world (Castells 1998).

Another potential source of dissatisfaction with globalization – a common one as I am hoping to show with certain counter-cosmopolitan perspectives – relates to its political character. Globalization is regarded as 'depoliticizing' the international public sphere (Boggs 2000: 69–70; see also Thornton 2004: 4; Appadurai 2001); however, as this volume argues, it also produces an anti-globalist, global politicization. Apart from the documented political resistance of new social movements (Bhagwati 2002: 4; Cohen and Rai 2000), the present collection testifies to the existence of an 'imagined community of the discontented that is paradoxically globalized in its own imagination' (see Theodossopoulos; Theodossopoulos & Kirtsoglou, this volume). These new imagined communities share many commonalities with the classic Andersonian ones, and especially what Anderson called a 'sense of simultaneity' (1983: 31), that is, confidence in the steady, anonymous, simultaneous activity of other people who are imagined to be equally dissatisfied with the new global regime. As we have argued (Kirstoglou and Theodossopoulos, this volume), this is precisely the case with Greek subjects. Imagination at the level of dreaming, as demonstrated by Edgar and Henig (this volume), is also related to a worldwide Islamic community united by prophetic dreams of jihad. Globalization, however, produces not only imagined worlds (Appadurai 1996). It also produces real interconnections of activists (Bhagwati 2002), young Muslims (Appiah 2007) and people who engage in politicized struggle seeking to 'control the conditions of their own action' (Melucci 1989: 45). In this sense, anti-globalism is a global project itself, carried out by interconnected social actors in a largely cosmopolitan fashion.

Inspired by the aforementioned observation, this volume has treated discontent with globalization and cosmopolitanism not as a sign of nationalism (see also Cheah and Robbins 1998), closure and backwardness, but as an alternative form of globalized thinking, produced by disenfranchised subjects who are concerned with political and ideological hegemony. Indeed, the volume has attested to various 'subaltern' notions of cosmopolitanism (Gledhill, this volume) and to types of resistance that emerge from alternative cosmopolitan visions. It has become clear, I think, that counter-cosmopolitanism concerns not only an array of discourses and practices of 'globalized resistance', but also the belief of many social actors that cosmopolitanism is a Western ideological product, designed to serve particular political interests. Discontent with it is a marker of a generalized discontent with processes of 'colonizing' indigenous consciousness so to speak. As we have demonstrated (Kirtsoglou and Theodossopoulos, this volume), for instance, when our Greek informants express their disaffection with cosmopolitanism, they are concerned with the power of some to create cosmologies that serve their own interests and then to hegemonically extend those cosmologies to the rest of the world in a naturalized fashion. On the one hand, cosmopolitanism professes respect for difference, but, indeed, as Appiah argues, it is rather difficult to 'have any respect for human diversity and expect everyone to become cosmopolitan' (2007: xx).

Globalization has been introduced as a new political project that would undermine nationalism and the nation, thus producing cosmopolitan forms of political identities (Chuang Ya-chung 2004: 19). Indeed, as Turner argues, nationalist ideology has been undermined, to a certain extent, while other institutions, like the World Bank and the World Trade Organization, 'exercise now considerable sovereignty beyond the borders of any state' (2004: 92; see also Mittelman 1996; Panitch 1996). Despite the transnational operation of such economic agents, a number of authors agree that the state does not seem to be replaced by any other form of political organization (Krasner 1988: 76; Sassen 1996; 1998: 199; Turner 2004: 91–92). Furthermore, as Billig (1995) has demonstrated, although banal nationalism is a quite widespread phenomenon, 'nationalist expressions' in the non-Western world are treated as pathological anomalies.

Discontent with cosmopolitanism has frequently been mistaken for nationalism (see also Cheah and Robbins 1998), as a pathology (Gellner 1997) 'of non-Western, primordial, irrational and backward Others' (cf. Wang Horngluen 2004: 30; Gledhill 2000: 14). Cosmopolitanism, however, is commonly distrusted for being an imposed idea that seeks to undermine cultural difference and to enforce upon various nations and peoples Western sovereignty and suzerainty. Hannerz distinguishes between cultural and political cosmopolitanism, arguing that, while 'the former is more often bottom-up', the latter tends to relate to top-down processes (2004: 79). He claims that the association between political cosmopolitanism and a global government – the reason behind many peoples' dissatisfaction with cosmopolitanism – is misguided, because political cosmopolitanism is related to global 'governance' and not 'government' (ibid). In turn, he goes on to describe governance as a form of global civil society (ibd.: 72). Nevertheless, global governance is easily (in practice) turned into a form of global government that disenfranchises less privileged groups in the configuration of global power.

Various authors have attested to the emergence of a global regime – economic or otherwise (Chuang Ya-chung 2004: 19; Friedman 2004: 57; see also Marcus 1999). In turn, civil society, according to Gellner, relates to the plurality of institutions that oppose and balance state power, ensuring 'the impossibility of ideological monopoly' (1994: 1, 3–4, 211). Concepts such as globalization, cosmopolitanism and multiculturalism however, have been almost naturalized in contemporary political discourse and presented in international forums as the only politically correct choices, as well as guides to strategic action and political intervention. The anti-cosmopolitan arguments sometimes wish to challenge precisely this kind of ideological monopoly and subsequently the political actions legitimized by it. Indeed, seen from a particular theoretical and analytical perspective, Turner's argument is difficult to resist:

> 'Disturbingly, the transnationalists' master trope, the binary classification of local societies and cultures as 'inertial' and lacking in dynamic capacities for resistance or change, while all agency, dynamism and effectively invincible force is ascribed to transnational processes of the global system, repeats the most ethnocentric and ideologically imperialist chronotope of all, the evolutionist vision of the dynamic historically innovative and spatially expansive West as the bearer of global progressive change to the historically inert, spatially closed and culturally traditional Others. The global system is US; local communities are Them; the myth of the historic 'break' constituted by transnationalism puts Them in the past and makes Us the bearers of history' (2004: 110–111).

Much like postmodernist, heterodox scholars (cf. Argyrou 2002), the uncritical advocate of cosmopolitanism seems, indeed, to occupy a space above the world, from which s/he is able to gaze down on the world liberated from various backward types of single identification, cultural, ethnic or racial, and thus capable of celebrating an 'enriched cultural territory' (Friedman 2004: 64), amidst, of course, bitter disputes and confrontations of nationalist/tribal/ethnic/racial character that torment virtually every continent of the world. Seen from this perspective, certain scholars who speak about 'elite' cosmopolitanism (Dirlik 1998; Robbins 1999; Friedman 2004) appear to have a strong point. Of course, cosmopolitanism is by no means the prerogative of elites (Hannerz 2004; Appiah 2007) and it does not come in direct confrontation with notions of belonging (Werbner 2006). The concepts of 'flexible citizenship' (Ong 1993), 'travelling cultures' (Clifford 1992, 1997), 'nomadic subjectivity' (Rapport 1997) and 'rooted cosmopolitanism' (Werbner 2006, 2008) are theoretically useful, analytically powerful and ethnographically substantiated.

The critique articulated here is not directed at cosmopolitanism as a discursive and practical political option, but to the imposition of cosmopolitanism as an ideology that is regarded by many as seeking to hegemonically legitimize Western ideological authority. Also, and perhaps most importantly, the need to address cosmopolitanism in a critical and reflexive manner is connected to its property as a 'grand narrative' that has the potential to 'Otherize', exoticize and ultimately create more dichotomies and oppositions than the ones it seeks to resolve. A similar argument is put forward by Zizek with reference to multiculturalist openness when this is juxtaposed to new forms of fundamentalism (1998: 1008). Multiculturalism, Zizek points out, can easily be seen as the opposite of 'self-enclosed, authentic' communities, creating an artificial distinction between the localist/fundamentalist, fossilized cultural subject and the multiculturalist who is observing, consuming and analysing it from the 'distance rendered possible by his privileged universal position' (Zizek 1997: 44).

Distrust in the concept of cosmopolitanism might also spring from the perception that it is largely unattainable and therefore an empty rhetorical tool in the hands of the powerful. The disbelief in the possibility of cosmopolitanism in practice itself has roots in the fact that the 'ideal of cosmopolitan democracy ... depends too much on the presumption of universal "world citizens", while the definition and classification of these citizens ... hinges on the institutions of the nation-state system' (Wang Horng-luen 2004: 31). This argument relates to my earlier point that although the nation state has been ideologically undermined, it remains the par excellence form of modern political organization. To corroborate this point I shall tentatively refer to Kymlicka, who argues that 'most important moral principles should be cosmopolitan in scope – human rights, democracy and environmental protection – and we should seek to promote these ideals internationally. But our democratic citizenship is, and will remain in the foreseeable future national in scope' (2001: 326). Multiculturalism is in turn treated with similar suspicion, often for much the same reasons. For it is vague enough to serve as 'an alibi' that 'exonerates the existing privileged inequities and class differences' (Miyoshi 2000: 44).

Discontent with globalization, cosmopolitanism and multiculturalism also relates, of course, for certain people to modernity's broken promises of transparency, equality, rationality, openness and trust. The flamboyant exhibition of power on behalf of states and coalitions, political unilateralism and the undermining of the importance of public debate (Beck 2000: 4) create a sense of worldwide political frustration. Social actors do not feel that they live in a more transparent (West and Sanders 2003) or a fairer (Kirtsoglou 2006) world and they are thus eager to pinpoint the problematic relationship between globalization, cosmopolitanism and power (Driessen 2005: 137). The cold war political legacy and the development of the global capitalist system have 'forced a partial abandonment of the post war social contract', led people to question the potential of political equality and intensified mistrust of the sincerity of the great powers (Turner 2004: 91; see also Marcus 1999; Kirtsoglou 2006). The presence of a hegemonic global empire (Stewart-Harawira 2005) that 'exports', so to speak, and imposes ideologies and policies alike is felt strongly in various parts of the world.

As we have argued (Kirtsoglou and Theodossopoulos, this volume) modernity produces disenfranchised subjectivities. Seen in this context, discontent with globalization and cosmopolitanism is emblematic of the people's struggle for agency and the power to produce and shape history. In this sense, some authors rightly point out that the identity politics of new social movements relate closely to the control of historicity (Touraine 1988; Chuang Ya-chung 2004; Trias I Valls, this volume). My observation here does not mean to offer support to Touraine's notion of 'levels of historicity' that distinguishes between post-industrial and developing societies (Escobar 1992; Chuang Ya-chung 2004: 15). I believe that political participation, contribution to historical processes and the power of self-representation are different dimensions and expressions of the same quest for agency. Hence I agree with Theodossopoulos (this volume) and others who extend the discussion of counter-cosmopolitanism to tourist practices and connect the latter with the presence of certain elites. Touching upon the concept of cultural difference, Friedman argues that 'cultural difference is consumed [by the elites] in the form of cultural products' (2004: 64–65). Despite the fact that some local communities succeed in turning this to their advantage by gaining visibility (Strathern and Stewart, this volume; Swain 1989; Tice 1995), some other actors are left disempowered by the process of consumerist exoticism (Kirtsoglou and Theodossopoulos 2004). The appreciation of 'difference' advocated by cosmopolitanism and multiculturalism is then closely related – analytically at least – to the standpoint of the respective actors and depends on whether we 'consume' each other from similar structural positions of power or whether this process generates further inequalities and frustrations.

Having said that cosmopolitanism has often been associated with elites (Hannerz 2004: 74) and an outward movement from centres to peripheries, I also wish to agree with Strathern and Stewart (this volume) when they argue that 'cosmopolitanism does not necessarily belong only to the multicultural metropolitan contexts of life'. Indeed, the authors are right to draw our attention to the ways in which people tend to exercise agency by creating 'new centres in which their peripheral status can be overcome' (ibid.). This last observation compels me to comment briefly upon the importance of space, place and locality in the appreciation of discontent with globalization, cosmopolitanism and multiculturalism.

Much of this volume has been devoted to discontent as the 'cosmopolitanism of the powerless and the disenfranchised'. Imagining the Other as sharing the same political predicament with oneself – that of being dispossessed – entails, of course, a certain degree of cosmopolitan empathy and interconnected, globalized thinking. To a great extent, this kind of cosmopolitan empathy utilizes – as we have shown (Kirtsoglou and Theodossopoulos, this volume) – 'analogical thinking' (Sutton 1998). Extending slightly Sutton's original concept of analogical thinking, we have argued that imagining oneself as another in the political sense requires a certain merging of the past, the present, the local and the global in terms of contexts, strategies, means and ends and ultimately in terms of the distribution and the effects of power diachronically. This argument is similar to Appadurai's appreciation of the relationship between local and global (2001), but it also has certain ramifications for the importance of space and locality. Space, place and locality are important references for the articulation of political discourse and the engagement in political practice (Buechler 2000) because, as Friedman argues, human experience is always localized (2004: 55) and to a great extent space- and place-specific.

The critiques of globalization can thus be better understood – in their distinctiveness – as local versions of global awareness (Theodossopoulos, this volume), which find their impetus in local histories and the politics of everyday life (Appadurai 2001). These localized versions of discontent that popular magazines like *Sabili* express (Watson, this volume) are nonetheless potent in expressing dissatisfaction with global processes. At this point, I would like to take the argument slightly further and claim that it is not only space and place that matter, but also embodiment as a 'version', so to speak, of locality. Our bodies can be seen as intersection points of different discourses and practices, the material loci from which we engage with the world (Kirtsoglou 2004). Discontent with globalization, cosmopolitanism and multiculturalism is also expressed in embodied ways, in demonstrations, protests, dress codes and violent confrontations. The body, then, is directly relevant to political practice although its importance has not been fully exploited analytically.

I started this last chapter of the volume by stressing the elusiveness of the terms it wished to discuss and by pinpointing a double impossibility: we can neither reduce the complexity of globalization and cosmopolitanism nor remain comfortable with the analytical vulnerability that comes as a result of their semantic vagueness. Acknowledging the internal differentiation of these concepts, at the level of both discourse and practice, and the inherent multiplicity in people's discontent with them is a way of dealing with our theoretical and analytical deadlock. Grounding our commentaries in ethnography is another means of capturing otherwise unstable political processes. Discontent has many faces, origins and expressions. Some of them are entirely valid and others are slightly far-fetched. Sometimes we tend to empathize with our informants, and others we indulge with a reserved scepticism about the validity of their claims and the effectiveness and wider consequences of certain extreme forms of political expression. In more than one way, we frequently find ourselves belonging to – or at least empathizing with – the imagined communities of the discontented. Above all, however, we consistently try to capture and convey the importance of local meaning, which in this particular case has, as we have all argued, global and cosmopolitan resonance. The excesses of power will not disappear with another academic publication. Nor shall we ever become capable of doing away with all forms of inequality and all kinds of dichotomies and oppositions in the wider political and public sphere. The task of ethnographic documentation and critical analysis itself has its own limits, but it is nevertheless a step in the desired direction. After all, democratic dialogue, public debate and attention to the importance of different opinions are the very political processes that cosmopolitanism promises to the world. In a sense, this volume is evidence that despite its faults and deficiencies, it also delivers.

References

Anderson, B. 1983. *Imagined Communities: Reflections on the Origins and Spread of Nationalism*. London: Verso.

Appadurai, A. 1996. *Modernity at Large: Cultural Dimensions of Globalization*. Minneapolis: University of Minnesota Press.

——— 2001. Grassroots Globalization and the Research Imagination. In A. Appadurai (ed.) *Globalization*. Durham N.C. Duke University Press, pp. 1–21.

Appiah, K.A. 2007. *Cosmopolitanism: Ethics in a World of Strangers*. New York: Norton.

Argyrou, V. 2002. *Anthropology and the Will to Meaning; a Postcolonial Critique*. London: Pluto Press.

Beck, U. 2000. *What is Globalization?* Cambridge: Polity Press.

Bhagwati, J. 2002. Coping with Antiglobalization: A Trilogy of Discontents. *Foreign Affairs*, 81 (1), 2–7.

Billig, M. 1995. *Banal Nationalism*. London: Sage.

Boggs, C. 2000. *The End of Politics: Corporate Power and the Decline of the Public Sphere*. New York: Guilford Press.

Buechler, S. 2000. *Social Movements in Advanced Capitalism: The Political Economy and Cultural Construction of Social Activism*. Oxford: Oxford University Press.

Castells, M. 1998. *End of Millennium*. London: Blackwell.

Cheah, P. and B. Robbins. 1998. *Cosmopolitcs: Thinking and Feeling Beyond the Nation*. Minneapolis: University of Minnesota Press.

Chuang Ya-chung. 2004. Re-Theorizing Social Movements in Changing Global Space. In Ya-chung Chuang (ed.) *Globalization*. Oxford: Berghahn, pp. 12–23.

Clifford, J. 1992. Travelling Cultures. In L. Grossberg, C. Nelson and P. Treichler (eds) *Cultural Studies*. New York: Routledge, pp. 96–117.

——— 1997. *Routes: Travel and Translation in the Late Twentieth Century*. Harvard: Harvard University Press.

Cohen, R. and S. Rai. 2000. *Global Social Movements*. London: Ahtlone Press.

Comaroff, J and J.L. Comaroff. 2001. Millennial Capitalism: First Thoughts on a Second Coming. In J. Comaroff and J. L. Comaroff (eds) *Millennial Capitalism and the Culture of Neoliberalism*. Durham, N.C: Duke University Press, pp. 1–56.

Driessen, H. 2005. Mediterranean Port Cities: Cosmopolitanism Reconsidered. *History and Anthropology*, 16 (1), 129–41.

Eriksen, T.H. 2003. Introduction. In T.H. Eriksen (ed.) *Globalization: Studies in Anthropology*. London: Pluto, pp. 1–17.

Escobar, A. 1992. Culture, Economics and Politics in Latin American Social Movements Theory and Research. In A. Escobar and S. Alvarez (eds) *The Making of Social Movements in Latin America: Identity, Strategy and Democracy*. Boulder, Oxford: Westview Press, pp. 62–85.

Friedman, J. 2004. Champagne Liberals and the New Dangerous Classes: Reconfigurations of Class, Identity and Cultural Production in the Contemporary Global System. In Ya-chung Chuang (ed.) *Globalization*. Oxford: Berghahn, pp. 49–82.

Gellner, E. 1994. *Conditions of Liberty: Civil Society and its Rivals*. London: Hamish Hamilton.

——— 1997. *Nationalism*. London: Phoenix.

Gledhill, J. 2000. *Power and its Disguises: Anthropological Perspectives on Politics*. London: Pluto Press.

Hannerz, U. 2004. Cosmopolitanism. In D. Nugent and J. Vincent (eds) *A Companion to the Anthropology of Politics*. Oxford: Blackwell, pp. 69–85.

Harvey, D. 1989. *The Urban Experience*. Oxford: Blackwell.

Kirtsoglou, E. 2004. *For the Love of Women: Gender, Identity and Same-Sex Relationships in a Greek Provincial Town*. London: Routledge.

——— 2006. Unspeakable crimes: Athenian Greek Perceptions of Local and International Terrorism. In A. Strathern, P. Stewart and N. Whitehead (eds) *Terror and Violence: Imagination and the Unimaginable*. London: Pluto, pp. 61–88.

Kirtsoglou, E. and D. Theodossopoulos. 2004. 'They are Taking our Culture Away': Tourism and Culture Commodification in the Black Carib Community of Roatan. *Critique of Anthropology*, 24 (2), 135–57.

Krasner, S.D. 1988. Sovereignty: An Institutional Perspective. *Comparative Political Studies*, 21, 66–94.

Kymlicka, W. 2001. *Politics in the Vernacular: Nationalism, Multiculturalism and Citizenship*. Oxford: Oxford University Press.

Marcus, G.E. 1999. Introduction to the Volume: The Paranoid Style Now. In G. Marcus (ed.) *Paranoia Within Reason: A Casebook on Conspiracy as Explanation*. Chicago: Chicago University Press, pp. 1–11.

Melucci, A. 1989. *Nomads of the Present: Social Movements and Individual Needs in Contemporary Society*. London: Hutchinson Radius.

Mittelman, J. 1996. (ed.) *Globalization: Critical Reflections. International Political Economy Yearbook*. Vol. 9. Boulder: Lynne Rienner.

Miyoshi, M. 2000. Ivory Tower in Escrow. *Boundary*, 2 (27), 7–50.

Ong, A. 1993. On the Edge of Empires: Flexible Citizenship among Chinese Diaspora. *Positions*, 1 (3), 745–78.

Panitch, L. 1996. Rethinking the role of the state in an era of globalization. In J. Mittelman (ed.) *Globalization: Critical Reflections. International Political Economy Yearbook*, vol 9. Boulder: Lynne Rienner.

Rapport, N. 1997. *Transcendent Individual: Towards a Literary and Liberal Anthropology*. London: Routledge.

Robbins, B. 1999. *Feeling Global: Internationalism in Distress*. New York: New York University Press.

Sassen, S. 1996. *Losing Control: Sovereignty in an Age of Globalization*. New York: Columbia University Press.

—— 1998. *Globalization and its Discontents: Essays on the Mobility of People and Money*. New York: New Press.

Schoppa, L. 2002. Globalization and the Squeeze on the Middle Class: Does any Version of Post-War Social Contract Meet the Challenge? In O. Zunz, L. Schoppa and N. Hiwatari (eds) *Social Contracts under Stress: The middle class of America Europe and Japan at the turn of the century*. New York: Russell Sage Foundation, pp. 319–44.

Stewart-Harawira, M. 2005. *The New World Order: Indigenous Responses to Globalization*. London: Zed Books.

Sutton, D. 1998. *Memories Cast in Stone: The Relevance of the Past in Everyday Life*. Oxford: Berg.

Swain, M.B. 1989. Gender Roles in Indigenous Tourism: Kuna Mola, Kuna Yala and Cultural Survival. In V.L. Smith (ed.) *Hosts and Guests: The Anthropology of Tourism*. Philadelphia: University of Pensylvania Press, pp. 83–104.

Theodossopoulos, D. 2007. Introduction: The 'Turks' in the imagination of the 'Greeks'. In D. Theodossopoulos (ed.) *When Greeks Think about Turks: The View from Anthropology*. London: Routledge, pp. 1–32.

Thornton, W. H. 2004. Civil Anti-Globalism and the Question of Class. In Ya-chung Chuang (ed.) *Globalization*. Oxford: Berghahn, pp. 1–11.

Tice, K. E. 1995. *Kuna Crafts, Gender and the Global Economy*. Austin: University of Texas Press.

Touraine, A. 1988. *Return of the Actor: Social Theory in Postindustrial Society*. Minneapolis: University of Minnesota Press.

Turner, T. 2004. Shifting the Frame from Nation-state to Global Market: Class and Social Consciousness in the Advanced Capitalist Countries. In Ya-chung Chuang (ed.) *Globalization*. Oxford: Berghan, pp. 83–119.

Wang Horng-luen. 2004. Mind the Gap: On Post-national Idea(l)s and the Nationalist Reality. In Ya-chung Chuang (ed.) *Globalization*. Oxford: Berghahn, pp. 24–36.

Werbner, P. 2006. Vernacular Cosmopolitanism. *Theory, Culture and Society*, 23 (1–20), 496–98.

———— 2008. Introduction; Towards a New Cosmopolitan Anthropology. In P. Werbner (ed.) *Anthropology and the New Cosmopolitanism: Rooted, Feminist and Vernacular Perspectives*. Oxford: Berg, pp. 1–29.

West, H.G. and T. Sanders. 2003. Power Revealed and Concealed in the New World Order. In H.G. West and T. Sanders (eds) *Transparency and Conspiracy; Ethnographies of Suspicion in the New World Order*. Durham and London: Duke University Press, pp. 1–37.

Zizek, S. 1997. Multiculturalism, or the Cultural Logic of Multinational Capitalism. *New Left Review*, 225, 28–51.

———— 1998. A Leftist Plea for Eurocentrism. *Critical Inquiry*, 24 (4), 988–1009.

NOTES ON CONTRIBUTORS

Iain R. Edgar teaches social anthropology at the University of Durham. His PhD study of meaning-making in dreamwork groups was published in *Dreaming, Anthropology and the Caring Professions* (Avebury, 1995). He researches and writes on dream and imagework in culture, politics, education and identity, including the *Guide to Imagework: Imagination-based Research Methods* (Routledge, 2004).

John Gledhill teaches social anthropology at the University of Manchester. He is a specialist on Latin America, with a particular interest in Mexico, Central America and Brazil. His thematic interests are in political, economic and historical anthropology and his publications include the books *Casi Nada: A Study of Agrarian Reform in the Homeland of Cardenismo* (University of Texas Press, 1991); *Neoliberalism, Transnationalization and Rural Poverty* (Westview Press, 1995); *Power and Its Disguises: Anthropological Perspectives on Politics* (Pluto, 2000); and *Cultura y Desafío en Ostula: Cuatro Siglos de Autonomía Indígena en la Costa-Sierra Nahua de Michoacán* (El Colegio de Michoacán, 2004).

Victoria Goddard teaches anthropology at Goldsmiths, University of London. Her research has focused on Europe, particularly southern Italy, and Latin America, specifically Argentina. Her research interests include gender, kinship and small-scale production, informal economies and political movements. She is author of *Gender, Family and Work in Naples* (Berg, 1996), editor of *Gender, Agency and Change: Anthropological Perspectives* (Routledge, 2000) and co-editor of *The Anthropology of Europe* (Berg, 1994).

David Henig teaches anthropology at the University of Kent. His research interests include the anthropology of Islam, post-socialism, social change and the epistemology and methodology of anthropological research. He has done research on Muslims in the Czech Republic, Egypt and the

Caucasus. From July 2008 he has been conducting doctoral fieldwork in the mountains of Central Bosnia.

Elisabeth Kirtsoglou teaches anthropology at the University of Durham. Her research interests focus on identity, gender and politics. She is author of the book *For the Love of Women: Gender, Identity, and Same-sex Relationships in a Greek Provincial Town* (Routledge, 2004).

Pamela J. Stewart and **Andrew Strathern** are a wife and husband research team with a long history of joint publications and research. They are based in the Department of Anthropology, University of Pittsburgh and are also Visiting Research Fellow and Visiting Professor, Department of Anthropology, University of Durham; Visiting Research Fellows in the Research Institute of Irish and Scottish Studies, University of Aberdeen; and have been, for many years, Visiting Research Fellows, at the Institute of Ethnology, Academic Sinica, Taipei, Taiwan. They have published many books and articles on their research in the Pacific region and in Europe (Scotland and Ireland), and in Asia (Taiwan and China). They are the editors of the Ritual Studies Monograph Series, and the Ethnographic Studies in Medical Anthropology Series with Carolina Academic Press. Their co-authored and co-edited books include *Witchcraft, Sorcery, Rumors and Gossip* (Cambridge University Press, 2004); *Asian Ritual Systems: Syncretisms and Ruptures* (Carolina Academic Press, 2007); and *Exchange and Sacrifice* (Carolina Academic Press, 2008).

Dimitrios Theodossopoulos teaches anthropology at the University of Kent. His earlier work examined people–wildlife conflicts and indigenous perceptions of the environment. He is currently concerned with ethnic stereotypes, indigeneity, authenticity and the politics of cultural representation in Panama and South-East Europe. He is the author of *Troubles with Turtles: Cultural Understandings of the Environment on a Greek Island* (Berghahn, 2003), and editor of *When Greeks Think about Turks: The View from Anthropology* (Routledge, 2006).

Àngels Trias i Valls has a 'Llicenciatura' in Social and Cultural Anthropology from UCB (Barcelona) and a PhD (2000) in Social Anthropology from the Queen's University of Belfast on the theme of economic anthropology in Japan. Àngels has been involved in anthropological research in Japan since 1995, focusing on the representation of economic exchange in areas such as gender, commodification of gifts, cosmopolitan sentiments and queer identities. A key theme of her research is the interpretation of visual aspects of gender politics and the anthropological understanding of contract and consent both in Japan and outside Japan. She has worked as a lecturer in

Social Anthropology in different institutions in the UK and has pioneered several e-learning anthropology programs.

C.W. (Bill) Watson teaches anthropology at the University of Kent. He is a specialist on Indonesia and has written about various aspects of Indonesian history and politics covering the last hundred years. His doctoral fieldwork on kinship and property was conducted in Kerinci in the central highlands of Sumatra, to which he has regularly returned over the last twenty-five years. Recently he has been writing about the role of Muslim institutions in the development of civil society in Indonesia. His most recent book, *Of Self and Injustice* (KITLV Press, 2006), looks at modern Indonesian autobiographies as sources for understanding indigenous perceptions of political life in Indonesia during the Suharto era.

INDEX